T0389036

TRANSFORMATIONAL PROCESSES IN CLINICAL PSYCHOANALYSIS

In this book, Lawrence J. Brown offers a contemporary perspective on how the mind transforms, and gives meaning to, emotional experience that arises unconsciously in the here-and-now of the clinical hour. Brown surveys the developments in theory and practice that follow from Freud's original observations and traces this evolution from its conception to contemporary analytic field theory.

Brown emphasizes that these unconscious transformational processes occur spontaneously, in the blink of an eye, through the "unconscious work" in which the analyst and patient are engaged. Though unconscious, these processes are accessible and the analyst must train himself to become aware of the subtle ways he is affected by the patient in the clinical moment. By paying attention to one's reveries, countertransference manifestations and even supposed "wild" or extraneous thoughts, the analyst is able to obtain a glimpse of how his unconscious is transforming the ambient emotions of the session in order to formulate an interpretation.

Brown casts a wide theoretical net in his exploration of these transformational processes and builds on the contributions of Freud, Theodor Reik, Bion, Ogden, the Barangers, Cassorla, Civitarese and Ferro. Bion's theories of alpha function, transformations, dreaming and his clinical emphasis on the present moment are foundational to this book. Brown's writing is clear and aims to describe the various theoretical ideas as plainly as possible. Detailed clinical material is given in most chapters to illustrate the theoretical perspectives. Brown applies this theory of transformational processes to a variety of topics, including the analyst's receptivity, countertransference as transformation, the analytic setting, the paintings of J.M.W. Turner, "autistic transformations" and other clinical situations in the analysis of children and adults.

Transformational Processes in Clinical Psychoanalysis will be of great interest to all psychoanalysts and psychoanalytic psychotherapists.

Lawrence J. Brown trained in adult and child psychoanalysis and is a faculty member and supervising child analyst at the Boston Psychoanalytic Institute (BPSI), USA. He is also a supervising and personal analyst at the Massachusetts Institute for Psychoanalysis. Brown has lectured internationally and published papers on a variety of topics, including the Oedipal situation, Bion, intersubjectivity, field theory and autistic phenomena.

PSYCHOANALYTIC IDEAS AND APPLICATIONS SERIES

Recent titles in the Series include

Art in Psychoanalysis: A Contemporary Approach to Creativity and Analytic Practice
edited by Gabriela Goldsteunb

The Female Body: Inside and Outside
edited by Ingrid Moeslein-Teising and Frances Thomson-Salo

Death and Identity: Being and the Psycho-Sexual Drama
Michel de M'Uzan

Unpresented States and the Construction of Meaning: Clinical and Theoretical Contributions
edited by Howard B. Levine and Gail S. Reed

The Ethical Seduction of the Analytic Situation: The Feminine–Maternal Origins of Responsibility for the Other
Viviane Chetrit-Vatine

Time for Change: Tracking Transformations in Psychoanalysis—The Three-Level Model and fufu
edited by Marina Altmann de Litvan

Hostile and Malignant Prejudice: Psychoanalytic Approaches
edited by Cyril Levitt

Freud and Culture
Eric Smadja

Play, Gender, Therapy: Selected Papers of Eleanor Galenson
edited by Nellie L. Thompson

Psychopathology of Work: Clinical Observations
edited by Christophe Dejours

Finding the Body in the Mind: Embodied Memories, Trauma, and Depression
Marianne Leuzinger-Bohleber

The Future of Psychoanalysis: The Debate about the Training Analyst System
edited by Peter Zagermann

The Analytical Process: Journeys and Pathways
Thierry Bokanowski

Psychotic Organisation of the Personality: Psychoanalytic Keys
Antonio Perez-Sanchez

Psychoanalytic Perspectives on Virtual Intimacy and Communication in Film
edited by Andrea Sabbadini, Ilany Kogan and Paola Golinelli

Transformational Processes in Clinical Psychoanalysis: Dreaming, Emotions and the Present Moment
Lawrence J. Brown

TRANSFORMATIONAL PROCESSES IN CLINICAL PSYCHOANALYSIS

Dreaming, Emotions and the Present Moment

Lawrence J. Brown

LONDON AND NEW YORK

First published 2019
by Routledge
2 Park Square, Milton Park, Abingdon, Oxon OX14 4RN

and by Routledge
711 Third Avenue, New York, NY 10017

Routledge is an imprint of the Taylor & Francis Group, an informa business

British Library Cataloguing-in-Publication Data
A catalogue record for this book is available from the British Library

Library of Congress Cataloging-in-Publication Data
Names: Brown, Lawrence J., 1946– author.
Title: Transformational processes in clinical psychoanalysis : dreaming, emotions and the present moment / Lawrence J. Brown.
Description: Abingdon, Oxon ; New York, NY : Routledge, 2019. | Series: The International Psychoanalytic Association ideas and applications series | Includes bibliographical references and index.
Identifiers: LCCN 2018025585 (print) | LCCN 2018027974 (ebook) | ISBN 9780429451140 (Master) | ISBN 9780429835827 (Web PDF) | ISBN 9780429835810 (ePub) | ISBN 9780429835803 (Mobipocket/Kindle) | ISBN 9781138323919 (hardback : alk. paper) | ISBN 9781138323926 (pbk.)
Subjects: LCSH: Psychoanalysis. | Psychiatry. | Clinical psychology.
Classification: LCC RC506 (ebook) | LCC RC506 .B696 2019 (print) | DDC 616.89/17—dc23
LC record available at https://lccn.loc.gov/2018025585

ISBN: 978-1-138-32391-9 (hbk)
ISBN: 978-1-138-32392-6 (pbk)
ISBN: 978-0-429-45114-0 (ebk)

Typeset in Palatino
by Apex CoVantage, LLC

This book is dedicated to the memory of
James Grotstein, MD
Teacher, mentor, friend

CONTENTS

ACKNOWLEDGEMENTS

I would like to thank my colleagues of the Klein/Bion Study Group in Boston and the Boston Group for Psychoanalytic Studies for creating and sustaining a rich and scholarly atmosphere which nurtured many years of collective study.

I would also like to thank my wife and family for supporting my efforts, granting me the time and space for thinking as well as to my children and grandchildren, who learned that I was unable to be with them at certain times because of "work."

I am indebted to the members of the IPA Publications committee for their interest in, and support of, this book, and a special thanks goes to Rod Tweedy of Karnac books for his help in navigating the initial publication process, which was then continued with generous assistance from the publication staff at Routledge.

I also wish to thank the *Psychoanalytic Quarterly* and John Wiley & Sons, Inc. for permission to use my (2015) paper "Ruptures in the analytic setting and disturbances in the transformational field of dreams," *Psa Q*, 84: 841–865. I appreciate permission from the *International Journal of Psychoanalysis* and John Wiley & Sons, Inc. to use my two papers: (2012) "Bion's discovery of alpha function: Thinking under fire on the battlefield and in the consulting room," *IJP*, 93: 1191–1214; and (2016) "The capacity to tell a joke: Reflections from work with Asperger's children," *IJP*, 97: 1609–1625.

Further thanks go to the American Psychiatric Association Publications for permission to use (2011) Countertransference. In G. Gabbard, B. Litowitz and H. Smith (Eds.) *Textbook of Psychoanalysis, Second Edition.* New York: American Psychiatric Publishing, pp. 79–92. I am grateful to *Rivista di Psicoanalisi* for permission to use my (2016) "The analyst's receptivity: Evolution of the concept and its clinical application," *Rivista di Psicoanalisi,* LXII: 29–49. Finally, thanks to Taylor & Francis, LLC for their permission to use my (2015) Notes on memory and desire: Implications for working through. In H. B. Levine and G. Civitarese (Eds.) *The Wilfred Bion Legacy*. London: Karnac Books, pp. 333–343.

SERIES EDITOR'S FOREWORD

The Publications Committee of the International Psychoanalytic Association continues, with this volume, the series Psychoanalytic Ideas and Applications.

The aim of these series is to focus on the scientific production of significant authors, whose works are outstanding contributions to the development of the psychoanalytic field and to set out relevant ideas and themes, generated during the history of psychoanalysis, that deserve to be known and discussed by present psychoanalysts.

The relationship between psychoanalytic ideas and their applications has to be put forward from the perspective of theory, clinical practice and research, so as to maintain their validity for contemporary psychoanalysis.

The Publication's Committee's objective is to share these ideas with the psychoanalytic community and with professionals in other related disciplines, in order to expand their knowledge and generate a productive interchange between the text and the reader.

Lawrence's Brown book is a much-welcomed study of the concept of transformation in psychoanalysis. Anchored in Wilfred Bion's theory and inspired by the work of different psychoanalytic cultures, in particular, the contemporary American psychoanalysts (James Grotstein and Thomas Ogden) and the work of South American psychoanalysts (José Bleger and Willy and Madelaine Baranger), the author offers an in depth and rich theoretical and clinical exploration of this concept. He stresses its important clinical implications, particularly in the way the analyst listens to the patient's free associations which, the author suggests, should be understood as part of a transformational process of emotional experiences into meaningful representations. All throughout this book, Dr. Brown has as a referential frame six concepts that are, in one way or another, present in the development of his ideas related to the theory and technique of transformations. The first concept refers to the speed at which the mind transforms emotional experience. The other five notions are: the notion of unconscious work (spontaneous production of symbols and metaphors), the concept of inter-subjectivity, the centrality of affect, the intersubjective field theory and the importance of the process of dreaming. These concepts are further elaborated, linking them to the various processes of transformation.

The 12 chapters present different facets, both clinical and theoretical, of the process of transformation. The study of these different aspects extends from defining key concepts such as the discovery of alpha function, to the illustration of transformations as seen in works of art, to

the clinical question of the type of receptivity necessary for the process of transformation to take place. Several clinical illustrations of adults and of children whose clinical picture rests within the autistic spectrum disorder, demonstrate the usefulness of the proposed theory of transformation.

Dr. Brown considers that the theory and technique of transformation suggests a new world view for psychoanalysis that, as he says, "emphasizes constant change, evolution and growth."

Lawrence J. Brown has brilliantly put together this new volume that enriches the Psychoanalytic Ideas and Application Series. The result is an important contribution which will surely be of interest to the psychoanalytic community and to all people interested in the complexity of the process of psychic transformations and their unquestionable value in clinical work.

Gabriela Legorreta
Series Editor
Chair, IPA Publications Committee

A PREFACE AND SOME "FROG" THOUGHTS

Giuseppe Civitarese

For several years now, a group of Boston psychoanalysts under the leadership of Lawrence Brown and Howard Levine has characterized itself by having introduced the study of analytical field theory in the United States. Developed in Italy by Antonino Ferro and Francesco Carrao, and expanded upon by their students, this theory represents, at least in my opinion, the most fertile and rigorous development of Bion's thought – not, to say, of the *Bion à la carte* type that is fashionable. Why Italy? Because it was Corrao himself who invited Bion to Rome to hold memorable seminars, which evidently left their mark. Currently the interest is vast and, in addition to Italy and Boston, especially popular in Brazil and on the Pacific Coast, both places where Bion lived and/or taught. It seems that even the French psychoanalytic culture – a traditional stronghold of metapsychology – is relatively opening up to accept Bionian psychoanalysis (but perhaps more correctly it should be called post-Bionian), as highlighted by the theme of their next (78°) Congress in Gêne: *Transformations et accomplissements psychiques*. Sometimes I wonder, what would we do with Bion without the tools that Ferro (and of course others, including mainly Ogden) made available to us in his theoretical and technical innovations in the application of Bion's heuristic ideas. I suspect that without the interpretations of Bion's work by these creative authors his writings would have remained obscure and out of reach for many analysts: that Bion would have been accused of mysticism or worse.

Then we have Ferro. I'd say that *he has passed the Rubicon* of which the reconstruction of historical truth of the patient's biography was required. I wouldn't want to exaggerate, but his contribution can be summed up in a very simple way: in contemporary psychoanalysis there is a *before* and an *after* Ferro. In my view, the same thing could not be seriously said for any other author, even though there are many other talented contemporary authors. What did he find across the Rubicon? Ferro's coherent and courageous application of Bion's concept of transformation in dreaming and its radical expansion. Seeing the session as a dream means that everything, but *everything*, can be heard virtually as the joint dream of patient and analyst, both committed to giving a meaning in the here and now of the session to the deep emotional experience that binds them in a bond of knowledge, love or hate.

This golden principle, which Bion militantly insists upon, aims to counteract the saturation of concepts and theories and instead keep ideas fresh and vibrant, rather than becoming meaningless clichés. I would say that this attitude *is the most disregarded even by those who are inspired by his thought*. So, as Bion writes in *Attention and Interpretation*, he worried his success would have made him a monument ("he was loaded down with honors and sank without a trace"), a psychoanalytic cliché to be easily forgotten. Similarly, sometimes I think that in the same way the post-Bionian theory of the analytical field risks collapsing from its success. Why? Because – and maybe this is inevitable, and even necessary – it becomes watered down, everything is related theoretically to a phantom "field," other presumed "field" theories are discovered, and in the mean time we forget the basic postulates that gave the original meaning value and which for the most part are derived from Bion. Which ones?

Bion elaborates a theory of dreaming that is alternative to Freud's: from the principle of oneiric "distortion" to the principle of "transformation"; Bion doesn't use the concept of instinctual drives but instead considers emotional drives (interpreting him, Grotstein adds the "truth drive"); historical reconstruction completely loses importance compared to favoring the emotional growth that takes place in the encounter between minds; each session is a first session and the patient is actually always a new patient; it is no longer a matter of the analysts interpreting the unconscious content to the patient but of holding with her a conversation that makes them both more true and real; the model of psychology within which the cure takes place is no longer unidirectional but bipersonal or intersubjective.

Furthermore, intersubjective is not synonymous with interpersonal, an adjective that still makes reference to two distinct subjects exchanging things between them; the concept of enactment, as well as that of countertransference, is not strictly considered as a field concept because it is used in a classical optics; the theory of the unconscious changes completely, as it is not anymore the "demoniac" unconscious but a psychoanalytic function of personality; compared to Freud, who according to Meltzer does not have a true theory of affects, since he mainly considers them as *manifestations* of meaning and not as *containers* of meaning. Bion puts emotion at the centre of psychoanalysis, the point being here that he never sees it as separated from a relationship; in this way emotion becomes the primary or more basic (as corporeal, semiotic, implicit or procedural) form of *social* elaboration (better: negotiation) of meaning, and meaning is the same as mutual recognition.

These rapid references should be enough to realize that we are facing a paradigm shift in the sense of Kuhn. Many, if not all, of the attempts to underline the continuity with classical psychoanalysis, that obviously does exist, and an endeavor that must be accomplished in order to give depth and perspective to the theoretical concepts, very often misunderstand the meaning of Kuhn's lesson. Many do not dare to allow themselves just a little bit of that courage, of that radicality, of that touch of madness that we recognize in Bion – otherwise he wouldn't have been accused of being a "deteriorated" person – and spend their time trying to normalize his puzzling theses and as it were give a blow to the circle and one to the barrel; or fetishize them, which basically is the same. On the contrary, in my opinion, psychoanalysis can remain vital and exciting if we show some of the courage of our most creative predecessors. As an example, is it not time to abandon completely the Freudian idea of the unconscious as a place inhabited by "a mob, eager for enjoyment and destruction" which he still expresses in 1932 in his text on Popper-Lynkeus (p. 221)? Is it not perhaps true that the unconscious conceived as hell ("*Acheronta movebo*") favors insidious moralistic and hypocritical attitudes, and also, consequently, not a few distortions in the functioning of psychoanalytic institutions, as they become more similar to churches than to universities?

That's why we can happily greet a book like Lawrence Brown's, which instead gives a balanced, lively, rich, captivating and accurate idea of the state of the art in Bionian and, I repeat, post-Bionian psychoanalysis. Through 12 chapters beautifully written, and that are read in a breath, never gray or heavy, Brown guides us with politeness, with confidence, with firm knowledge among some of the concepts I mentioned above and makes them familiar to us. Recurring for a while to some Bionian slang, the "vertex" he himself proposes to approach this psychoanalysis is the concept of transformation. Whether it is understood as an element of the theory of psychoanalytic observation, according to Bion's explicit intention, or of a new psychoanalytic theory as such, for Bion the concept of transformation is linked to a model of psychoanalysis in which it is relevant to focus on unconscious emotional experience lived by the analytic dyad in the present of the session. This experience is understood as belonging neither to the patient nor to the analyst, but as an expression of the couple that is constantly generated between the two in the intermediate area that constitutes the meeting of unconscious and conscious minds; in the dialectical-negative movement of recognizing each other as subjects. That transformations are the object of the analysis, which for Bion means fostering the development of psychic containers over the identification of repressed contents.

From this point of view, what interests Bion is how the something that arises between analyst and patient is transformed with respect to the complex psychic movements schematized in the Grid, the scheme (a "psychoanalytic play") that he invented to assign a value to the facts of the analysis. The vertical axis of the rows defines the level of development of a given psychic content, from proto-sensory and proto-emotional elements to the most sophisticated forms of logical-rational thinking; the horizontal axis of columns specifies how such content is being used, not what it means in itself. For example, Bion writes, "if the content is oedipal material I do not concern myself with this but with the transformation it has undergone, the stage of growth it reveals, and the use to which its communication is being put" (1965, p. 35). In other words, every time a certain event of the analysis occurs, he assigns it ideally to a Grid's box to deduce the direction of the psychic, whether it goes towards the development of concepts and effective action or towards regression. It is worth emphasizing again that for Bion the concept of transformation only makes full sense within his new theory of the unconscious, affects and dream. But what is transformed? What is the process of transformation in itself? What is the engine? What is the purpose? It is obvious that what interests us as analysts are the transformations that lead to the birth of the mind and then nourish its growth. What we would like is to better grasp its essence, get a more precise idea of it and develop a more successful technique to promote it.

If, then, the transformations that interest the analyst are those that nourish and grow the mind, it is important to know how to recognize them for at least two good reasons even when they are not evident. First, because only in this way is it possible to map the analytical field and intuit where to meet the patient; and, second, because the perspective that the unconscious has on things is always richer than that of the conscious since it is much more capable of thinking about infinity. As Ogden (2010, p. 328) writes,

> the predominantly unconscious psychological work that we do in the course of dreaming [. . .] is our most encompassing, penetrating, and creative form of thinking. We are insatiable in our need to dream our lived experience in an effort to create personal, psychological meanings (which are organized and represented in such forms as visual images, verbal symbols, kinesthetically organized impressions, and so on).

Following these premises, we distance ourselves from the idea of an interpretation that is exact in the same way a measurement in physics can be said to be. Interpretation takes more and more the character of an aesthetic transformation, because it is made in accordance with our theoretical understanding of how meaningful the aesthetic elements intrinsic to communication are and with our technical effort to "play" them in the relationship. Bion insists on the metaphor of artistic creation in all of his work. The analyst must be like a painter. As a painter, he must know how to use his palette of colors, his emotions and dreams. Only in this way will he be able to give an "integrated" or "somato-psychic" interpretation of the facts of the analysis. "Integrated" here means not split, not only rational or intellectual nor exclusively intuitive; directed not only to what can be translated into words (in linguistic meaning), but also to what is only of the order of sense.

To formulate a theory of transformations that would be "superior to those already used consciously and unconsciously" (Bion, 1965, p. 42), what is needed is to develop precise conceptual devices to recognize phenomena when they occur. For example, if we didn't have the concept of it, we couldn't recognize a transformation into hallucinosis. As we said, strictly speaking, the theory of transformations is a theory of psychoanalytic observation. In his stated intentions Bion says that he wouldn't want to add other theories to those already existing in the body of psychoanalysis. What he aims at is to find terms (invariants) that can summarize in themselves the variety of (psychic, relational) psychoanalytic configurations that are substantially similar. He thinks that in this way he could avoid the multiplication of different terms, which then lead to as many theories as the patients and as many theories as the therapists. These terms should be precise, clear, communicable and uniform. Bion makes an example discussing claustrophobia and agoraphobia. They are two fundamentally equal types of situations, which in essence could correspond to the experience that "an infant might have when the breast is withdrawn, of facing emotions that are unknown, unrecognized as belonging to himself, and confused with an object which he but recently possessed" (1965, p. 124). *In fact, however, Bion founds a new psychoanalytic theory*. Otherwise we would not even mention the notion of paradigm shift. Could a theory of observation ever be "pure," that is, separate from theoretical premises and axioms? It is true that at least at the beginning Bion only understands it as a higher level of formalization of the discipline; as a way to arrive at a concept/abstraction of several concepts expressed by different psychoanalytic theories. And yet, what do O and invariants mean? How do they relate to the key concept of transformation?

There are no comfortable doors to enter into Bion's world, but here Brown is a magnificent Virgil. So, page after page he brings us from O's hell to purgatory of invariance and then to the paradise of alpha function, container/content and reverie. One perceives distinctly the style of the author, which I would define as rigorous but gentle. You always feel in the background the great clinical experience and the humor. The parts I personally prefer are when he illustrates concepts with clinical examples, especially with young patients. It is then that not only his professional qualities and vast theoretical knowledge, but also his skill in getting in a profound emotional contact with patients comes clearly to the fore.

There are many appealing treats, like delicacies at a restaurant, that await the reader of this book. The menu features many offerings that characterize Brown's conception of analysis: the rapidity of mental processes of digesting the emotional experience, the concept of the unconscious's work, the intersubjective or field perspective, the centrality of affect, the new conception of the dream, the relevance of intimacy, the value of surprise, (*the "frog" thought* that jumps. . .), the idea of the analytic process as a flux, the role of deferred action, receptivity and the idea of the sublime as a possible narrative of emotional experience in the encounter with the other.

Brown reveals a great teaching ability because he is scholarly without being sterilely academic. The chapters on the concepts of countertransference, receptivity and alpha function are brilliant. Especially in the last he manages beautifully to keep together the theoretical plan, some of the most dramatic events in Bion's past (the experience of war) and his current situation of life (the marriage with Francesca seen as a containment function), and so he gives the reader a glimpse of what original thinking can stem out from. He also guesses what Bion's most personal source of a certain way of seeing the patient as enemy, which is in shocking contrast with his sceptic attitude, can be. The dramatic scene in which dying Sweeting desperately asks Bion to contact his mother becomes the paradigm of the deep need every human being has to face anguish for a containment function and for another mind.

This heart-breaking scene is also an example of what Bion means with "think under fire," an expression that reminds us of the famous British "grace under fire." The same expression is also useful to describe the chapter in which Brown deals with *Transformations.* The third of Bion's major books is the one that remains the most difficult to understand. Most readers and scholars look at it with the greatest scepticism (a "challenging book . . . excessively dense and nearly impenetrable . . . too open, too pro- and -vocative, and weakened by riddling meanings"). Personally, I share the judgment about the difficulty, but I believe that *Transformations* in some respects is still to be discovered. In this book the theoretical vision of Bion is at its zenith and requires an expert reader. It is, however, the book in which, among other things, Bion reformulates the concept of conscious and unconscious as finite and infinite; explains why with respect to the Freudian idea of distortion the concept of transformation marks a paradigm shift; in speculative terms, gives a psychoanalytic account of what is meant by the dialectic between being and being-there and consequently a theory of temporality; finally, with the conceptual triad of O, invariance and transformation he draws a complex theory of knowledge which is absolutely in accordance with the principles of contemporary epistemology.

The use Bion makes in the book of graphic signs taken from geometry is also a very courageous and interesting way to show, not only enunciate, how the process of formalization of sensoriality takes place. Brown doesn't hide the fact that he often remains puzzled, or that he feels a certain doubtfulness, and yet with passion and honesty he draws his path – there may be different ones – through *Transformations*. The reader will be grateful to him. If I can add one last annotation: it is not possible to understand Bion without reading deeply through *Transformations* or without realizing that the Grid is at the very heart of his theoretical thought and that *in no way* it can be overlooked. Moreover, if one reads *Transformations* carefully, the idea of a mystical Bion sounds ridiculous, a coarse misunderstanding. But it is true that he asks much from the reader and does not always, in fact almost never, provides maps on the sources of some of his most difficult concepts. For example, one cannot really discern the distinction between

God and Godhead without a minimal knowledge of Hegel's thought and his criticism of Kant.

The next chapter, on the analyst's receptivity, touches on a central theme. The analyst's mind becomes somehow the main place of the cure. Brown once again demonstrates his great teaching ability. I find his idea of the three imaginary consultations with Freud, Reik and Bion wonderful, and I am honored to have published it during my direction at the *Rivista di Psicoanalisi*. Here Brown demonstrates, beyond his great expertise as scholar, his unique playfulness, a rare quality. The distinction between models is an essential step to grasp how our discipline evolves. Brown is laudably clear in underlying the elements of continuity but also those of discontinuity. In fact, he honestly admits, "My 'supervision' with Bion left me somewhat off balance."

There is not enough room here to deal with all the remaining chapters in detail. I will therefore limit myself to just a few points that I believe are important. I am very much in tune with the beautiful chapter on Bleger's concept of setting (Civitarese, 2004), a theme with which I inaugurated my own psychoanalytic production. Bleger's reflection, now available also in English in a recent translation in his book *Symbiosis and Ambiguity*, is precious to understand that identity is also a matter of semiotic schemes, of what the body knows, of somatic intentionality (Merleau-Ponty), of institutions, of habits (Hegel). Consequently, it is essential to theorize this level and to know how to address it in the session. Otherwise, the risk could be of making just intellectualized interventions, without really reaching the patient.

The chapter on the Sublime also arouses my enthusiasm, because it touches on an issue that I have been trying to clarify for a while (Civitarese, 2017a). In fact, I believe that the aesthetics of the sublime has deeply inspired Bion and that it is also in itself an inspiring theory of subjectivation. The concept of Sublime hides in itself the secret of the negative pleasure of representation, a pleasure that arises, as in Turner's paintings, which Brown comments on in his text, when an infant faces the seductive but frightening aspects of the mother. For each subject the struggle is to find the right distance from the O/other. The theme of Sublime also allows us to link aesthetics in art to aesthetic experience in analysis. The first constitution of human subjectivity takes place in fact at an aesthetic and intersubjective level, and it never ceases to occur also at *this* level, not even when the most sophisticated tools of logical-rational thought will be available. Another great value of the paintings inspired by the sentiment of the Sublime is that they allow us, through the aesthetic experience that they evoke, to "suffer," Bion would say, the pleasure of negotiating the right distance from the object; in other words, to have an emotional, lived experience of what we "just" theorize in more abstract terms, so to say from the inside, both spiritual and physical.

But where Brown becomes irresistible for me it is when he shows himself in action as a therapist for children, which is the theme of the last chapters. Among the many other reasons to recommend these chapters to the reader – sensitivity, respect, competence, experience, ability to love etc. – there are some beautiful illustrations of what it means for him to work within the frame of the post-Bionian theory of the analytical field. Immediately, and with very difficult patients, we are transported in fascinating stories, as if we were children listening to fairy tales told by a grandmother around the fireplace. Wonderful characters tell us about the volcanic emotions that light up with the "accelerating rapidity" that Brown mentions in the introduction. A partial list should at least be attempted: I find impressive *Brown-the-second-caveman*, that I imagine dressed as a character in a BC comic strip, in lion leather and holding a club: in fact here there is a delightful fragment of his personal analysis, an occasion in which his own analyst allowed himself to *play*. In analysis a joke can be much more than an explanation that unveils the unconscious functioning of the mind, more like the equivalent of a felicitous metaphor or a micro-dream that the patient can continue to interrogate her whole life, with a mixture of pleasure, humor, affection and gratitude. By the way, it is fantastic that Brown writes that he has felt the impulse to recontact his analyst to ask him how the joke had come to his mind, because this act in itself is the best illustration, if taken as an allegory, of the contact function that play can have in analysis – what I called transformations in play (Civitarese, 2017b). As we know, nothing is more serious than play, i.e. being in transitional space. Moreover, the text has been propitiated by the writing of the chapter: one can see how writing is also a way of dreaming oneself into existence.

The central question becomes: "whose joke was this?" in the sense that it is always a shared joke (or dream), and consequently the goal becomes to develop "the capacity to tell a joke" as we see in one of the chapters on autistic transformations. So, we are witness to the extraordinary transformations that Brown himself undergoes in analyzing these autistic spectrum children: *Brown-the-caveman* becomes the uniquely talented *Mr. Fixit*; and then there's *Brown-Batman*, or *Brown-Doc*, the only one who seems to have the spiritual strength to face *The Angry Man!* In other words, we have beautiful sequences of the dance of analysis: we read about Sean, a three and a half-year-old patient affected by psychogenic autism, and we see how his autism "infects" the analytic couple; how gradually the ability develops to play or rather to dream O, the emotional unconscious experience of an analytic hour. Another astonishing character of the dream is the *Permian Extinction* or, better, of the terrible nightmare Brown must suffer in order to help Sean recover from his infantile catastrophe. The metaphor can be seen as a reverie, even if it does not come directly from the clinical work, but in fact *is* part of the work of the mind (of the minds) to transform an unsustainable experience of psychic agony. I loved reading that Bollas characterizes the mother as *the First Clown*, which relates to a former patient of mine, a clever but silent woman with severe autistic nuclei, whose treatment challenged me to remain alive in the analytic relationship. I used to say that I played the clown with her and that it worked beautifully, though I sometimes felt I had to conceal that I had played the clown with her from *the-Severe-Psychoanalytic-Super-They.*

So, it's not by chance that in the last summarizing chapter Brown quotes from Ferro's interview *The New Analyst's Guide to the Galaxy*: we need to unload much of the old stuff, and remain faithful to the spirit of our best guides from the past, not to sacralise their contributions. That happened and still happens too frequently and it is the reason why in a very honest but disquieting passage Brown reveals his feelings about what for a while he felt as a "moribund" atmosphere at the annual psychoanalytic meeting of his national Society. The astonishing fact is that we *do* have great new guides. Why then do we feel so obliged to repeating and repeating the sterile exercise of affirming that everything is implicit (*sic*) in Freud's work? Why don't we feel that this is a way to kill any new idea that could stem out from the beautiful psychoanalytic method of investigating the essence of humanity that he *did* invent? Why do not we take seriously Kuhn's great work on scientific paradigms? As we saw, Lawrence Brown has a lot to say in this matter, and that's why once again I manifest here my enthusiastic appreciation for this beautiful book, at the end of this brief note, just with a small but significant Italian word: *bravo!*

References

Bion, W. R. (1965) Transformations. Change from Learning to Growth. London: Tavistock.

Civitarese, G. (2004) The symbiotic bond and the setting. In The Intimate Room: Theory and Technique of the Analytic Field. Pp. 22–49. London: Routledge, 2010.

Civitarese, G. (2017a) Sublime Subjects. Aesthetic Experience and Intersubjectivity in Psychoanalysis. London: Routledge.
Civitarese, G. (2017b) Traduire l'expérience: le concept de transformation dans Bion et la théorie post-bionienne du champ analytique. Bulletin de la Société Psychanalytique de Paris, in press.
Ogden, T. H. (2010) On three forms of thinking: Magical thinking, dream thinking, and transformative thinking. Psychoanal. Q., 79(2): 317–347.

CHAPTER ONE

Introduction

To write a book about transformations is a preposterous undertaking, akin to writing about the nature of life on earth. One would begin writing and never finish since the transformations occurring during the process of writing would require additional chapters to address the unanticipated new developments. In a sense, the author would have embarked on a quixotic mission chasing the infinite. This book is about the topic of transformations in psychoanalysis; although this is a considerably narrower focus, anyone who has studied our field soon learns the immensity of scope within the purview of our profession. Indeed, psychoanalysis has always been about transformations, but what do we mean when we say something has undergone a "transformation?" There are many definitions of the word *transformation* and it is a widely used noun with unique meanings depending on the context: various fields of study such as Linguistics, Biology, etc., have highly specific usages. The general definition listed in the Oxford English Dictionary is "a marked change in form, nature or appearance" and, more specifically, "a metamorphosis during the life cycle of an animal." The meaning in Physics is given as "the induced or spontaneous change of one element into another by a nuclear process." Though there is no official definition of "transformation" in psychoanalysis, it seems to me that these three definitions come closest to what an analyst means when he uses this word.

When Freud (1933) stated "where id was, there ego shall be," in essence he described "a marked change in form, nature or appearance." Similarly, when we speak of a child as father to the man we are referencing "a metamorphosis during the life cycle of an animal" and, furthermore, when the analyst experiences a sudden and surprising association to a patient's material we may say he is experiencing an "induced or spontaneous change of one element into another." Bion (1965) was the first to propose a very specific psychoanalytic definition of transformation that is derived from the clinician's observations of the evolution of an emotional experience that arises and then is developed over the course of an individual analytic session. He asks us to be mindful of the metamorphosis of an affect from its unanticipated appearance in the session and through its evolution as the analyst and analysand, by means of their spontaneous associations, "transform" the emotional experience into a narrative. I believe that what is unique to Bion's contribution is his stance toward those associations: he does not search these to uncover the hidden unconscious meanings, but rather his focus is on *the free associations as the transformative process by which meaning is created.*

Recently I was reading a biography of Basho (Reichhold, 2013), the great Japanese poet who originated *haiku,* which the author stated "capture[s] both the momentary and the eternal in a small poem" (p. 9) and it struck me that the same may be said about an individual psychoanalytic session. A single clinical hour is a snapshot of a moment together uniquely shared by a particular analyst with a particular patient, colored by the shadings of affects that enliven the hour, which in turn are generated by the unconscious communications between their respective minds; each psyche populated by the unique demographics of their personal representational worlds (Brown, 1996). Thus, the "snapshot" aspect of the session also opens to experiences that border on the eternal and I believe that we can say the same about an analytic hour that Freud (1900) said about a dream:

> There is often a passage in even the most thoroughly interpreted dream which has to be left obscure; this is because we become aware during the work of interpretation that at that point there is a tangle of dream-thoughts which cannot be unraveled and which moreover adds nothing to our knowledge of the content of the dream. This is the dream's navel, the spot where it reaches down into the unknown.
>
> (p. 525)

But what is the *session's* navel which in Freud's view about a dream may be approached but never fully grasped? Following Bion (1965), it is an unknown emotional experience from which the associations of the patient and analyst emanate; furthermore, each association in itself is a link in the process of *transformation* that occurs within each member of the analytic dyad. That is to say that the analyst and patient are equally affected by the ambient emotion of the session but that each partner transforms it through his own storehouse of personal experiences and internal objects. Bion (1965) distinguishes between the *process of transformation* and a *representation* which is the endpoint of that process. In my view, a free association in the patient or the analyst *is a point in the transformational process that yields a representation of the shared emotional experience alive in the clinical hour at a particular moment.* When the patient and analyst are actively engaged in an analytic encounter, what we call an *analytic process,* their minds are generating mutual associations that aim to represent, and give meaning to, the here-and-now emotional atmosphere. The respective associations of analysand and analyst draw from an undercurrent of projective and introjective processes and activation of areas in each that resonate with the emotional experience being transformed; thereby creating a complex skein, "a tangle of [waking][1] dream-thoughts which cannot be unraveled," but about which the analyst may offer an approximated guess, i.e., an interpretation.

Some foundational assumptions

This book rests on five basic concepts that underpin most or all of the chapters. I will review each of these briefly in the following paragraphs and these concepts will be further developed in the various chapters. In my previous (2011a) book, *Intersubjective Processes and the Unconscious: An Integration of Freudian, Kleinian and Bionian Perspectives,* I related Thomas Friedman's (2005) publication, *The World Is Flat,* which captured the interconnectedness of the world made smaller by globalization and the internet, to intersubjectivity in psychoanalysis. It struck me that Friedman's discussion of the inescapable impact of nations on each other paralleled the realization in analysis of the inevitable psychic interdigitation between analyst and analysand. In his most recent (2016) work, *Thank You for Being Late,* Friedman goes beyond the "flat world" and addresses the sense in Europe and North America that our world is *accelerating rapidly,* leaving many people feeling that it has already spun out of control. A potent combination of ever-advancing technology, financial markets on a hair trigger and the quickening effects of climate change are frighteningly unsettling.

I put "accelerating rapidly" in italics to denote the **first underlying assumption** for this book in order to accentuate *the incredible speed with which the mind transforms emotional experience into meaningful representations*. In my clinical work, I have been increasingly impressed with the alacrity that new associations are created and may appear in a surprising flash of reverie, an unexpected spontaneous interpretation, a quip or joke, the appearance of a long-forgotten memory or a night dream that brings further meaning to something left unfinished in the remains of the day's session. All of this happens unconsciously and presents the analyst with a valuable ally if he or she can train oneself to attend to these experiences which often seem "irrelevant" or mental jetsam. However, in my view these phenomena are the products of our "unconscious psychological work" (Ogden, 2009, 2010), which are produced spontaneously and in a microsecond.

A **second foundational principle** of this book is the notion of *unconscious work* and the speed with which it is achieved. This concept itself links with unconscious phantasy, dream work, alpha function, free association and reverie; processes that do their "work" within the blink of an eye. Theodor Reik (1927, 1934; Chapter 5) was a pioneer in advocating the analyst have his mind receptively open to "surprise," a product of our unconscious work. Later, in the early 1950s, Kleinian analysts inspired by the work of Paula Heimann (1950)[2] promoted the use of countertransference as an "instrument of research" into the *patient's* unconscious.[3] North American analysts, beginning in the 1970s through their studies of enactments (Jacobs, 1986, 1999) and intersubjectivity, highlighted the role of the analyst's unconscious in co-constructing joint narratives, though these approaches did not attend to the detailed and instantaneous unconscious work always at play beneath these more conscious phenomena. I hope that the readers of this volume will come away with an appreciation of the ubiquity of these processes: the nature of unconscious work in the analyst and analysand that gives meaning to emotions operative in the session, the speed with which this occurs and the therapeutic utility of learning to use these phenomena in one's clinical work.

A **third guiding principle** in this book is the concept of *intersubjectivity* and the related perspective of *intersubjective field theory*, both of which comprise a broad area of study that has been written about extensively from various points of view. In my (2011) book on this topic I emphasized the *unconscious processes* that underpinned intersubjective manifestations: unconscious to unconscious communication fostered by mutual projective and introjective identifications between analyst and patient that serve to bring meaning to emotional experiences evoked by their therapeutic encounter. In this present study, I advance these ideas further by expanding on the concept of unconscious work as the spontaneous production of symbols and metaphors that transform and represent the emotions active in the session. Since these occurrences unfold spontaneously in the session, the analyst must train himself to attend to reveries, random thoughts, etc., and learn to use these "messengers" as an instrument of his or her clinical technique. Intersubjective field theory that combines the notion of the unconscious intersubjective connection between the analyst and analysand with a study of the emotional field that arises from that interconnection. The concept of an analytic field denotes the creation of a third psychic presence from the unconscious intersection between the minds of patient and analyst, like a child born to two parents who, though carrying the lineage of each parent, is its own psychic agency that has a subsequent impact upon the parents.

Furthermore, a **fourth fundamental principle** inherent in what I have been saying is the *centrality of affect*. Where classical analysts placed greatest importance on listening for drive derivatives as revealed when reading between the lines of the patient's associations, many contemporary analysts follow the twists and turns of emotional experience in the session.[4] I find focusing on the evoked affects of the session and how these are given meaning by the analyst and patient through their respective transformations of those emotions in the immediacy of the clinical hour to be an *additional* way of approaching the clinical data separate from the classical technique of ferreting meaning from the patient's associations. Bion (1965) stated this difference when he said:

> For a greater part of its [psychoanalysis] history it has been assumed that a psycho-analytic interpretation has as its function the rendering conscious of that which is unconscious . . . [and that] The differentiation I wish to introduce is not between conscious and unconscious, but between finite and infinite.
>
> (p. 46)

Finally, a **fifth guiding premise** is the importance of the process of dreaming, whether awake or asleep. Freud's (1900) comprehensive study of dreams and the process of dreaming addressed night dreams and in many respects this colossal work was the core for much of his later writings. Similarly, Bion (1962b, 1992) formulated the notion that the processes of dreams described by Freud also operated constantly, whether we were awake or asleep, and this theory was a primary kernel from which many of his subsequent contributions developed.

An analytic session

A patient began a session by saying he had seen his old lover on the street and was pleased to no longer experience the deep agony that pained him after their break-up. His mood took a nostalgic turn as he mournfully spoke of her irresistible beauty and sculpted body: even at her age, no longer young, her body is perfection for him. He remembered how peaceful he felt being with her during their good moments. He pinched the tips of his fingers together, brought them to his lips and then quickly pulled them away in an audible kiss as though saluting her magnificence. I think of his recent life-threatening illness and say that her youthful perfection must have felt like it helped to repair his frightening brush with death, like a fountain of youth. He goes on to tell me of her allure, that no one could resist her. Suddenly I find myself in a reverie, thinking of a scene from the movie, *Interview with the Vampire*, in which Christian Slater, a reporter who interviews Brad Pitt's vampire, begs to be turned into a vampire after hearing about the cruel beauty of that world to which he has now been seductively drawn.

I associated my reverie with the analysand's longing and, knowing that he enjoyed the cinema, said that as he was speaking a scene from the film *Interview with the Vampire* came to mind, which I think was my mind's way of depicting something about the pining he felt in the moment, and I shared it with him. He quickly talked about how he enjoys his time alone though he also values and needs intimacy, but the romance with his girlfriend came with a very high price tag. He went on to elaborate his longing and his thoughts then turned to seeing his favorite nephew who was coming to town the next day; he's like a son. However, his thoughts soon returned to his ex-lover and the painful intimacy between them. I thought of the word "sublime," which in Romantic period art was viewed as a mixture of awe, beauty and terror, and said that he was telling me he felt helplessly drawn to the mixture of awesome beauty alongside terror that she evoked in him. My comment elicited many more associations from the patient about the mixture of awe and fear of his former paramour and it was at this point that I felt we had made emotional contact, which I did not especially feel during the earlier part of the session.

The reader will note that this session is presented shorn of history, age of the patient, details about his lover, review of the analytic relationship, which transferences are active, etc., and instead consider it in its raw form. The idea here is for the analyst to start each session, as both Freud (1912) and Bion (1965, 1967b) have suggested, with a clear mind free of any particular agenda in order to achieve a state of mind that is maximally receptive (Brown, 2016a, Chapter 5) to communications from the analysand and/or from within the clinician. I think this may be what Basho was getting at when he wrote:

old pond:
a frog jumps into
the sound of water
(1681–1682)

An "old pond" may be seen as the stilled listening surface of the analyst's mind awaiting a "frog" thought, emanating from within himself or from the patient, to impact that surface; or, perhaps, how repetitive "old pond" material requires the emergence of something new, a "splash" or unexpected shock to animate a stagnant surface.[5] I experienced such a surprise when the *Interview with the Vampire* reverie crossed my mind: until that point much of what the patient had to say was dynamically accurate, reflecting important insights gained during the analysis, but now deployed repetitively as an infertile "old pond." Why did this particular reverie spring to mind at this moment or, put another way, what emotions were being transformed by this reverie? It is unusual for me to reference vampires since they carry little interest to me: there are many other films I might have unconsciously employed instead, such as *Black Widow* about a woman in serial marriages to wealthy husbands who "mysteriously" die.

On reflection, my unconscious could not have come up with a more accurate representation of what the patient and I had been lulled into ignoring by his paeans to his former lover. The analysand began the session announcing that he was pleased to have seen his ex-girlfriend and was not overly upset; however, his longing for, and idealization of, her body upended his calm. I found his pining for her both charming and sad: after his initial comment about feeling free of her, he was drawn back into the familiar orbit of worshipping her beauty. Feeling somewhat frustrated, I tried to cajole him out of this ensorcelled state by interpreting its defensive purpose – that he immersed himself in this blissful state, a "fountain of youth," to defend against his recent serious illness. (I might have been more empathic instead and tuned into his longing, but it felt familiarly repetitive and so I turned to the defense interpretation.) Suddenly the *Interview with the Vampire* reverie floated into my mind and I thought it was my unconscious transformation of his longing and the toll it took on his present life, so I shared the scene of Christian Slater begging to be made a vampire. My patient instantly replied that that intimacy "came with a very high price tag," which introduced a new element, i.e., the emotional cost of his continued immersion in his idealizing phantasy.

I suspect that the phrase, "came with a high price tag," registered unconsciously with me and initiated a transformational process that eventuated in the word "sublime" coming to mind. At that time, I was working on Chapter 7 in this book on the sublime in J. M. W. Turner's paintings, a theme in much Romantic period art that captures the amalgam of terror and beauty in nature. Thus, the analysand's phrase, "high price tag," was like a day residue that instigated my unconscious work to produce the word "sublime" as a reverie. I then offered an interpretation that underscored his being captivated by her dangerous beauty, which had the very positive effect of the patient recognizing and intensely feeling his profound fear of the woman that he also held in awe. In retrospect, it seems that the emotional navel of this session had to do with the analysand's deep longing for, and terrible fear of, his girlfriend that was kept forcibly at bay by the idealization of his lover. Slowly this realization first came to my mind in the *Interview with the Vampire* reverie that introduced the notion of longing and my interpretation addressed his desire for some irresistibly macabre beauty. However, his mention of the "high price tag" of being with her initiated a transformational process in me that created the word "sublime," which referred to her beauty *but also introduced his profound fear of his girlfriend*. My "unconscious psychological work" (Ogden, 2009, 2010) gave representation to the fear component of the analysand's experience and furthered the process of transformation from my first interpretation that emphasized his longing; thus deepening our shared appreciation of the emotions that seemed to be at the heart of this session.

A proposed model of the psychoanalytic process

In his last paper, James Grotstein (2014) spoke of the ancient Greek concept of *flux*, which holds that the only thing that is constant is change and that the change itself may be imperceptible. As Heraclitus, a leader of that school of thought, famously said, "No man ever steps in the same river twice, for it's not the same river and he's not the same man." The same may be said about psychoanalysis – ever evolving as a body of knowledge and clinical practice – and so too the clinical hour. It is in this spirit that I suggest the following model of the psychoanalytic process that develops between the analyst and patient as an overarching theory for this book; that analytic treatment involves

> *the active here-and-now process of continuous transformations of affects arising in the intersubjective field to create new meaning, which is achieved through a perpetual, unconscious, joint process of dreaming and* Nachträglichkeit (après-coup), *made possible through the linked alpha functions of patient and analyst – all of which is enabled by, and depends upon, a stable analytic setting/frame.*

I realize this is quite a mouthful of psychoanalytic theory, dense and tightly woven, and one of my aims in this book is to unpack this assertion in the book's chapters. But first, how are these factors evidenced in the clinical vignette above?

"The active here-and-now process of continuous transformations of affects arising in the intersubjective field to create new meaning . . ." This material from the clinical hour focuses exclusively on what is happening in the immediacy of the encounter between my patient and me and my emphasis is on the unconscious dimensions of this engagement. Addressing what is occurring in the moment is not a new perspective and has been central to clinical practice in most analytic approaches. Even classical analysts who emphasize an infantile neurosis as the source of the transference, find that the repetition of the transference neurosis makes its appearance as "not an event of the past, but as a present day force" (Freud, 1914, p. 151). Klein and her followers have underscored the value of interpreting in the here-and-now (Steiner, 2017) and making linkages to the past (Spillius, 2007), but also offer a model of transference that is based upon the externalization of the analysand's internal world into the therapeutic relationship that configures the transference and countertransference active in the present. Technical innovations by contemporary Ego Psychologists (Busch, 2011; Gray, 1996), what they term *close process monitoring*, focus on showing the workings of defensive maneuvers to patients as these arise in the session. Betty Joseph (1985), too, has aptly demonstrated her skill in "showing" the patient how his or her pathology is being played out at a particular point in the clinical hour.

I am suggesting another component to working in the here-and-now which views the therapeutic couple as engaged in actively transforming emotional experience that is unknown (unconscious) to both of them because the affects are repressed and/or unrepresented. The patient began the session by speaking mournfully about his former lover, but this was familiar territory as he saluted her beauty. I felt there were affects that this repetitive talk kept at bay, thus I consciously searched my memory to connect his thoughts with something more "significant" and suggested that fantasies about her on this day were like a "fountain of youth" that served to quell his recent serious health scare. While this interpretation was surely correct on a dynamic level, it did not reach him emotionally. In contrast to my deliberative effort in crafting the fountain of youth interpretation, the *Interview with the Vampire* reverie appeared unbidden and signaled that my unconscious was at work to represent the *affect of longing* (Christian Slater longing to be turned into a vampire). Later in the session, cued by the patient's saying that the romance came with "very high price tag," a one word reverie, "sublime," came to mind, which broadened the unconscious terrain in which my analysand and I were traveling. It was through this ping-ponging of unconscious communications that the patient and I progressively transformed the previously unknown emotions permeating the session into an understanding that he struggled with longing for his former girlfriend *and* his terror of her.

"*. . . which is achieved through a perpetual, unconscious, joint process of dreaming and Nachträglichkeit (après-coup). . .*" However, it was Ogden's (2004a, 2005) and Ferro's (2002b) emphasis on the relevance of Bion's theory of dreaming/reverie formation to generating these elements of the field that moved our understanding forward of how these "thirdness-es" arose between analyst and analysand. Ferro, more than other authors, applied Bion's (1965) *theory of transformations* to help the clinician appreciate the moment-to-moment shifts of how emotional experience in the session was actively and unconsciously being worked on to create reveries, i.e., waking dream thoughts. Finally, in this very brief review, both Cassorla (2005, 2008) and I (Brown, 2011a, 2015b) have carefully explored the process of mutual dreaming in the analyst and patient by which the shared unconscious phantasy of the couple (analytic third) is formed and then subsequently transformed within the analytic field. This process of shared and interactive dreaming in the formation of representations *in statu nascendi* in the session is a central background concept for this book. In my opinion, Freud's concept of *Nachtraglichkeit* is a special type of dreaming by which a (usually) past traumatic experience lays fallow – split off or dissociated – in the mind and awaits a mind capable of dreaming to give it representation.[6]

We can see this constant process of mutual dreaming at work in the session above: when my patient talked about his near helplessness in the presence of his paramour's allure and how my unconscious represented that emotion with the *Interview with the Vampire* reverie which I shared with him as a sort of interpretive comment. His response was to think about the "high price tag" emotional cost of being with his girlfriend which brought the concept of the "sublime" to my mind and my conscious association to beauty *and* terror. I was able to dream/represent an experience which had remained unknown to both of us; that he was truly terrified of this woman and it was through a mutual unconscious process that the recognition of his terror was achieved.

Until the word "sublime" spontaneously came to me, the emotional depth and strength of his fear had not been sufficiently appreciated. This process is yet another bedrock concept in this book.

"*. . . made possible through the linked alpha functions of patient and analyst . . .*" The concept of mutual dreaming by the analyst and patient depends upon the rapid mutual unconscious communications between their linked alpha functions. In another publication, I (Brown, 2012; Chapter 2) refer to alpha function as the "engine of transformations" and in an optimally functioning analytic process the analyst and analysand dream/transform the ambient emotions of the intersubjective field; what Cassorla (2008) terms "dreams for two." The subject of dreaming is discussed more extensively as follows.

"*. . . all of which is enabled by, and depends upon, a stable analytic setting/frame.*" The analytic setting has been discussed by many analysts from Freud to Klein to Winnicott, Bleger and Andre Green, just to name a few contributors. The setting (or frame) refers to the physical aspects of one's office and other practical qualities such as fees, appointment times, vacations and other absences, etc. But beginning with Winnicott (1955) we have focused on the deep unconscious significance the analytic frame carries for both the analyst and analysand. Bleger (1967/2013; Chapter 6), in particular, has addressed the ways in which the stable frame holds in abeyance the more primitive anxieties that the analytic couple are not ready to face and that disruptions to that setting/frame can "release" these disorganizing anxieties. Thus, an unstable or destabilized setting may lead to a sudden influx of primitive emotions that threaten to overrun the analytic process.

Transformations and dreaming

I have been describing a process by which unnamed (repressed or unrepresented) emotional experience is gradually transformed from a purely affective state to one that is conceptual in nature and how this transformation is achieved through a complex *intersubjective* operation. In my (2011a) previous book, *Intersubjective Processes and the Unconscious: An Integration of Freudian, Kleinian and Bionian Perspectives,* I offered a theory of intersubjectivity that emphasized its unconscious aspects. Briefly put, I built on Freud's (1912) famous metaphor of the telephone as a model for unconscious communication and suggested that Freud's (1894) notion of projection elaborated by Klein's (1946) concept of projective identification, Bion's (1959) proposal of *communicative* projective identification together with Ferenczi's (1909) contribution of introjection, could account for how one unconscious communicated with another (Freud, 1915a). Further, I asserted that Bion's theory of alpha function could explain how unconscious experiences in the analyst or patient were both encoded and decoded by the sending and receiving unconscious.

In addition, this transformational process is akin to, and enabled by, Bion's (1962b, 1992) elaboration of Freud's (1900) theory of dreaming. Freud introduced the term *dream-work* to describe how the unconscious wish, pressuring for expression in consciousness yet barred by the *censor,* was disguised in order to allow a partial expression in consciousness. It was dream-work which offered a *representation* of the censored wish by creating a symbol[7] that could later be decoded to reach the unconscious wish contained within it. Bion did not take issue with Freud's dream theory but instead expanded upon it by broadening Freud's dream-work to include the notion that we are always dreaming, while awake and asleep (this is discussed in much greater depth in Chapter 2). Bion's elaboration of dream-work evolved to his promulgating *alpha function* as the structure responsible for representing raw emotional experience as "thinkable thoughts" that were suitable for unconscious communication. Reveries, in this model, are the transformational products of the unprocessed affective experience in the here-and-now of the clinical hour and are living phenomena born from the communicating alpha functions of the analyst and patient actively engaged in unconsciously giving representation to their shared emotional experience.

This book is divided into 12 chapters (including this Introduction) in which the concepts described earlier are further elaborated and discussed in greater detail from a variety of different perspectives. I am aware that to explore the topics outlined in this Introduction would require several volumes since the collective chapters touch on much of the body of psychoanalytic thinking and practice; however, my focus is on the various processes of transformation that are addressed in the individual chapters.

Most chapters include extensive clinical material to illustrate the theoretical points and ground the concepts in clinical practice. Chapter 2, "Transformational aspects of countertransference," traces the concept of countertransference from Freud's writings through the present and follows the transformation of this concept over nearly 100 years of psychoanalytic thinking. The discussion begins with Freud's early observations about "countertransference" and follows how subsequent generations of analysts viewed and clinically applied the analyst's emotional responses. This overview concludes with a discussion of concepts of intersubjectivity, field theory and other contemporary theories. This chapter also sets the stage for subsequent chapters that deepen our understanding of the emotional engagement between analyst and patient.

Chapter 3, "Bion's discovery of alpha function: The engine of transformations," examines the development of alpha function, which I consider among Bion's most important contributions. I explore how Bion's "discovery" resulted from the intersection of several tributaries in his life: his war experiences in World War I, his expansion of Freud's theory of dreaming, clinical work with psychotic patients and his marriage to Francesca Bion. Chapter 4, "Bion's *Transformations* and clinical practice," is a close reading of his third major book that focuses on the clinical implications of this difficult work. Interestingly, he hardly mentions his two previous books, *Learning from Experience* and *Elements of Psychoanalysis*, in *Transformations*; Chapter 3, therefore, is necessary and foundational for fully understanding Chapter 4.

Chapter 5, "The analyst's receptivity: Evolution of the concept and its clinical application," is a somewhat whimsical exploration of the analyst's receptivity, a central clinical concept that has not received much attention in the literature. I present a clinical vignette which I bring to three imagined "supervisions" with Freud, Theodor Reik and Bion to illustrate their clinical views on this subject, highlighting the evolution of the concept of the analyst's receptivity across the years as revealed in their consultations with me. Chapter 6, "Ruptures in the analytic setting and disturbances in the transformational field of dreams," investigates Bleger's (1967/2013) classic paper on the subject of the analytic setting and discusses current views on this subject. I also discuss the analysis of the patient in Chapter 5 ("analyst's receptivity") through the lens of attacks on the analytic setting. Additional clinical material is given regarding the analysand's propensity to disrupt the analytic setting by abruptly ending the analysis. Thus, Chapters 5 and 6 together offer a "binocular view" of different aspects of the analytic process with the same analysand.

Chapter 7, "The unbearable glare of living: The Sublime, Bion's theory of 'O' and J. M. W. Turner, 'Painter of Light'," is a short biographical study of the British landscape painter J. M. W. Turner, through the lens of Bion's theory of "O," which is the ineffable origin of that which is transformed. In addition to the usual attention to the subject's family, etc., I also suggest that a motive in many of his paintings seemed to be an attempt to explore the essence of light itself, which held great meaning in his personal life and his work. In Chapter 8, "Three unconscious pathways to representing the analyst's experience: Reverie, countertransference dreams and joke-work," I explore three means of representing the unconscious experience of the analyst in the clinical hour and propose a common process by which each of these transformations is created. Extensive clinical material from the analysis of a man is given to illustrate the spontaneous appearance of a reverie, countertransference dream and a joke in my mind and how these phenomena were used technically to foster the treatment.

Chapters 9, "From ashes to ashes: The heroic struggle of an autistic boy trying to be born and stay alive," and 10, "The capacity to tell a joke: Reflections from work with Asperger's children," explore the concept of "autistic transformations" in analytic work with Autistic Spectrum Disorders. These transformations are characterized by a flattening out of emotional experience, a sense of a black hole where a self ought to be and a relative absence of understanding metaphor, including a blunted or absent sense of humor. Both chapters are anchored by extensive clinical material to illustrate autistic transformations and in Chapter 10 I describe my young patient's growing ability to comprehend and tell a joke as a pathway to greater cognitive and interpersonal flexibility. In Chapter 11, "'Notes on memory and desire': Implications for working through," I raise the question of how can we understand the process of working through if we practice analysis with an emphasis on the here-and-now and "without memory and desire." This approach seems at odds with the usual analytic perspective of the slow, step-by-step working through. Clinical material from the long analysis of a young man from latency into late adolescence is offered to illustrate changes that occur on the immediate and more long-range levels. In the final Chapter, "Conclusion: On Freud's "the question of a *Weltanschauung*" – a world of perpetual transformation?", some of the main themes of the book are reviewed in the light of the question "whether the ideas and concepts adumbrated here, as well as their clinical applications, suggest a new *Weltanschauung* for psychoanalysis; a world view that emphasizes constant change, evolution and growth."

Notes

1 I inserted "waking" in reference to Bion's (1962b) notion of "waking dream thought," also known as "reverie."
2 Her first analyst was Theodor Reik.
3 Heinrich Racker (1951) simultaneously in Buenos Aires advocated much the same stance, though Heimann's and his work were unknown to each other.
4 Contemporary French (Green, LaPlanche, Miller, etc.) analysts have proposed a "return to Freud" and have reinterpreted drive theory in creative directions; however, these developments are being the scope of this book.
5 I assume that the reader may also have his or her own interpretations of Basho's haiku.
6 This mind capable of dreaming may be another person or, perhaps, a part of the patient's mind in which the capacity for dreaming has not yet matured. This may be the case with Freud's (1918) "Wolfman" who experienced a trauma at 18 months that exceeded his representational capacity, but which he was able to literally dream at four and a half years old; ostensibly because his ego capacities had further developed.
7 A process also referred to as *figurability* by many authors, e.g., Green (1999), Botella and Botella (2005).

CHAPTER TWO

From countertransference to *Transformations*[1]

> No one who, like me, conjures up the most evil of those half-tamed demons that inhabit the human breast and seeks to wrestle with them, can expect to come through the struggle unscathed.
>
> (Freud, 1905a, p. 109)

In this chapter, we follow the development of the concept of countertransference from initially being seen as a hindrance to psychoanalytic progress to its current use as an important tool in clinical practice. I cover a wide swath of theories on this subject from American, British, South American and Italian authors with an eye on how each has been a step in the evolution toward an appreciation of transformational processes in contemporary psychoanalysis. Although there is no clinical illustration in this chapter, I discuss a 1909 letter from Karl Abraham to Freud in which he reveals an interesting "symptomatic reaction" in his practice, which I "analyze" from the various perspectives on countertransference.

There has been an awareness from the earliest days of psychoanalysis that the analyst is deeply, sometimes disturbingly, affected by engagement with the patient's unconscious experience. Freud (1910) coined the term *counter-transference* to refer to the therapist's *unconscious* reaction to the analysand's transference and noted that handling one's emotions toward the patient presented the analyst with a significant challenge. It was recommended that the clinician use the countertransference as a stimulus to his self-analysis so that one's capacity to listen to the patient's concerns could proceed without interference from the analyst's private reactions. In this chapter, we will review the development of the concept of countertransference from its initially being seen as a hindrance to later perspectives that view it as a means by which to better understand the patient, which thereby goes on to enhance the therapeutic process.

In a letter to Freud, dated April 7, 1909, Abraham referred to taking on two new patients and remarked that with each new treatment his understanding of analysis increased. He also observed that

> I have tracked down a symptomatic reaction in myself. While I am analyzing and am waiting for the patient's reply, I often cast a quick glance at the picture of my parents. I know that I always do this when I am following up the infantile transference in the patient. The glance is always accompanied by a particular guilt feeling: what will they think of me? This has of course to do with my separation from them, which was not too easy. Since explaining this symptomatic action to myself, I have not caught myself at it any more.
>
> (p. 88)

Abraham's next thoughts are of his two-year-old daughter to whom he gave enemas recently and on each following day she expressed hope there would not be another. However, he noted that the plea was offered "with a rather arch smile. So obviously she wants to get the injection. Apart from this, she does not show any analerotic tendencies" (p. 88).

There is a sense of Abraham's prideful accomplishment in this note to his good friend in having "tracked down a symptomatic reaction in myself" and not having "caught myself at it any more." This has been achieved through the analyst's observation of his reaction to the patient's infantile transference; a reaction he has had with other patients that is considered to be a distraction from his task of listening carefully to the analysand's associations. Abraham then engages in a piece of self-analysis: he realizes his guilt is connected to his "not too easy" separation from his parents and this insight has subsequently freed him from similar diversions. In essence, he has succeeded in three ways: first, by recognizing his distracting personal reaction stirred by the patient's "infantile transference"; second, by engaging in self-analysis to remove this "symptomatic reaction"; and, finally, to return his attention to the analysand's narrative.

This brief vignette is a veritable goldmine that contains within it the multitude of potential meanings that will be given to the term *countertransference* from its inception as an inevitable, albeit distracting, factor in analysis to contemporary perspectives that consider it an essential ingredient of the psychoanalytic process. For Abraham and his cohort, emotions evoked in the analyst were expectable (e.g., the quotes from Freud and Bion) and served to foster his own self-reflections from which his personal growth as analyst and individual developed. It was, therefore, very clear from the earliest days of psychoanalysis that powerful, even deeply disturbing, emotions were a common side-effect of this work and it was unrealistic to "expect to come through the struggle unscathed."

If we scratch the surface of Abraham's communication with Freud there are many other layers of meaning that await our discovery and raise important questions about the analyst's subjective reactions. Why, for example, does Abraham look at the picture of his parents and feel guilt precisely during the interim between interpreting and the patient's response? Is there some sort of unconscious need for approval, and worry of making an error, that is being evoked in this analyst by this particular patient at this single moment in the analytic work? Abraham does not feel this guilt with every analysand: does his contriteness surface with all facets of the patient's infantile neurosis or with certain themes? Does the analysand "sense," unconsciously or not, the analyst's anxious anticipation of the patient's reply and, if so, might he/she withhold associations to the interpretation? Is there some ambient, though unarticulated, emotion permeating the session that has to do with being a "good" boy, analyst or patient that is expressed in various ways, such as Abraham's report to Freud that he is a dutiful analyst or his glancing over to the picture of his parents? Finally, what are we to make of Abraham's thoughts turning next to his constipated daughter and her ambivalence about the enemas? Is this an "association" that is relevant to his "symptomatic reaction" and to the analysis?

Thus, much of the "raw material" from which additional definitions of countertransference have been crafted is implicit in the letter from Abraham to Freud and it has been left to subsequent generations to expand upon. I will begin with a discussion of Freud's views of countertransference, which were often seemingly at odds with each other, and the perspectives of the early analysts; moving from there to later contributions in order to highlight the development of our understanding of the analyst's subjective reactions and how these are employed in the analytic encounter.

Freud and the early analysts on countertransference (pre-1940)

The question of the countertransference and how it should be handled was initially discussed informally as in Abraham's (1909) letter and appears for the first time in Freud's (1910)[2] publications when he stated that such feelings arise in the analyst

> as a result of the *patient's influence on his unconscious feelings*. . . [and that the analyst should] recognize this counter-transference in himself and overcome it
>
> (p. 144) [italics added]

and that

> no psychoanalyst goes further than his own complexes and internal resistances permit.
>
> (ibid, p. 145)

These brief quotes are very significant in that they state that (1) the countertransference results from the impact of the patient's difficulties *upon the analyst's unconscious*; (2) since such emotions in the analyst are unconscious, he must strive to become aware of his reaction "and overcome it"; and (3) that the progress of an analysis also depends upon the analyst being aware of his "complexes and internal resistances." Thus, Freud is describing psychoanalysis as an intense interpersonal process in which encounters with the patient's unconscious deeply impact the unconscious of the analyst, an effect that the clinician must overcome. Failure to do so may impede the course of the patient's analysis and, furthermore, it is implied that the personal growth of the analyst may be hindered.

The growing realization that countertransference was an inevitable, and sometimes destructive, phenomenon led to the requirement that all analysts have a personal analysis as part of their education. This became one of the three pillars of training, in addition to seminars and seeing analysands under supervision, that was introduced by Max Eitington (the "Eitington Model" of training) when he founded the Berlin Psychoanalytic Polyclinic in 1920. Indeed, as Balint (1954) observed, Eitington may have received the first "training analysis" as described in a letter from Freud (22 October, 1909) to Ferenczi, "Eitington is here. Twice weekly, after dinner, he comes with me for a walk and has his analysis during it." These strolls must have had a very positive effect that stayed with Eitington and contributed to his instituting the necessity of a training analysis.

However, Freud also offered other views that suggested countertransference feelings could be of benefit in an analysis. The vignette from Abraham's letter points to how the therapist's subjective reactions may be a stimulus to self-analytic work and personal growth in the analyst. In addition, Freud (1912) also recommended that the analyst "use his unconscious . . . as an instrument of the analysis" (p. 116), though he did not instruct us as to how this is achieved. In the same paper, he proposed that the free associations of the patient and the "evenly suspended attention" of the analyst are linked phenomena; however, Freud and his contemporaries only explored the impact of the analysand's unconscious upon that of the clinician, leaving aside the effect of the analyst's unconscious upon the patient. In connecting the subjective emotions of the analyst and patient, Freud may have been suggesting that the therapist can use his unconscious "as an instrument of the analysis" by paying attention to his countertransference feelings.

These early analysts also examined how successful work on the countertransference was necessary for unlocking the analysand's life-constricting conflicts. If Abraham had not become aware of his "symptomatic reaction" that was stirred by his patient's infantile neurosis and had instead blocked recognition, then this denial could have thwarted the analytic progress. Freud (1910) noticed this tendency when he wrote that unrealized "internal resistances" in the analyst can limit his emotional freedom, thereby tying the analysand's emotional development to the clinician's capacity to manage one's countertransference. Some years later, Theodore Reik (1924) expanded on this point by introducing the notion of *counterresistance* that is a subtype of countertransference in response to an obdurate resistance in the patient characterized by "a decrease of interest in the case or even a change in the mode of treatment" (p. 150). Glover (1927) subsequently added that a counterresistance was an expression of the analyst's *negative* countertransference, that is, his aggression towards the patient.

Freud is often faulted for having advocated that the analyst should remain opaque and manifest the surgeon's dispassionate attitude of "emotional coldness" (Freud, 1912, p. 115). However, it is important to note that these first psychoanalysts struggled with the heat generated by the transference-countertransference matrix and I suspect that the goal of "emotional coldness" was likely a fantasied state aimed at cooling down the necessary, but searing emotions of the analytic consulting room. Freud (1913a) seemed to be saying as much in a letter to Binswanger when he stated that the problem of countertransference was "among the most intricate in psycho-analysis" (20 February, p. 112) and that the analyst must display to the patient "spontaneous affect, but measured out consciously at times" (p. 112). He implies that some patients may require more of this than others, "but never from one's own unconscious" (p. 112). Thus, Freud appears most concerned about the heat of the analyst's unconscious affecting the analysis negatively; hence, his advocacy of "emotional coldness" is meant to help the clinician keep his "cool" rather than to promote an air of aloofness.

Before leaving this section, there is a statement by Freud (1912)[3] that deserves our attention: it is as contemporary as any offered by current writers and lays the groundwork for the contributions of many recent analysts:

> he [the analyst] must turn his own unconscious like a receptive organ towards the transmitting unconscious of the patient . . . so the doctor's unconscious is able, from the derivatives of the unconscious which are communicated to him, to reconstruct that unconscious, which has determined the patient's free associations.
>
> (Freud, 1912, pp. 115–116)

Though Freud does not elaborate on this observation, he is offering a model of unconscious communication as an additional perspective from which to understand countertransference. Implicit in this vertex is the notion that the patient's unconscious *actively* conveys a communication for the "doctor's unconscious" that functions like a "*receptive organ*" to receive and then "reconstruct that [communicating] unconscious." Perhaps Freud had in mind Ferenczi's (7 February, 1911) letter a year earlier in which he suggested that the countertransference was "being induced" (p. 253) by the patients, thus implying a purposeful function to this emotional induction?

Freud (1923) introduced the *structural theory* (id, ego, superego) that subsumed the previous *topographical theory* (conscious, preconscious and unconscious) and also outlined a new *theory of anxiety* (Freud, 1926) that placed great importance on the role of defense mechanisms in the ego's armamentarium for managing anxiety. This important evolution in psychoanalytic theory also signaled a shift in emphasis away from the study of *unconscious [id] fantasy contents* toward the workings of the *unconscious ego* in defense. Consequently, the exploration of countertransference, which was defined as the unconscious reaction to the analysand's unconscious expressions, faded and tended to be seen as "unscientific" (Lothane, 2006) as compared to the examination of the ego's functioning that could be more easily observed. Ego psychology subsequently became the predominant theoretical orientation in the United States and was galvanized by the influx of orthodox Freudian analysts from the European diaspora of World War II. However, ego psychology did not achieve the prominence in Europe, and especially South America, that it was accorded in institutes under the aegis of the American Psychoanalytic Association (Brown, 2009a, 2011a). Consequently, most American analysts were trained to adhere to Freud's (1910) admonition to "recognize this countertransference and overcome it" (p. 253) even though he (Freud, 1912) had hinted at the relevance of countertransference for understanding the patient's unconscious communications.

Use of the countertransference as "an instrument of the analysis" (1940–1960)

There was a significant shift in the understanding of countertransference during this period: from viewing it as an encumbrance to treatment that must be overcome to seeing countertransference as an essential "instrument of the analysis." The 1930s ended with Alice and Michael Balint's (1939) paper that debunked the notion there could be a "sterile" manner of analyzing free from effects of the analyst's personality; indeed, they argued that there was an interaction between the transference and countertransference "complicated by the reactions released in each by the other's transference onto him" (p. 228). They also observed that patients adapt to the analyst's countertransference and go on in analysis to "proceed to their own transference" (p. 228). In addition to normalizing the presence of countertransference feelings, the Balints also brought for our consideration the effect of the analyst's subjective experiences on the analysand; however, their view was that the patient worked around the countertransference and they did not discuss in detail its effect on the analysand's transference. Robert Fliess' 1942 paper, "The Metapsychology of the Analyst," examined in great detail the nature of the analyst's *work ego* that depended upon a capacity for *trial identification,* which required the analyst "to step into his [patient's] shoes and obtain in this way an inside knowledge that is almost first hand" (p. 212). It was through this process that the analyst could use his countertransference as an instrument of the analysis by obtaining a "taste" of the analysand's struggles through a transient identification in which "he becomes the subject himself" (p. 215). Now armed with the "firsthand" knowledge, the clinician may make a more accurate interpretation to the analysand; however, Fleiss cautioned the analyst take care "to guarantee that no instinctual additions of our own distort the picture" (p. 219), a view that appears to partially espouse the outlook that the countertransference is something to be "cleansed." Nevertheless, Fleiss' perspective represents a significant departure from the first analysts who considered the countertransference as a distraction to listening to the patient, albeit a potentially helpful one to the analyst in his self-analysis.

Though Fliess does not use the term "analyzing instrument," he is essentially offering us an insider's look at the process occurring in the analyst's mind. Thus, by introducing trial identification, the work ego, and other concepts into our lexicon, contributions that Schafer (2007) states "helps launch psychoanalysis towards its contemporary form" (p. 698), Fliess expanded the range of conceptual tools to apply to our understanding of how one uses the countertransference. As discussed, beginning in the 1930s there was a divide between the ego psychologists' attempts to develop techniques that sought to "cleanse" a patient's material from being alloyed with countertransference, while another group (Balints, Fliess) viewed countertransference as a pathway to the analyst's empathic understanding. In my opinion, we can see in Fliess the tension between these two perspectives: his open advocacy of the relevance of the analyst's subjective experience on the one hand and, on the other, his wish to be "able to guarantee that no instinctual additions of our own distort the picture." Jacobs (2007) comments:

> One suspects that issues of loyalty to Freud, as well as fears of Ferenczi's influence and of wild, undisciplined behavior on the part of colleagues, influenced Fliess and others who held this idealized and sanitized view of the analyst's functioning.
>
> (p. 717)

The Kleinian School and projective identification

Melanie Klein (1946) introduced the term *projective identification* to describe how the attribution (by projection) of aspects of the self to the internal image of an object (in the projecting subject's inner world) changes the inner experience of that object. The internal object thereby becomes *identified* with what has been projected into it and the patient's behavior toward the actual external object is governed by his inner experience of that object. In more disturbed patients, such as psychotic and severe borderline individuals, the distinction between inner and outer reality may be erased; while the neurotic patient is capable of understanding his distortions that create the feeling, for example, of "it's *as if* you are my father." Klein's followers saw in projective identification a way of explaining countertransference: that the analyst's subjective reactions, in addition to his transference to the analysand's transference (the classical explanation), may have been created by projective identification. In this regard, countertransference could be partly explained by the patient's unconscious placement of painful emotions into[4] the therapist; thus, not only does the patient's subjective experience of the clinician change, but *the analyst is emotionally affected by what is projected.*

However, though Klein acknowledged it was sometimes difficult for the analyst to be the recipient of such projective identifications (Spillius, 2007) because of his associated inner objects stirred by the projection, like Freud she stressed that the countertransference was to be dealt with by the analyst in one's self-analysis. Despite the fact that many of her devotees regarded countertransference, induced by the patient's projective identification, as a useful tool of analytic work, she remained skeptical of its relevance as a guide to emotionally understanding he analysand. She held this position firmly to the end of her career: witness her comments to a group of young analysts in 1958 (quoted in Spillius, 2007):

> I have never found that the countertransference has helped me to understand my patient better. If I may put it like this, I have found that it helped me to understand myself better.
>
> (p. 78)

Paula Heimann (1950) was the first of Klein's followers to apply the concept of projective identification to the study of countertransference and asserted that it "is an instrument of research into the patient's unconscious" (p. 81) and also that it is "the patient's creation, it is part of the patient's personality" (p. 83). Thus, she linked Freud's (1912) recommendation that the analyst use his unconscious "as an instrument of the analysis" to Klein's projective identification, seeing the latter as the means by which the patient's unconscious communicates with that of the therapist. By asserting that the countertransference is a *creation* of the patient, Heimann effectively explained the mechanism by which the countertransference is *induced* (see Ferenczi's and the Balints' earlier comments) as well as how the analyst *becomes* a part of the patient (Fleiss). Perhaps Brenman Pick (1985) said it best when she noted that

> The child's or patient's projective identifications are actions in part intended to produce [emotional] reactions.
>
> (p. 157)

Roger Money-Kyrle (1956) advanced Heimann's ideas and elaborated them further. Like others before him, he observed that there are inevitable periods when the analyst fails to understand the analysand, which occur when an aspect of the patient disturbingly coincides with an unanalyzed portion of the analyst's psyche. Money-Kyrle added an original element to this situation by stating that one task of the analyst is to interpret the effect of the countertransference on the patient; however, it is important to note that *he did not favor disclosing one's feelings directly to the patient*. Instead, he suggests that the analyst deal with the patient's comments about his mood, whether accurately perceived or not, by interpreting it as psychic reality that has personal meaning to the analysand. Money-Kyrle's perspective, therefore, squarely places the emphasis on the unconscious meanings both the analyst and patient attribute to their interaction. He argues that while acknowledging the analyst's conscious feelings toward the patient may "confirm" the accuracy of the patient's perceptions, it does little to address the unconscious meaning the patient has attached to the perception (accurate or not) of the analyst. Betty Joseph (1975/1989) summed up this stance when she stated that

> It is important to show, primarily, the use the patient has made of what he believes to be going on in the analyst's mind.
>
> (p. 80)

Simultaneous with these applications of projective identification by Heimann and Money-Kyrle in London, analysts in Argentina and Uruguay were exploring similar territory. The cultural ambience of the Argentine Psychoanalytic Association (APA), which was formed in 1942, was one that combined psychoanalysis (with a primary Kleinian orientation) with input from Kurt Lewin's "field theory," studies of dream-like states, and probes into the nature of psychosomatic states (de Leon de Bernardi, 2008). Heinrich Racker was one of the leading figures in the early days of the Argentine Society and, like Heimann, believed that the capacity to identify with the patient is the "basis of comprehension" (Racker, 1953/1968, p. 134) of the analysand. His investigation of the role of identifications in countertransference was considerably more detailed than contribution on the subject from any previous authors.

Racker (1968) delineated what he termed *concordant* and *complementary identifications* that comprise important elements of the countertransference. Concordant identifications denote the analyst's introjection of an aspect of the patient's self ("sent" by projective identification), in which case the analyst unconsciously feels "this part of me is you" (pp. 134–135).

In contrast, a complementary identification signals that the analyst has identified with an internal object of the patient. Racker, more stridently than Money-Kyrle and Joseph, asserts that the analysand is attuned to the countertransference and that the patient's awareness of the fantasied and real countertransference is a determinant of the transference. Thus,

> Analysis of the patient's fantasies about countertransference, which in the widest sense constitute the causes and consequences of the transferences, is an essential part of the analysis of the transferences.
>
> (p. 131)

However, the clinician must be attuned to the possible development of a *countertransference neurosis* in which the patient, in the analyst's unconscious, is equated with a disavowed part of the analyst. In such a situation, for example, the analysand may become identified with the therapist's projected aggression and, now experiencing the patient as embodying hostility, there may be a misrecognition by the analyst that guides his interventions.

We can see how Racker has deepened our understanding of variations in the countertransference that assists the therapist in using one's feelings toward the patient as "an instrument of the analysis." It is an important differentiation for the analyst to be able to discern countertransference feelings resulting from an identification with a disowned segment of the patient's self (concordant) or whether from an identification with a figure from the analysand's inner world (complementary). Leon Grinberg, a colleague of Racker, coined the term *projective counteridentification* to describe the impact of the analysand's violent projective identifications upon the analyst's subjectivity. As we have seen, it is essential that the analyst *become* through a temporary identification what the patient is projecting; however, there are certain situations when the analyst "ceases to be himself and turns unavoidably into what the patient unconsciously wants him to be" (1990, p. 84). He contrasts the concept of projective counteridentification with Racker's idea of the complementary countertransference. When the analyst is under the impact of a complementary countertransference his identification with the projected internal object of the patient stirs a personal reaction, based upon the analyst's idiosyncratic conflicts similar to that which is projected. By contrast, with projective counteridentification

> the same patient, using his projective identification in a particularly intense and specific way, could evoke the *same countertransferential response* (projective counteridentification) in different analysts.
>
> [author's italics] (Grinberg, 1990, p. 90)

Wilfred Bion and communicative aspects of projective identification

Wilfred Bion, a strikingly independent thinker, was trained in the London Kleinian (second analysis with Melanie Klein) tradition and creatively expanded on some basic Kleinian concepts. Grinberg's (1990) notion of projective counteridentification was based on the idea of *violent* projective identification, which denotes the effect on the analyst of a patient's relentless barrage of accusations, for example, that the analyst hates the analysand. As such an attack continues, sooner or later the therapist will come to hate his patient independent of the analyst's attempts to remain composed or "neutral." Winnicott (1949) wrote convincingly about the necessity of the clinician coming to hate certain kinds of patients, which was an essential part of the treatment. Thus, violent projective identification *creates* an experience in the analyst of being passively taken over by a patient whose sole interest is to *evacuate* his own frightening emotions into the analyst.

Bion, who worked analytically with many psychotic and borderline patients, wrote a series of papers in the 1950s (1957, 1958, 1959) in which he described the *communicative* aspects of projective identification. In essence he was asserting that while projective identification may serve the function of emptying out the psyche of unwanted elements, *it was also a means of emotional communication from one psyche to another.* In this connection, even the most violent expression of projective identification that leaves the therapist feeling battered is also a communication of the nature of the patient's anguish. Bion deeply believed in this, a conviction that led him to claim the patient as our best ally because even in his most disturbing interactions the patient was attempting, however feebly or ferociously, to communicate something of his own inner suffering. Thus, he (Bion, 1973) came to observe (cited in the quote at the beginning of this chapter) that "we, patient and analyst alike, are certain to be disturbed" (p. 4).

In proposing the communicative component of projective identification, Bion, although he did not say it directly, was in effect telling the analyst how to use one's unconscious as "an instrument of the analysis." Communicative projective identification, therefore, was the means by which "the transmitting unconscious of the patient" (Freud, 1912, p. 115) communicated with the "receptive organ" of the analyst's unconscious. However, we may also wonder about the fate of that which is projected into the therapist: what becomes of it once it has been successfully communicated and taken in, or *introjected*, by the receiving unconscious of the analyst? Bion (1958) commented that in addition to its communicative aspects, projective identification also aimed to "put bad feelings in me and leave them there long enough *to be modified by their sojourn in my psyche*" (p. 146) [italics added]. The conception that feelings are "modified by their sojourn" in the analyst's mind became the cornerstone of Bion's later theories and furthered our understanding of countertransference: thus, another facet of countertransference was its role in modifying what has been transmitted to the clinician's unconscious.

Bion's researches into how the psyche modifies the projection led to his discovery of *reverie*, but first a detour back to Abraham's (1909) letter to Freud will be a useful illustration. As a thought experiment, I suggest we place ourselves as Abraham's supervisor as he tells us about his treatment of the patient with whom he experiences the need to look over to the picture of his parents while awaiting the analysand's reply to an interpretation. Abraham tells us that, in the classical mode, he has successfully stopped this "symptom" of gazing at the picture. Applying the notion of communicative projective identification, we may wonder whether this analyst's (Abraham) unconscious has received some communication from the patient's unconscious and that looking at the picture of his parents was this analyst's unique way of unconsciously registering in his own metaphor the patient's communication. Furthermore, we might also consider Abraham's next thoughts about his daughter's constipation and her "rather arch smile" about the enemas as further data, encoded in the analyst's personal experience, about what the analysand is unconsciously communicating. Employing the analyst's seemingly "unimportant" side remarks as his unconscious representation of the patient's subliminal communication furthers the analyst's ability to use his unconscious "as an instrument of the analysis."

Further elaborations of countertransference: enactments and the concept of a "two person" psychology (1960–1990)

Bion's (1962a, b; 1997b; Ogden, 2003a, b, 2004a) concept of *reverie* refers to a wide range of experiences (visual images, seemingly irrelevant thoughts, random tunes) that spontaneously come to the analyst's mind while listening to a patient and signal that his unconscious is quietly working to transform the analysand's unconscious communication and "re-register" it in the therapist's personal idioms. If the clinician applies this stance, then what we consider clinical "material" that is relevant to the patient's difficulties is greatly broadened. Thus, within this frame of reference, Abraham's thoughts (associations?) about his daughter's constipation are viewed as a "legitimate" potential source of information about what the patient is communicating in this session. We may therefore formulate a hypothesis that Abraham's gaze over at his parents' photograph for approval that is followed by thoughts about his daughter's bowel difficulties are a reverie that indicates his unconscious reception of a communication from the analysand that is transformed into these particular thoughts. Furthermore, his unconscious may be a lightning rod for the patient's emotions about being good (Abraham's looking toward his parents), being withholding (his daughter's constipation) and perhaps an enticement to draw Abraham into some sado-masochistic struggle ("the arch smile").

I can imagine at this point that the reader may be wondering whether these extrapolations from the analyst's countertransference are at best extremely fanciful and, at their worst, a gross misuse and misapplication of countertransference. Indeed, this was the objection in most American psychoanalytic circles in the beginning of the 1960s regarding the use of countertransference "as an instrument of research into the patient's unconscious" (Heimann, 1950, p. 81). For example, Ross and Kapp (1962) wrote a very interesting paper in which they recommended that the analyst pay attention to *his* visual images stirred by listening to a patient's dream because these images could offer clues to countertransference feelings of which the therapist was unaware. While for Bion or Heimann such images might be considered vital data about the patient, Ross and Kapp considered these images as confirmations of "when a countertransference problem has already been suspected" (p. 645), that is, information about the analyst and *not* the patient.

There were, however, a number of American analysts who earlier advocated using the countertransference as a means of better understanding the patient in addition to oneself, but their ideas did not gain much traction. Indeed, Theodore Reik's (1948) book, *Listening with the Third Ear: The Inner Experiences of a Psychoanalyst*, which argued for the value of the analyst's subjectivity (his "third ear") in understanding the patient, was widely read among the general population but seemed to have much less impact on the mainstream of American psychoanalysis.

Otto Isakower (1957/1992, 1963/1992) of the New York Psychoanalytic Institute gave a series of lectures in the late 1950s and early '60s that dealt with supervision in which he emphasized the importance of teaching candidates to use their countertransference as a component of the "analyzing instrument." He reported his supervision of an analytic trainee who shared with an analysand a spontaneous visual image he experienced while listening to him, which Isakower discussed as having had a positive treatment effect. This presentation was met with many negative responses from the audience (Wyman and Rittenberg, 1992), including the comment by Martin Stein that questioned whether the candidate's sharing of the visual image

> has to do with some unanalyzed personal problem? To use an analogy from medieval times – when a person had a vision to tell, was the vision sent by God or the Devil?
>
> (p. 221)

Kernberg (1965) published a groundbreaking (for American psychoanalysis) paper in which he detailed two currents in thinking about countertransference: one was the "classical" definition that regarded countertransference as the analyst's unconscious reaction to the patient's transference and the second use was the "totalistic" one, characterized by a broader view of countertransference as something that "should be certainly resolved . . . [and also] useful in gaining more understanding of the patient" (p. 39). He described various countertransference difficulties that may await those who undertake the treatment of seriously disturbed patients and warned that the analyst should take care to recognize the possible development of "chronic countertransference fixation" that arises from the "reappearance of abandoned neurotic character traits" (p. 54) in the analyst triggered by primitive aspects of the patient. It is important to note that this article was written during the time when he was investigating the intensive analytic treatment of patients with "borderline personality organization" (Kernberg, 1967) and narcissistic disorders and this publication argued that the analyst adopt the "totalistic" approach to countertransference as a necessary tool for treating such individuals. Although this paper did not offer new innovations in understanding the phenomenon of countertransference, its linkage of particular emotional reactions in the analyst to specific severe diagnostic states and the fact that it was published in the *Journal of the American Psychoanalytic Association* introduced most American psychoanalysts of that era, largely under the sway of then-prevalent ego psychological models, to a broadened ("totalistic") view of countertransference.

Kernberg's advocacy of the "totalistic" approach to countertransference helped to foster an evolution from a "one person" to a "two person" psychology in American psychoanalysis that began in the mid-1970s. Though Modell (1984) is generally credited with coining this distinction, the term "two person psychology" is first mentioned by John Rickman (1951), who defined it as "the psychological region of reciprocal relationships" (p. 219) that takes into account the interaction between the psychologies of the analyst and patient. In this regard, Joseph Sandler (1976)[5] introduced the idea that the transference has an intended purpose of *actualizing* an internal object relationship of the analysand in the analytic relationship. The patient assumes a certain role in accord with an internal fantasy and also deliberately, though unconsciously, acts to evoke in the analyst a complementary role of that fantasy. Sandler emphasizes that this *role responsiveness* is not just a fantasy existing in the patient's psyche, but an actual state of emotional affairs that permeates the subjective experiences of the analyst and analysand. He treads familiar ground to what Racker had earlier described, but emphasizes the *pressure brought to bear on the therapist to behaviorally step into a role that is scripted by the patient's internal fantasy.* Sandler advised the clinician to maintain a *free-floating behavioral responsiveness*: a receptive capacity to being placed in a variety of roles that pull him in the direction of specific actions delimited by the nature of the role he has been pushed to assume. The analyst may find himself placed into a role that causes some distress and Sandler cautions him not to simply view this upset as a mere "blind spot," but to consider his reaction as a "compromise-formation" between his own proclivities and his reaction to the nature of the role forced upon him.

Sandler moved the classical analytic understanding of countertransference forward to include the patient's pressure on us to take on a role in his inner world and the effect upon the analyst in acquiescing. It is through Sandler's technical suggestion that the analyst *become* one of the patient's inner objects or a disowned aspect of the analysand, what he terms "role responsiveness," that we are able to gain knowledge of the patient's inner workings. Thus, Sandler expanded upon the analyst's use of his unconscious as an instrument of the analysis by giving privilege to the pull on the analyst to *act* in a particular role that may offer insight into the nature of the analysand's inner drama that is played out in the therapeutic situation.

The emphasis in Sandler's paper on the patient's pressure for us to assume a role and act it out provides a central theoretical grounding for the focus on *enactments* beginning in the analytic literature in the 1980s. In Sandler's concept of role responsiveness it was the patient's inner world, and its externalization into the analytic situation, that spurred the analyst's involvement; i.e., *that the analyst's psyche was viewed as reactive rather than an active participant in initiating the interaction.* Beginning in the late 1970s, Theodore Jacobs (1991) has written extensively about the actualizing component of enactments, adding a two-person dimension that was essentially absent in Sandler's discussion, bringing us closer to the "region of reciprocal relationships." The patient and analyst may engage in an unconscious mutual enactment that serves resistance:

> the enactments carried out by both patient and analyst . . . Their investigation opened the way, not only to uncovering an essential piece of history that had not yet surfaced, but to bringing to the fore certain crucial aspects of the interaction between patient and analyst that, arousing anxiety in each and strongly defended by both, had until then been insufficiently explored.
>
> (p. 40)

For Jacobs, the analyst is typically drawn into an enactment because of his unconscious resonance with an aspect of the conflict that the patient is manifesting. Not uncommonly, the analyst identifies with an internal object of the patient who may represent a figure in the analyst's inner world or a split-off piece of himself (Jacobs, 1983). In this situation, personages from the analysand's representational world (Sandler and Rosenblatt, 1962) may become unknowingly linked with presences in the analyst's mind. Invariably, however, for Jacobs an enactment and its successful analysis allows for the emergence and clarification of unconscious conflicts in the patient; thus, *an enactment is considered within the framework of the classically established goal of making the unconscious conscious.*

Like Jacobs, most American analysts have tended to view enactments as an avenue toward the goal of making unconscious conflicts in the patient conscious. Boesky (1990) suggests that, in addition to helping to foster the conscious awareness of previously unconscious elements, another benefit to the analyst's being drawn into an enactment is that the analysand senses the analyst's engagement with him:

> If the analyst does not get emotionally involved sooner or later in a manner that he had not intended, the analysis will not proceed to a successful conclusion.
>
> (p. 573)

Here Boesky is making an important point about the *patient's awareness of the analyst's countertransference*: where Money-Kyrle (1956) addressed the unconscious meaning the analysand gives to the perception of the countertransference, Boesky is additionally underscoring that the patient may find conscious reassurance in the clinician's emotional engagement. By the early 1990s, the role of the analyst's subjectivity in the analytic encounter was becoming an increasingly prominent area of study and we now turn to this development.

Countertransference: the analytic field, intersubjectivity and a new theory of dreaming (1990–present)

One of the criticisms of classical analytic technique (Mitchell, 1998; Renik, 1995) has been that it relied upon the analyst as an "authority" figure who sifts through the analysand's associations to discover the hidden meaning and then offers his interpretive pronouncements. Renik (1993) introduced the notion of the analyst's "irreducible subjectivity" to highlight the inevitable involvement of the analyst's personality in his interpretations and that, therefore, insight is not a commodity given by the analyst to the patient but rather

> that analytic truths are co-created by analyst and patient, rather than unveiled by means of the analyst's objective observations of the patient's projections.
>
> (Renik, 2004, p. 1056)

These comments, distilled from the study of the analyst's involvement in enactments, further shifted the concept of countertransference away from an artifact to be "sanitized" to an "irreducible subjectivity" and thereby promoted a diminished emphasis on the analyst's authority.

The theme of analyst and patient co-creating insight is closely allied to the exploration of the *intersubjective analytic field* by other authors whose works are influenced by the writings of Melanie Klein and Bion (Brown, 2011a). The analytic field concept has an ancestry of its own (Brown, 2011c) that stretches back to *Gestalt psychology* in the early twentieth century and, somewhat later, Kurt Lewin (1935) coined the term *field theory* to denote the idea that the whole (as in Gestalt psychology), created from the sum of its parts, is greater than the sum of those parts. Bion and Rickman (1946) applied this model to the study of group processes in the 1940s and somewhat later Bion (1952) introduced Klein's ideas of primitive mental functioning to his understanding of group phenomena. He proposed the idea of the *basic assumption*, which is a shared unconscious phantasy, assembled from aspects of each group member, that permeated the group and affected each member individually in accordance with his or her psychological make-up. This was an important step forward in psychoanalytic field theory because it represented the idea of an unconscious psychic entity constructed from the group members, yet having an independent existence of its own, which suffused the group with an emotional experience. Other authors further developed the idea of a third psychic presence through their unique contributions, most notably Willy and Madeleine Baranger (1961/2008) who wrote about the *shared unconscious phantasy of the couple,* and stated that

> This structure [shared unconscious phantasy] cannot in any way be considered to be determined by the patient's (or the analyst's) instinctual impulses, although the impulses of both are involved in its structuring . . . Neither can it be considered to be the sum of the two internal situations. *It is something created between the two, within the unit that they form in the moment of the session, something radically different from what each of them is separately.* [italics added] (p. 806).

Other notable contributions to the idea of a third subjectivity forming from the deep unconscious interaction of the patient and analyst are Ogden's (1994) *intersubjective analytic third,* and Ferro's and Civitarese's (1992) important work on the concept of *characters in the field.*

This model of the analytic relationship adds a new dimension to our comprehension of countertransference: the analyst's emotional experience in the session is a conduit to a shared unconscious experience that is built from aspects of the patient and himself. It is "something radically different from what each of them is separately" or, put another way, it represents "something fascinating about the analytic intercourse; between the two of them, they do seem to give birth to an idea" (Bion, 2005, p. 22). From this perspective, therefore, it is less important to sort out "whose ideas was it" (Ogden, 2003a), than for the analyst to regard his countertransference as tuned into a shared emotional experience that he and the patient, each in their own way, are attempting to come to terms with. Returning once again to Abraham's (1909) letter to Freud, I began the last section (1960–1990) by speculating that Abraham's looking at the picture of his parents for approval and his associations to his daughter's constipation may indicate that he was unconsciously resonating with some emotion stirred by his patient. If we add the perspective of the "shared unconscious phantasy," we may also consider the possibility that *both Abraham and his patient* were under the sway of an unconscious phantasy (i.e., a wish to receive parental approval and defiance against that authority) that permeated the communal analytic mood.

The literature on the analyst's and patient's mutual contribution to enactments, Renik's (and others) thoughts about the co-creation of meaning (insight) in the analytic pair and the idea of a shared unconscious fantasy all fall under the umbrella of *intersubjectivity*. This topic is discussed in another chapter in this textbook, but it seems important to note that the study of countertransference appears to have been subsumed in recent years by investigations into the nature of intersubjectivity (Brown, 2011a). It is my impression that countertransference still carries a somewhat pejorative association; for example, countertransference dreams are not generally spoken about and candidates are loath to discuss these in supervision (Brown, 2007). On the other hand, the term "intersubjectivity" does not have the history of stigmatizing the analyst's feelings that countertransference has carried and instead normalizes the therapist's experience, however troubling it may be.

Before closing, there is one last perspective on countertransference that deserves attention: that *the analyst's experience of the analytic hour is a dream*. Bion (1992) expanded Freud's theory of dreaming (the reader is referred to Grotstein's (2009c) paper dealing with Freud's and Bion's dream theories) when he asserted that we are always dreaming, while awake and asleep. He viewed dreaming as the mind's way of processing raw emotional experience and giving it meaning with one's personal stamp. Ogden (2003b, 2004a, 2007) has written extensively about Bion's views on dreaming and describes how the analyst's waking dream thoughts (or reveries) are the means by which our psyches unconsciously transform experiences of the patient (conveyed to us through projective identification) that are too unbearable for the analysand to "dream" on his own. Furthermore, the clinician is not only transforming an unmanageable emotional experience for the patient but his waking dream thoughts are also "unconscious work" he is doing to represent the shared unconscious phantasy active in the analytic hour.

The Italian analysts Antonino Ferro and Giuseppe Civitarese also place great importance on the concept of "waking dream thoughts" (Ferro, 2002b, 2005, 2009b) in both the analyst and patient as indicators of the analytic *couple's fertility*, which is an important component of the analytic field and related to the question of analyzability: can this analyst/patient dyad engage in a mutual unconscious process that transforms unrepresented emotional experience? One offspring of the analysand and analyst unconscious interaction is the appearance of new *characters* in the patient's narrative that is a barometer of aliveness in the analytic field. Abraham's (1909) letter to Freud is a fascinating collection of characters: the picture of his parents, the infantile transferences from his patients, and the constipated daughter. Each of these for Ferro and Civitarese (1992) are representatives that carry important meaning in the context of the here-and-now of the session. Ferro views the development of a jointly constructed narrative as the vehicle for transformation of the unconscious elements of analytic field (Ferro, 2009a). He stresses that a chief task of the analyst is to adopt a stance of *transformational receptiveness*, which means that we must be open to experience what the patient needs us to feel and only then can we use our reverie function to give possible significance to the analysand's communications. Ultimately, analytic progress depends on

> the deep emotional level of the couple, on which the projective identifications are used to establish the emotional foundation which needs to be narrated through the characters and transformed by working through, and which must be shared by way of a story.
>
> (Ferro, 2002, p. 25)

This overview of the ways in which our understanding of countertransference has transformed over the first hundred years of psychoanalytic history brings us to Bion's *theory of transformations*. It is a complex theory that moves contemporary analytic thinking away from its prior emphasis on making the unconscious conscious to considering what is unknown and ephemeral; from the importance of understanding the meanings of an analysand's utterances to a focus on how meaning is created jointly by analyst and patient; a rediscovery of Freud's (1912) advice that the analyst not have an agenda for the session, now couched as beginning each session "without memory and desire"; from a more panoramic view of following the development of the transference in the course of an analysis to a focus on the individual session as a means of tracking micro-transformations in the evolution of a session; and from an emphasis on drive theory and its derivatives to a near exclusive focus on emotional experience that is alive in the here-and-now of the session. But before exploring the theory of transformations (Chapter 4), we must first discuss Bion's discovery of alpha function (Chapter 3), which is necessary to fully understand *Transformations* (1965).

Notes

1 Previously published as Brown (2011b) Countertransference. In G. Gabbard, B. Litowitz and H. Smith (Eds.) *Textbook of Psychoanalysis, Second Edition.* NY: American Psychiatric Publishing. Pp 79–92.

2 In a letter to Jung, Freud (31 December, 1911) wrote "I believe an article on counter-transference is sorely needed; of course we could not publish it, we

would have to circulate copies among ourselves" (p. 476), thus expressing an attitude that the analyst's emotional reactions to the patient were best kept from the public view.

3 I (Brown, 2011, p. 20) have called this comment "the big bang statement from which the universe of intersubjectivity has emanated."

4 Painful affects cannot literally be placed *into* an object because they "are not palpable entities with weight and mass to be transferred over a physical distance . . . [and] the notion that something is projected *into* an object rests upon an understanding of [Klein's view of] the concrete nature of unconscious phantasy" (Brown, 2011, p. 51).

5 I have earlier cited contributions from London Kleinian analysts (such as Joseph and Brenman Pick) whose techniques in the 1970s were also increasingly aimed at helping the patient see the pressure being placed on the analyst to participate in an interaction that is an externalization of an unconscious internal phantasy template.

CHAPTER THREE

Bion's discovery of alpha function

The engine of transformations[1]

Evolution of the concept of alpha function: 1940–1960

I visited Sarajevo several years ago and stood on the famous Latin Bridge, now modernized and quite ordinary, where Archduke Ferdinand and his wife were shot dead by a Bosnian Serb assassin; an event that lit the fuse for the horrendous conflagration of World War I. Just around the corner from the bridge was a souvenir shop in which tourists could have their picture taken while sitting in a cardboard replica of the Archduke's open-air limousine; cheerful faces inserted into the cut-out photographs of the two assassination victims. There was a sense of manic excitement at the opportunity to be photographed as the royal couple, yet to survive and email that picture home, sanitized of any recognition that these murders unleashed an unprecedented degree of barbarous violence.

However, on other streets one could discover the "Sarajevo Roses," created from the small pockets that were gouged out of the pavement by thousands of bombshells that rained down from the city's surrounding hills during the four-year siege in the 1990s. The shells left imprints that resembled macabre flowers and some of these were filled in and painted red to commemorate the fallen citizens. Walking through the city, you would come upon these and feel intensely solemn as though stepping on holy ground; the red "petals" of the roses as painful reminders that the blood of innocents was splattered where you were standing. There were neither antiseptic tourist sites here nor surreal photo ops; instead there was the arresting chill at knowing that someone was blown to pieces where you stood.

I was reminded of these two images from Sarajevo's war torn past when thinking about Bion's (1962a, 1962b, 1992) discovery of alpha function upon which the psyche depends in order to make psychological meaning of raw emotional facts so that we may learn from experience. When the emotional truth of what we must endure in order to develop personally is too great, that truth may be trivialized and transformed into a thrilling sideshow attraction that sweeps away awareness of the 15 million soldiers who perished in World War I. But how are we to memorialize horrific trauma in a manner that conveys to the observer something true about the nightmarish event yet evoking a tolerable "taste" of that unbearable tragedy, i.e., the "Sarajevo Roses," to stimulate reflection and promote emotional growth?

The discovery of alpha function

This paper traces the development of Bion's theory of thinking and explores the various trends in his personal and psychoanalytic experiences that contributed to the discovery of alpha function which, in my view, was his greatest achievement. I have come to regard his proposal of alpha function, formulated during an especially fertile period of approximately two years from 1958 through 1960, as the culmination of several seemingly disconnected facets of his life all of which had to do with how the mind may process unthinkably painful feelings. I argue that his articulation of alpha function was the final common pathway of three areas of "research" that Bion simultaneously had undertaken: (1) the immensely personal and riveting (Bion, 1997) account of the 1918 Battle of Amiens written between 1958 and 1960; (2) the seemingly "scientific" elaboration of the theory of alpha function (Bion, 1992) detailed in *Cogitations* from 1959 through 1960; and (3) the winding down of what Hinshelwood (2011) has called the second major phase of Bion's work, the papers on schizophrenia during the 1950s. In addition, in my view Bion's marriage to Francesca in 1951 served an essential and invaluable role that provided him the necessary containment in order to confront the demons from his own traumatized past as well as those in his psychotic patients, which eventuated in his proposing alpha function.

There has been a growing recognition in recent years that Bion's World War I traumatic experiences have been a hidden order in his published psychoanalytic writings (Roper, 2009, in press; Souter, 2009; Symington & Symington, 1996; Szykierski, 2010). The theme of war and references to the military became apparent to me as an organizing motif beginning in Bion's first publication in 1940, "The 'war of nerves': Civilian reaction, morale and prophylaxis," and continuing through his last (1979/1994) article nearly 40 years later, "Making the best of a bad job,"[2] in which we are witness to his awareness of disrupted thinking while under fire, either in the cacophony of battle or in the analyst's consulting room "When two personalities meet, [and] an emotional storm is created" (p. 321). The individual soldier, whether infantryman or officer, is subjected to a "war of nerves" and that the

> object of the combatant is to exploit unconscious phantasies, both in the enemy and in himself, in such a way that the enemy is discomfited and he himself benefited.
>
> (Bion, 1940, p. 180)

Later (1958–1960/1997), in recounting his mental state during the 1918 Battle of Amiens in which he was a 20-year-old tank commander, Bion writes "Bion felt sick. He wanted to think . . . He tried to think . . . He tried to think" (p. 254).[3] In his final paper, Bion (1979) likens the encounter with some patients to combat:

> In war the enemy's object is to terrify you that you cannot think clearly, while your object is to continue to think clearly no matter how adverse or frightening the situation.
>
> (p. 322)

As if to remind us that his World War I experiences have not faded from memory, it is striking to me that he closes "Making the best of a bad job" with his final published sentence, "That war has not ceased yet" (p. 331).

There is a curious divide between Bion's personal journals (1982, 1985, 1990, 1997a), published after his death in which his encounters in battle are described in often gruesome terms, and his "professional" writings, which make only oblique mention of these experiences, if at all. Nevertheless, it was Francesca Bion (1997) herself who succinctly stated that Bion's war actions "all formed part of the real personal emotional experience on which his theories lie" (p. 311). Two recent papers by Szykierski (2010) and Souter (2009) offer close readings of Bion's accounts of World War I in his diaries, especially the Battle of Amiens, and convincingly link these to his theory of the *container/contained* (Szykierski) and to "the horrors of psychic abandonment" (Souter, p. 795). In other writings, I (Brown, 2005, 2006, 2011a) have suggested that Bion's (1957) notion of the psychotic part of the personality may also derive from his military exploits in which he was exposed to the structure of split-off parts of the self in severely traumatized individuals.[4]

In preparing to write this paper, I became aware of a period for over a year from 1959 through 1960 during which Bion's ideas about alpha function slowly evolved through a long series of entries in *Cogitations* (Bion, 1992) and wondered whether this intense focus might have been associated with some important events in his concurrent life. I learned (Tarantelli, 2011) that this was the same period in which Bion was engaged in writing his Amiens memoir; thus, it became clear that Bion's development of alpha function was partly stimulated by his work on the war recollection and that this autobiographical writing in turn was fostered by his growing understanding of the processes involved in alpha function; that these two synchronous endeavors enabled each other.[5] Just as Isaac Newton had to invent calculus in order to study planetary movement, so Bion formulated alpha function, which gave him the tools to understand psychotic thinking as well as to assist in working through his World War I trauma.

Bion began writing the Amiens diary in 1958 after he and Francesca visited the site of that battle and stopped, mid-sentence, in 1960. Francesca Bion (1997) attributes this stoppage to "other more pressing commitments [that] intervened. He was working on *Learning from Experience* at the time" (p. 214). During this period, we can trace in *Cogitations* an especially creative time beginning in July, 1959, and ending at some point in 1960[6] in which he formulated his theory of dreaming and alpha function. I suggest that *Learning from Experience* (1962b) was the capstone of these two simultaneous projects (writing the diary and formulating the theory of dreaming/alpha function) which extended some implicit concepts in his schizophrenia papers and were nurtured in the embrace of an emotionally safe, replenishing marriage.

Bion met Francesca in 1951 and after a short courtship they were married several months later.[7] From the outset there was something remarkable about their deep emotional connection that provided Bion an experience of what he would later call *containment*, which permitted him to emotionally revisit his traumatic World War I horrors that had remained fallow for more than 30 years and had left "an abiding impression of unrelieved gloom and profound dislike of himself" (F. Bion, 1985, p. 6). This "unrelieved gloom" most likely was a conglomerate of past trauma that had been fused together into a bleak amalgam that remained unmetabolized: the death in childbirth of his first wife while he was on assignment in World War II; the scars from his immersion in the daily deadly horrors of World War I; and a feeling about his own childhood as expressed by the following:

> How people can think of childhood as 'happy' I do not know. A horrible bogey-ridden, demon-haunted time it was to me and then one has not the fortitude, or callosities, with which to deal with it.
>
> (1985, p. 76)

Bion must have sensed in his future wife a remarkable capacity for understanding and tolerating his despair, a woman who had enabled "a renaissance she had brought about in his life" (Bleandonu, 1994, p. 102) at a time when he felt emotionally deadened. This awakening had partly to do with the freedom he felt to share his World War I affective scars with Francesca in a letter to her shortly after their first date (Bion, 1985) in which he spoke movingly about his experiences in battle that he had not recounted since writing his earlier memoirs in 1917–1919. This initial encounter contrasted with his preliminary analytic meeting with Melanie Klein who "did not understand, or chose not to know – the enormous significance of the DSO[8] . . . [that felt like] a cosmetic cover for my cowardice" (1985, p. 67). In addition, Bion had found the challenge of raising his infant daughter, Parthenope, on his own after the death of his first wife to be very daunting and believed "I had lost my child" (1985, p. 70) because he was "numbed and insensitive" (p. 70) to her needs. This anesthetized state also papered over his profound guilt that he had "begged Betty [his first wife] to agree to have a baby; her agreement to do so had cost her her life" (p. 70) when she died shortly after Pathenope's birth.

Francesca was "a miracle that has happened to me" (1985, p. 82), who had drawn him out from his somnambulistic existence and had "given Parthenope back to me and made me feel what it is like to have a child" (p. 85). In a letter to Francesca, Bion also wrote that "I felt so happy when you spoke of a nursery" (p. 85); a happiness that must have felt an especially joyous release from his gloom because of Francesca's eagerness in contrast to his pressuring Betty to become a mother that "had cost her her life." I also believe that the safe comfort in his marriage provided Bion with the necessary emotional grounding to tolerate the stresses in analyzing psychotics and also taught him about the need for the psyche under extreme pressure to have another available mind to help carry the affective burden. Thus, his papers on schizophrenic thought in the 1950s were partly sponsored by the "background of safety" (Sandler, 1960) of a loving marriage; an on-going presence of emotional stability that enabled Bion in 1958 to literally return to the physical site of the Battle of Amiens as well as to revisit the painful memories in writing that memoir[9].

With regard to Bion's work in *Cogitations*, we see in this span of approximately one year (1959–1960) his gradual departure from Freud's (1900) theory of dreaming that dealt with how dreams conceal instinctual wishes in order to achieve wish-fulfillment to Bion's development of his ideas about the function of dreams in the service of making sense of reality. *I believe that Bion's expansion in* Cogitations *of Freud's theory of dream-work that eventuated in the proposition of alpha function ought to be considered as one of psychoanalysis' greatest advancements because of the profound implications this holds for theoretical and clinical analysis.* The notion that we are constantly dreaming while awake and asleep to transform the emotional reality of experience redefined how we view the analyst's subjective experiences as his/her unconscious processing of the patient's unconscious communicated affects. Where Freud viewed dreams as operating in the service of the *pleasure principle* (Freud, 1911b), Bion offered an additional perspective that emphasized the importance of the *reality principle.* Freud considered disguise as the main role of *dream-work* and Bion used the same term (dream-work) to describe an additional function of the dream as a "mental digestive process" (1992, undated, p. 42). Bion asserted that conscious experience must be subjected to dream-work in order for it to become personalized: conscious experience remains an "undigested fact" until it is processed by dream-work and turned into a memory that may be linked with other memories in an individual's self-narrative. Thus, Bion accorded to dream-work a central role in one's capacity for dealing with conscious experience, thereby broadening the "domain of the dream" (p. 45) to include the notion that dream-work also performs its function while we are awake:

> Freud says Aristotle states that a dream is the way that a mind works in sleep: *I* say it is the way it works when awake.
>
> (p. 43) [italics in original]

At about the same time Bion was framing in *Cogitations* this new view of dreaming, he was also facing the emotional reality of his war trauma through writing in the *Amiens* diary. Bion (1917–1919/1997a) had previously written to his parents after the war about his experiences but left this reflective chronicling aside and the traumatic facts were "carried over almost unchewed and apparently undigested" (F. Bion, 1997, p. 309) until he returned to them 40 years after the events. Bion (1997a) recounts an episode the night before the deciding battle in which he and his companion, Asser, each had restless nights with bad dreams, stating that

> one gets the most appalling dreams, and then when you wake up you don't know whether it wouldn't have been better to go on sleeping. The dreams are much nicer than the actual reality we have to face now.
>
> (p. 236)

One has the impression of hearing about a mind that is struggling to dream a horror that cannot be dreamed in the sense of turning it into a memory that may perhaps be repressed; the boundaries between wakefulness and sleep are blurred and "the most appalling dreams . . . are much nicer than the actual reality." Bion has a firsthand sampling of the unending mental agony that can result when dream-work not only fails to disguise (in the Freudian sense) but also is unable to function at all.

Bion's experiences also taught him about the importance of dreaming in the ability to distinguish between reality and phantasy. Endless bombardment and the deafening roar of battle resulted in sleep deprivation so that even though one might manage to sleep "when you awoke you wondered whether you were dreaming" (Bion, 1997a, p. 94).[10] Thus, it was difficult to see how Freud's wish-fulfillment theory of dreams applied to combat situations "when the most appalling dreams . . . are much nicer than actual reality." In normal situations, the "digestive" function of dreams allows the individual to metabolize experience by "dreaming" it, but when an overwhelming reality disables (Bion's version of) dream-work the "emotion-recording apparatus" of which Graves (1929) spoke fails and reality becomes an interchangeable nightmare with phantasy.

It seems to me that this entry in the Amiens diary that describes the failure to dream leads in *Cogitations* to explore the psychic danger of inoperative dream-work and, in a kind of Mobius strip, Bion's ability to theorize about the functions of dream-work circles back to enable him to continue the emotional work in the diary. When dream-work is attacked, Bion states in *Cogitations*, there is a subjective sense of being dead and what should have been given meaning instead is felt as lifeless. In this connection, being dead may be more appealing than being alive; that is, it can be preferable not to be able to feel than to have to endure unbearable pain as he vividly expresses in Amiens:

> I wish I was a dummy stuffed with straw now. Unfortunately, if I'm hit it hurts and I hate being hurt. I don't think anybody knows how afraid I am of physical pain. If I could be sure that I should be killed, I don't think I would mind, but the ghastly and terrible thing, the awful thought of one's shins crumbling up inside one's legs at the burst of shells and the flying splinters, is more than I can stand.
>
> (1997a, p. 240)

In contrast to the failure of dream-work and the feeling of being dead, Bion states in *Cogitations* that "the true dream *is* felt as life promoting" (p. 67) [italics in original] and one can detect in the quote of being an unfeeling dummy an empathy for those who are unable to manage reality and must resort to dismantling dream-work in order to survive. Bion (1982) himself knew this when he said about the Battle of Amiens, "Oh yes, I died on August 8th 1918" (p. 265).

Beginning in early 1960, Bion's *Cogitations* entries took an important step forward by drawing a distinction between Freud's definition of dream-work and his own concept of *dream-work-α*. Freud's dream-work addressed how an unconscious wish was masqueraded to hide its true nature from the censor so it could achieve partial satisfaction and was related to dream interpretation, i.e., detecting the camouflaged hidden wish. Bion's dream-work-α denotes *the capacity to dream*, which rests upon the ability of dream-work-α to transform undigested facts into dream thoughts (*α elements*) that may be linked together in a dream narrative. From a clinical point of view, the analyst may be neglecting an important factor if he insists only on interpreting the dream from a Freudian axis: the patient may be unable to dream dreams that are "life promoting" and if this is the case then the treatment focus must redirect its efforts away from interpretations that assume the existence of a symbolic (dream-work-α) capacity. Sometime later Bion replaced dream-work-α with simply *alpha function*, therefore breaking further with Freud's pleasure principle derived theory and establishing his own viewpoint that emphasized the dream's function in service of the reality principle – i.e., the dream as a mental digestive process that operated while we are asleep and also while awake. However, Bion did not reject Freud's theory of dreaming, but instead offered an additional perspective.

It seems appropriate at this point to consider some aspects of the psychoanalytic understanding of *war neuroses*[11] at the end of World War I to contextualize Bion's later formulations about the effects of battle upon alpha function. Many considered the war neuroses to represent a challenge to Freud's sexual etiological theory of the neuroses and this question was discussed at a Symposium held at the Fifth Psycho-Analytical Congress in Budapest in September, 1918, just two months before the armistice, at which Freud gave an introduction to papers by Ferenczi, Abraham, Jones and Ernst Simmel. Abraham's (1921) statement that "the war neuroses are not to be understood without taking the sexuality into consideration" (p. 20) captured the prevailing view that contemporary analysts might find somewhat pejorative. The psychosexual issue arose mainly in response to the question of why some soldiers fell ill while others did not, and this was typically considered from a vertex of pre-existing susceptibility to breakdown resulting from childhood conflicts, often around passive homosexual longings:

> Many of the patients show themselves as completely female-passive in their surrender to their suffering.
>
> (Abraham, 1921, p. 18)

Little attention was paid in these reports either to the ferocity of battle and the nightmarish realities of the war front or to the possibility that "regressive" cries for mother by injured infantrymen were desperate pleas for comfort from their anguish. Jones (1921), however, emphasized the instinctual need to survive more than the sexual instincts per se:

> but that in war the conflict between the instinct for self-preservation and the ego-ideal [not to kill] is enough to lead to a neurosis.
>
> (p. 41)

Finally, regarding the repetitive traumatic dreams of the servicemen, Ferenczi (1921) importantly noted that these terrors may be "spontaneous attempts at cure on the part of the patient" (p. 15) accomplished through abreaction.

I think this last comment by Ferenczi links very directly with Bion's attempts in the 1950s to understand the psychological mechanisms that must be in place in order to withstand and mentally "digest" overwhelming emotional experience, whether arising internally or invading the psyche from external sources as in war. As early as 1940 in his first paper, "The 'war of nerves,'" Bion was attuned to the primary interpersonal importance of belonging to a group during the war as a potential bulwark against becoming traumatized.[12] Just after the Budapest conference, Freud (1920) proposed the concept of a *Reizschutz*, or "protective shield," a neurophysiologically conceived rind buffering the psyche to protect it from "any excitations from outside which are powerful enough to break through the protective shield" (p. 29) and therefore cause trauma. Current thinking is that this shield is constructed from internalized object relations. For example, Khan (1963) considered the internalized mother functioning as an auxiliary ego to be a prime component of this shield, while others have likened it to a membrane which enfolds the ego as a kind of 'second skin' (Anzieu, 1993; Bick, 1968, 1986) or what Gerzi (2005) has termed a 'narcissistic envelope.' In other publications (Brown, 2005, 2006, 2011a), I have extended the definition of the protective shield to include those internal objects, such as the container/contained relationship[13], as well as the capacity to dream, which operate to abate and metabolize excessive "excitations from outside" (or emerging from internal sources). Unlike Ferenczi, I think Bion would see the repetitive traumatic dream as a failure to digest frightening experience, i. e., an evacuation of unmanageable raw emotion, and not a "true dream . . . [that] "is felt as life promoting" (Bion, 1992, p. 67). Nevertheless, Bion, like Ferenczi, was struggling to understand how the mind contends with terrifying phenomena that threaten to disassemble the psyche's protective shield.

Nowhere is this "war of nerves" more prominent than in Bion's (1997a) description of his entrapment in a shell-hole during the battle of Amiens[14] with his young runner, whom he calls Sweeting. It illustrates not only the sheer horror of war, but also Bion's attempts to think in the midst of overwhelming sensory bombardment and his ultimate failure to do so. The pair had taken shelter from the German attack with Sweeting holding close to Bion when the runner asked, "Why can't I cough, why can't I cough, sir?"

> Bion turned round and looked at Sweeting's side, and there he saw gusts of steam coming from where his left side should be. A shell splinter had torn out the left side of his chest. There was no lung left there. Leaning back in the shell-hole, Bion began to vomit unrestrainedly, helplessly.
>
> (p. 255)

Sweeting started incessantly to beg Bion to be sure to write to his mother and these appeals appeared to grate on Bion's already frayed nerves: "'Oh, for Christ's sake shut up', shouted Bion, revolted and terrified" (p. 255). Then, later, "I wish he would shut up. I wish he would die. Why can't he die?" (p. 256).

I would like to suggest that the episode of Sweeting's horrific injury and his panicked, desperate entreaties for Bion to contact the boy's mother confronted Bion with an overwhelming *in vivo* experience from which he learned about the nature of alpha function and its limitations. The incident is described in vivid sensorial language and begins with the German artillery barrage:

> At first all was a silent fiery curtain, and then came the sound, a rushing, pulsating sound which came in gusts against the skin of face and hands as well as ears.
>
> (1997, p. 252)

In the shell-hole with Sweeting, the drumming din of the explosions blended together with the boy's begging to create a composite sensory missile that crashed through Bion's protective shield: "never have I know such a bombardment like this" (p. 256). This "bombardment" by sensory fragments reduced Bion to vomiting in order to evacuate the sensory overload and must also have taught him, in retrospect, how the desperate mind madly discharges experience that cannot be abstracted. Perhaps, as well, surviving this showering fusillade of shell splinters served as a template for Bion's (1957/1967a) description of the psychotic state of mind when he said "the patient feels surrounded by minute links which, being impregnated now with cruelty, link objects together cruelly" (p. 50).

Writing in *Cogitations* before he introduced the concept of alpha function, Bion observed the link between dreaming and *introjection*: that conscious, sensory experience must first be introjected in order for dream-work to process the raw emotional material. Bion (1958) had earlier described in the paper "On arrogance" how a patient projects into the analyst who then must introject the projection and permit it to "sojourn" in the analyst's psyche and we can see in the Sweeting incident Bion's inability to tolerate his runner's agony. It is too much to bear the "bombardment" of the admixture of Sweeting's horrible injury, the "gusts of steam" billowing out of his side, with the noise of the German barrage: these stay as sensory events that overload Bion's alpha function and his mind can only expel (vomit out) these unmanageable experiences.

It seems likely to me that Sweeting's insistent appeals to Bion to contact his mother, as well as hearing dying soldiers call for their mothers on the battlefield, made Bion aware of a mother's central role in helping her child manage emotional pain; an awareness that was later realized in his marriage to Francesca. This brings us to the threshold of Bion's introduction of his model of the *container/contained* that was proposed after the creative period discussed here between 1958 and 1960 when he wrote the Amiens diary and developed the theory of alpha function in *Cogitations*, which extended in new and important ways ideas that were implicit in his papers on schizophrenic thinking.

Before moving on to an exploration of the container/contained conception, I would like to offer a speculation about Bion ending the Amiens diary in mid-sentence. Bion and another officer were speaking about someone who had "cracked up" under pressure and the officer commented that Bion showed no signs of this, to which Bion (1997a) writes

> Bion did not believe him. He felt that people who cracked up were merely those who did not allow the rest of the world to . . .
>
> (p. 308)

Francesca Bion (1997) believes that "other more pressing commitments intervened" (p. 214) such as his work on *Learning from Experience*. Szykierski (2010) writes

> it reads as though Bion were about to formulate the great unknown of mental catastrophe, but could not find the words, and went on an intellectual journey to find the elements and factors determining the transformations that determine whether a mind will *learn from experience* or "crack up.
>
> (p. 959) [italics in original]

Souter (2009) questions whether we should even attempt to complete this sentence because it would be an artificial closure and that

> it seems wrong to conventionalize this final utterance into collected prose, to demand that the bloodied gap be closed.
>
> (p. 806)

Each of these opinions has important merit and, from a close reading of his entries in *Cogitations* written during the same period (1958–1960) in which he wrote the Amiens diary, it seems more than coincidental to me that he would end the diary at the same time his speculations in *Cogitations* led him to introduce the concept of alpha function (in 1960). This formulation also signaled Bion's amending of Freud's theory of dreaming (by emphasizing that the processes of dreaming are also active while one is awake) and represents a quantum step forward in his independence as a psychoanalytic thinker. Therefore, Bion's discovery of alpha function was a milestone reached by having traveled the dual carriageway of the Amiens dairy and *Cogitations*, an achievement opening up new creative avenues that led to crafting the invaluable theories of thinking, the container and the contained, etc., that began with *Learning from Experience* in 1962 and which I view as a coalescence [a kind of selected fact] of these earlier threads into an impressive new pattern. It may be that he stopped writing in the diary because he suddenly realized that he *had* "found the words . . . [to continue] on an intellectual journey" (Szykierski, ibid) and those words were "alpha function."

Further refinements of alpha function: theory of container and contained[15] and its elaboration (1960–1970)

How does alpha function develop? The container and the contained

Although Bion's concepts of alpha function and the container/contained relationship are usually linked together, it is important to note that his articulation of alpha function preceded the development of the theory of container and contained. I consider alpha function a part of the unconscious ego (Brown, 2009a, 2011a) by which affective experience is transformed from its sensory roots to an emotional experience that is also a thought or, put another way, from existing as an undigested fact to becoming a memory. "Alpha function" describes the psychic process by which this transformation occurs and also the agency that performs the operation. We have seen how Bion's ideas about alpha function slowly evolved as a means by which to understand his clinical experiences with psychotics as well as a tool to assist him in coming to terms with his World War I trauma. Alpha function has its theoretical roots in Freud's (1900) concept of dream-work, which Bion then built upon to create a distinctly unique and original proposition. Though we have traced the arc of Bion's thinking that brought him to theorize alpha function, the question still remains of how this capacity forms in the individual psyche and this query brings us to Bion's formulation of the container and the contained.

I suggest that while Bion's working through his World War I trauma by writing in the Amiens diary and in *Cogitations* largely addressed the "emotion-recording apparatus [that] seems to have failed" (Graves, 1929) in the tumultuous roar of battle (alpha function), that his marriage to Francesca Bion as well his clinical work with psychotic patients in the 1950s contributed significantly to his understanding the kind of relationship with another person that is required to be able to think under fire, i.e., his theory of container and contained. Szykierski (2010) links Bion's use of the word "containment" with its military implication, as in "containing" the enemy, and sees its roots in his war experiences. Though this connection seems very relevant, as in Bion's inability to "contain" Sweeting's terror (if, in fact, such horror can be bearably contained at all), I think his experiences in the intimacy of a satisfying marriage and in the difficult closeness of analytic work with psychotics taught him more about the vital importance of containment than the chaos of the battlefield. We can see the kernels of ideas in his psychoanalytic writings in the 1950s on schizophrenic thought that would eventually lead him to propose the theory of container and contained.

Bion seems to have used the term "contained" for the first time in his 1956 paper "Development of schizophrenic thought," in which he described psychotic patient's projection of "expelled particles of ego" (p. 39) into objects which are then experienced as "containing," perhaps even being taken over by, the projection. A year later, he (Bion, 1957) observed the futility of the analyst's attempt to put the projection back into the patient through an interpretation. Unlike the analyst's experience with healthier analysands, the psychotic portion mind feels assaulted and painfully impinged upon by these traditional analytic interventions. This realization that simply interpreting the projection often served to increase the analysand's sense of persecution collided with Bion's (1958) stated conviction in "On arrogance" that in analysis the patient and analyst were "required to pursue the truth." How is one to help a patient in this pursuit if the conventional analytic tools leave the patient feeling bludgeoned? In response this dilemma, Bion turned his focus away from the patient's difficulties and trained his attention on the task challenging the analyst, which was "to tolerate the stresses associated with the introjections of another person's projective identification" (p. 88). *This shift in perspective from the patient to the analyst represents, in my view, a radical departure from the extantemphasis on the analysand's disturbed ego as a limiting factor in "analyzability" to considering the vital role of the clinician's emotional capacities in the treatment of very ill individuals.* Bion had learned that the capacity to "tolerate the stresses" of introjecting the analysand's projective identification depended upon

> the ability [of the patient] to put bad feelings in me and leave them there long enough for them to be modified by their sojourn in my psyche.
>
> (p. 92)

This last statement[16] signals Bion's recognition that allowing the projection to "sojourn in my psyche" could result in some "modification" of the patient's "bad feelings," though the process by which that metamorphosis is achieved awaited further explanation and anticipated his soon-to-arrive thoughts about the *container* and *contained*.

In reading Bion's (1962a) brief paper, "The psycho-analytic study of thinking," one has the impression of watching an engaging movie trailer that whets our appetite for seeing the entire show, which in this case was the publication of *Learning from Experience* (1962b) in the same year. In the paper on thinking, he takes an important first step forward to further develop the nascent theme in his schizophrenia papers that suggested the part played by the analyst's thinking in transforming the patient's projections. He takes an impressive theoretical leap forward in our understanding of alpha function through connecting the process by which projected feelings are modified by their "sojourn" in the analyst's psyche with an activity "between mother and infant, a relationship in which normal projective identification is possible" (p. 115). This still leaves the reader wondering what precisely occurs during the transformational sojourn *inside* the mother (or the analyst), and Bion proposes a procedure between a mother and her baby in which maternal receptivity to the infant's projected emotions plays a central role:

> The mother's capacity for reverie[17] is the *receptor organ*[18] for the infant's harvest of self-sensation gained by its conscious.
>
> (1962a, p. 116) [italics in the original]

The infant requires a mother who is *receptive* to, and can tolerate the stress of, its projective identifications and through her capacity for *reverie* "pre-chews" the baby's unmetabolized emotional experiences into manageable psychic events (alpha elements). Thus, this short paper about the roots of thinking is an important transitional step to significantly enlarge the theory of alpha function by proposing its intimate link with the object relations of very early development.

Learning from Experience, factors of alpha function and intersubjective processes

In *Learning from Experience*, Bion (1962b) deconstructs alpha function into its various *factors*[19] and accords a primary role to reverie, which "is a factor of the mother's alpha function" (p. 36) and also an expression of love for her baby through her "reception of the infant's projective identifications whether they are felt by the infant to be good or bad" (p. 36). Bion regards this notion as a "*digestive model*"[20] (p. 42) of alpha function in which "the alimentary system [is used] as a model for the processes of thought" (p. 62). Accordingly, through her reverie (a factor of alpha function) the mother converts "uncooked" (Ferro, 2005) emotional experience (β elements) into mentally "digestible" morsels (α elements) that the infant's undeveloped psyche can absorb without feeling oppressively choked by some foreign body too large to swallow. Maternal reverie also seems to involve, with the ascendancy of the *depressive position*, a capacity to spontaneously link together disparate α elements into a *selected fact* that forms a coherent narrative. Over time the infant introjects its mother's alpha function, and the associated capacity for reverie, which forms the core of its own developing[21] ability to metabolize experience.

It is only in the last few pages of *Learning from Experience* that Bion introduces the concept of container and contained along with an *intersubjective* (Brown, 2009a, 2011a) perspective on the relationship between the two, which I have termed a *procreative* model and Sandler (2000) has called the "reproductive" point of view. Interestingly, Bion decides to represent the container with the sign "♀" and the contained with "♂," thereby implying a sexual connotation[22] about which he later comments in *Attention and Interpretation* (1970):

> The use of the male and female symbols is deliberate but must not be taken to mean that other than sexual implications are excluded . . . [and is] the sexual relationship ♀♂
>
> (pp. 106–107)

Bion additionally underscores the intersubjective aspects of container and contained by using the word *commensal* to describe the interaction between the mother as container and the baby as contained, which he characterizes as a model from which

> the mother derives benefit and achieves mental growth from the experience: the infant likewise extracts benefit and achieves growth.
>
> (p. 110)

Furthermore, he offers an observation that I believe many analysts have overlooked: that the infant incorporates this shared commensal activity of "thinking" together with its mother, represented by ♀♂, as its alpha function. Most writers view alpha function originating in the infant through introjection of the maternal alpha function; however, from the *procreative* point of view, alpha function also is formed by the internalization of an intersubjective relationship:

> *The activity that I have here described as shared by two individuals becomes introjected by the infant so that the ♀♂ apparatus becomes installed in the infant* as part of the apparatus of alpha-function.
>
> (p. 91) [italics added]

Moreover, Bion stresses the shared experience of mutual emotional growth in both container and contained; development that depends upon a milieu of *tolerated doubt* between mother and infant and, finally, this "Growing ♂♀ provides the basis of an apparatus for learning by experience" (p. 92).

In summary, Bion's discovery of alpha function represents a selected fact that brought together several strains of his thinking during an especially fertile period from 1958 to 1960. This period followed on the heels of his writings in the 1950s about schizophrenic thinking and it was also a time in which he developed his theory of dreaming while simultaneously writing the Amiens diary. These themes coalesced within the context of his marriage to Francesca Bion that appears to have provided him with the necessary background of safety to deal with his war trauma, the stresses of working with psychotic patients and provided him with a profound experience of personal containment. I suspect that he gleaned from his own individual experience and from clinical encounters with psychotic states of mind an appreciation of the necessary presence for another containing mind to absorb and modify by some unspecified process the emotional turmoil that the troubled psyche cannot manage on its own. His continued exploration of the means by which this metabolizing operation occurred led Bion to appreciate the vital role of the mother's capacity to withstand taking in her baby's projections and subject these to her reverie, which he viewed as a factor of alpha function. Bion first considered this process from a digestive model in which the "infant depends on the Mother to act as its α-function" (Bion, 1963, p. 27) to effectively pre-masticate experience, but later added an intersubjective framework when he (Bion, 1962b) introduced the notion of the container (♀) and the contained (♂). The ♀♂ may be seen as the first couple,[23] mother and infant, who grow together through the ability to tolerate doubt until some meaning is ascribed to unprocessed emotions and this collective activity is introjected as the "apparatus for thinking" (Bion, 1963, p. 31), a central component of alpha function, by which we are able to learn from experience. Thus, *alpha function is the overarching concept of which reverie and the container/contained (♀♂) are factors* (Brown, 2013). Bion uses the sign ♀♂ to refer to two phenomena: the container/contained relationship between mother and infant and also to denote the "apparatus for thinking." This may seem confusing at first, especially for a writer like Bion who is so precise, but it seems his intention is to convey an intricate connection linking these two factors of alpha function, i.e., between the early mother/baby relationship and the apparatus for thinking.

Further constituents of alpha function and the Constellation for Thinking

Though Bion's work after the publication of *Learning from Experience* explored many areas of great importance, I want to stay with the focus on how his further researches led to a more complete understanding of the constituent factors of alpha function. In addition to the factors of reverie/dreaming, container/contained and the apparatus for thinking which comprise alpha function, Bion adds the Ps↔D balance and tolerated doubt as additional components in *Elements of Psychoanalysis* (1963). Some of these factors duplicate each other's functions and/or may be represented by the same denotation (e. g., the use of ♀♂ for both "container/contained" and the "apparatus for thinking"), which can be confusing to the reader. Thus, I suggest bringing these together under the catchphrase of a *Constellation for Thinking*.

Having outlined a general theory of alpha function in *Learning from Experience* (1962b), Bion began at the end of that book to elaborate in greater detail the factors that comprised it when he launched the study of the container/contained. In the following year, *Elements of Psychoanalysis* (1963) was published in which he elevated the "dynamic relationship between container and contained" (p. 3) from its appearance in the closing pages of *Learning* as a near afterthought, to be the foremost element in psychoanalysis, thereby according a primacy to the analytic dyad, its link to the early mother/infant dialogue and the development of the apparatus for thinking. To these phenomena he added a second element, the Ps↔D balance, which refers to the oscillation between moments of coherence (D signifying the depressive position) and of relative disintegration (Ps standing for the paranoid-schizoid position). His unique interpretation of Ps and D represented a creative elaboration of Klein's original concepts and now, for Bion, the fluctuations between these states indicated an analytic engagement that was alive and evolving. In what may appear to be a blurring of terms, Bion links the concepts of Ps↔D and ♀♂ and views these factors as working collaboratively: the existence of a container (♀) is a necessary presence to gather up the psychic bits of experience (♂) that enables coherence (D) to emerge out of fragmentation (Ps). As a corollary, the ♀♂ depends upon the mind's capacity to tolerate swings in the Ps↔D balance[24] (tolerated doubt) and Bion states that these are "mechanisms each of which can at need assume the characteristics of the other" (p. 44).

Many of these factors that comprise alpha function overlap and are redundant, which can easily appear confusing to the reader. Nevertheless,

I believe that Bion's model actually captures the intricate connections and redundancies upon which rests the capacity to transform (think) raw emotional experiences into elements of thought. I suggest that these various factors may be gathered together under the rubric (schematized here)[25] of a *Constellation for Thinking*, all of which are subsumed by the super-ordinate concept of alpha function, which is the engine that drives transformations:

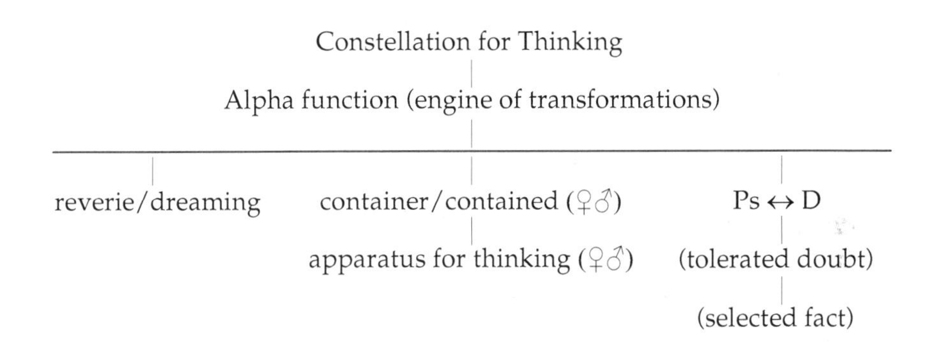

Moving from left to right, the three columns map the growth of the concept of alpha function. We will recall that in his work with psychotic patients Bion observed that their capacity for reverie had been severely impeded and he concluded that there was psychological meaning to this symptom: that these individuals had dismantled their capacity to know reality. This led Bion to amend Freud's theory of dreaming by claiming that dreams function to give emotional meaning to reality experiences. Furthermore, he needed a theory about how the capacity to dream (as an act of transforming experience) developed in the individual psyche that brought him to propose the model of the container/contained (♀♂), or how the early mother/infant pair "thought" together, which, when introjected into the baby's psyche, became the "apparatus for thinking." Bion (1963) accorded the container/contained relationship the primary place in the psychoanalytic encounter and added, secondarily, the Ps↔D balance and its oscillations between states of relative disintegration with experiences of integration. Finally, and most importantly, emotional growth in both the patient and analyst depended on being able to tolerate the doubt and turbulence (Ps) of not knowing until some selected fact appeared (D) to bring coherence to what had been disjointed and incomprehensible.

Summary

This chapter has traced Bion's discovery of alpha function and its subsequent elaboration. His traumatic experiences as a young tank commander in World War I (overlaid on, and intertwined with, childhood conflicts) gave him first-hand exposure to very painful emotions that tested his capacity to manage. Later, in the 1950s, after his analysis with Melanie Klein and marriage to Francesca Bion, he undertook the analysis of psychotic patients and learned how they disassembled their ability to know reality as a defense against unbearable emotional truths in their lives. This led Bion to identify an aspect of dreaming that was necessary in order for reality experience to be given personal meaning so that one may learn from experience. Simultaneous with working out this new theory of dreaming, Bion also revisited his World War I experiences that had remained undigested and all these elements coalesced into a selected fact – his discovery of alpha function. In subsequent writings, Bion explored the constituent factors of alpha function, including the container/contained relationship, the Ps↔D balance, reverie, tolerated doubt and other factors I have termed the *Constellation for Thinking*.

Notes

1 Previously published as Brown (2012) Bion's discovery of alpha function: Thinking under fire on the battlefield and in the consulting room. *IJP*, 93: 1191–1214.
2 Bion (1997) used this phrase in the *War Diaries* while comparing the common plight of the frontline soldier, whether British or German, who "live in the same danger, the same vile conditions . . . [to the] "war profiteers [who] are sitting at home in Germany or England *making the best of a very bad job*" (p. 292) [italics added].
3 Compare with Robert Graves comment that "These daydreams persisted like an alternate life and did not leave me until well in 1928. The scenes were nearly always recollections of my first four months in France; *the emotion-recording apparatus* seems to have failed after [the battle of] Loos" (Graves, 1929) [italics added].
4 The relationship between trauma and psychosis is a very complex one that goes beyond the scope of this paper. Though Bion rarely, if ever, mentions trauma in his psychoanalytic writings, many of the characteristics of the traumatized and psychotic mind are similar: the blunted capacity for abstract thought and dreaming and the tendency to fragmentation are two

examples. Additionally, I propose the existence in severely traumatized patients of a *traumatic organization* that rigidly holds together a shattered psyche and can feel impermeable to analytic access just like the psychotic part of the mind (Brown, 2005, 2006). Much of what Bion ascribes to the psychotic mind also applies to the severely traumatized individual.

5 Sandler (2003) regards Bion's (1997a) *War Memoirs* (of which the Amiens Diary is a part) as an "autobiographical counterpart" (p. 59) to *Cogitations*, though he does not link these together as a joint project to work through war trauma.
6 Some of these entries were undated, but are thought to have been written in this period.
7 Bion's analysis with Melanie Klein ended in 1952. One might speculate that his analysis "readied" him for the intimacy with Francesca. It is interesting that most writers attribute Bion's capacity to work through his war trauma to Francesca's empathic gifts, yet there is little mention of the analysis with Klein as a factor in this process.
8 The Distinguished Service Order medal awarded to Bion for meritorious service during combat in World War I.
9 It is interesting to note that Bion and Francesca did not take their honeymoon until seven years after their marriage (Bleandonu, 1994) and it appears that a visit to the site of the Battle of Amiens was part of their itinerary.
10 Similarly, Roper (2009) quotes Hankey (1917), "The weird thing was that I couldn't wake up properly" (p. 91).
11 It was common at the time to distinguish between the *peace neuroses*, that is, ordinary neuroses, and the *war neuroses* (also known at the time as *shell shock*).
12 The Italian analyst, Francesco Corrao (1981), proposed the existence of a *gamma function* in groups, analogous to alpha function in the individual, which task is to transform the shared traumatic emotions that have permeated the group. Thus, Carrao's formulation goes a long way in explaining the therapeutic effectiveness of the group's power to help the members bear and "digest" (transform) experience as well as the affective cement that bonds the group together.
13 The container/container relationship is a factor of alpha function.
14 Bion wrote several accounts of this battle and I am using the 1958 version because it "is altered in such a way as to sharpen the aspect of failed containing" (Roper, in press).
15 The subject of alpha function covers a wide range of phenomena including the differentiation of the conscious and unconscious, the nature of psychotic thinking, the relationship between dreaming and hallucination, to

name a few. My focus here, however, is to investigate the development of Bion's theory of alpha function and his subsequent formulation of the container and contained as well as the interconnection between these concepts.

16 Bion (1959) also reports this assertion in "Attacks on linking," but does not explore this idea further.

17 Bion (1957) had earlier referred to stunted capacity for *reverie*, i.e., an absence of freely imaginative thinking, in the psychotic part of the personality.

18 The use of this phrase, "receptor organ," seems to be a direct reference to Freud's (1912) statement that the analyst "must turn his *own unconscious like a receptive organ* towards the transmitting unconscious of the patient" (p. 115) [italics added]. Thus, I believe that Bion appears to be associating the capacity to tolerate the stress of accepting the patient's projections and the analyst's openness to reverie with Freud's description of unconscious communication (see also Brown, 2011a, Chapter 4).

19 Bion (1962b) defines a *factor* as "the name for a mental activity operating in consort with other mental activities to constitute a function" (p. 2).

20 Bion also offers what I (Brown, 2009, 2011a) call a "procreative model" of alpha function.

21 Grotstein (2007) asserts that there is an inchoate alpha function at birth; thus, the introjection of maternal alpha function enables and strengthens this inborn capacity.

22 In the Commentary section of *Second Thoughts* Bion (1967a) alludes to ♀♂ as a "sexual model" (p. 140), but does not elaborate this further.

23 I would suggest that the container/contained couple represents an earlier stage of "couple-hood" that is foundational for the Kleinian (1945) early Oedipal situation which itself scaffolds the classical Freudian Oedipus Complex.

24 Though Bion does not connect his earlier (1962b) concept of "tolerated doubt" with the Ps↔D balance (1963), it seems to me that these are nearly interchangeable ideas and that the latter replaced the earlier notion.

25 This schema is an expanded version of what I (Brown, 2011) have previously proposed.

CHAPTER FOUR

Bion's *Transformations* and clinical practice

In the last chapter, we examined the development of Bion's theory of alpha function, which I termed the "engine of transformations," and in this chapter I will explore in detail his *theory of transformations* (1965) with an eye toward separating out the clinical implications of this challenging book. When the topic of *Transformations* arises in conversation, the response is frequently that the book is excessively dense and nearly impenetrable. Interestingly, as far as I can tell, the book has never been reviewed in the analytic literature and it is met with mixed reactions among contemporary psychoanalysts. Until very recently many analysts in the UK have tended to regard *Transformations* as evidence of Bion's radical departure from the essential Kleinian tradition, while non-British analysts interested in his work have tended to embrace aspects of the ideas contained in the book. This divide was evident in a series of papers (2005) in the *IJP*, "Whose Bion?" in which Edna O'Shaughnessy, Elizabeth Bianchedi and Antonino Ferro offered their opinions about the value of the so-called "late Bion" period that began with the publication of *Transformations*. O'Shaughnessy (2005) offered that

> his late thinking becomes less boundaried, the defects of these very qualities make the texts too open, too pro- and e-vocative, and weakened by riddling meanings.
>
> (p. 1525)

while Ferro (2005) emphasized the ever evolving process of transformations of emotional experience in both the analyst and analysand and that, quoting Bion (1970), "Analysis is a probe that expands the very field it explores" (p. 1538)."[1]

The theme of transformations had already been significant in Bion's work in various iterations since the late 1950s when he (1958) noted in "On Arrogance" that the analyst, like the mother, is obliged to introject the analysand's projective identification and allow it to "sojourn" in his psyche. As I (2012, Chapter 3 here) discussed in the previous chapter, his introduction of *alpha function* (1962) described the transformative process that the patient's projection undergoes in the analyst's/mother's psyche. To summarize: the transformation of $\beta \rightarrow \alpha$ elements required some activity (α function) to act on raw emotional experience (β element) and transform it into what Bion terms a "thinkable thought" (α element) that is suitable for secondary process thinking. It was also in this period leading up to 1965 that he gradually formulated the theory of alpha function, which grew out of Bion's (1958–1960) extension of Freud's theory of dreaming while he simultaneously worked through his World War I traumatic experiences (Brown, 2012; Chapter 3). This combined activity of developing the theory of alpha function and working on his war diaries offered Bion an *in vivo* experience of transforming his own unprocessed emotional experiences ($\beta \rightarrow \alpha$) from the Great War.

In his brief introduction to *Transformations*, Bion stated that he had hoped this book could be read as a contribution independent of his previous books, *Learning from Experience* (1962) and *Elements of Psycho-Analysis* (1963), but realized that there was an undeniable continuity to these three volumes. It was in his paper "The Grid" (1963)[2] that Bion first referred to the notion of *transformation* as a process, "whatever it is," (CW **V**, p. 106) by which a raw emotional experience is represented; this representation may be an artistic work, a scientific achievement, ordinary conversation or the field of psychoanalysis in which "the communication of both patient and analyst is about an emotional experience" (ibid, p. 106). In addition, in my view *Transformations* should be considered in the context of themes that were developing in his work in the mid-1960s and evident in two unpublished papers, "Memory and Desire" (1965)[3] and "Catastrophic Change" (1966)[4]. Briefly put, these two papers, together with *Transformations*, all deal with the necessity for the analyst to embrace uncertainty, the deceptive allure of believing one *knows* the analysand that forecloses *understanding* him, the inevitability of emotional turmoil in the analytic endeavor, the requirement that the clinician tolerate what is unknown in order for emotional growth to occur and the immense value of viewing each session as a unique event. Furthermore, I cannot escape thinking that these psychoanalytic works were embedded in, and intertwined with, some personal turbulence percolating within Bion, that eventuated in his move to Los Angeles in early 1968 after giving several lectures there the previous year (Aguayo, 2015). Indeed, uprooting oneself at the age of 70 to move to another country[5] seems the embodiment of facing the unknown, exposing oneself to barely tolerable doubt and to the challenge of learning from (potentially catastrophic) experience.

The subtitle of *Transformations* is "Change from Learning to Growth," which links this book to *Learning from Experience* (1962) and also underscores Bion's shift in focus to mental growth and the processes that occur between analysand and analyst to promote or forestall psychic development. He narrows the object of his study to *what occurs in a session* within each member of the analytic dyad and between their psyches as they are engaged in transforming the emotional experience that arises as a result of that engagement. Bion's attention to the individual session as a window to the widening analytic process is a powerful tool, like a microscope on high magnification that reveals what is ordinarily unseen. He rarely refers in *Transformations* to the traditional analytic concepts of transference and countertransference; indeed, the different status of analyst and analysand is blurred and we are left with two individuals each engaged in transforming and giving meaning to their emotional experiences. Interestingly, though most of what Bion addresses in *Transformations* are processes that occur unconsciously, he considers the time honored technique of making the unconscious conscious as lacking:

> For a greater part of its [psychoanalysis] history it has been assumed that a psycho-analytic interpretation has as its function the rendering conscious of that which is unconscious. The relatively simple division of elements into conscious and unconscious has proved extremely fruitful, but it no longer provides a satisfactory criterion of an interpretation to regard it as either making or failing to make that which is unconscious conscious.
> (p. 135)

I do not believe that Bion means to discard traditional concepts of transference[6] and making the unconscious conscious, but rather his aim is to reconceptualize these ideas within the framework of his *theory of transformations*. But what does Bion mean by a theory of transformations? He offers the following summary:

> The theory of transformations and its development does not relate to the main body of psycho-analytic theory, but to the practice of psycho-analytic *observation*. Psycho-analytic theories, patient's or analyst's statements are representations of an emotional experience. . . . The theory of transformations is intended to illuminate a chain of phenomena in which the understanding of one link, or aspect of it, helps in the understanding of others. The emphasis of this inquiry is on the nature of the transformation in the psychoanalytic session.
>
> (p. 34) [italics in original]

In asserting that the theory of transformations does not "relate to the main body of psycho-analytic theory," I believe Bion is reorienting the analyst away from content analysis and making the unconscious conscious to instead observing the process by which that content is actively created and is a *representation* of an emotional experience alive in the clinical moment. Regarding the content of the hour, Bion would refer the analyst to the theories of Freud and Klein in order to ferret out the unconscious meanings (Brown, 2016a, Chapter 5 here). Similarly, Bion does not discuss instinct or drive theory but directs his attention to what is observable – i.e., emotional experience in the patient and/or analyst. To a possible objection that affects are derivatives of the drives in order to bolster the importance of instinctual/drive theory, my impression is that Bion would reiterate his interest in remaining an observer.

Invariance, representation and O

Regarding specific analytic theories, Bion states, "I am therefore ignoring here, and throughout this book, any discussion of psycho-analytic theories" (p. 16).[7] He seems to be offering a more general theory about how meaning evolves in an individual session out of the analytic engagement between analyst and analysand that is relatively independent of the analyst's allegiance to one analytic school or another. Since his focus is on "the practice of psycho-analytic observations," he cautions the observer to be wary of making inferences of causation about phenomena that frequently appear together, what Bion calls a *constant conjunction*, which is a function of consciousness. He warns against assuming causation between elements in a constant conjunction because that may lead to foreclosing the consideration of a variety of points of view. The pressure to attribute causation is "derived from forces within the observer and not necessarily having a part in the conjunction observed" (p. 71). This pressure to reach a conclusion about the causative relationship between various elements in a constant conjunction has to do with the analyst's difficulties in tolerating doubt and in maintaining faith (Bion, 1970) that understanding will eventually emerge.

Bion repeatedly emphasizes the importance of keeping ideas *unsaturated*, which means that we dissuade the patient and ourselves from attributing meaning to a constant conjunction until it is better understood. It was his effort to promote unsaturated concepts that led Bion to employ various symbols (e. g., α, β, ♂, ♀) and that we should leave these symbols as unknowns whose value is to be determined. This is in contrast with the use of existing psychoanalytic concepts because such well worn ideas carry a "penumbra of associations" (1962b, p. vi) that lead the analyst away from understanding what currently is under observation. Instead, he encourages us to tolerate the uncertainty of not knowing and allowing a phenomenon to slowly accrue meaning; that is, to become *saturated*. But what is it about the constant conjunction that we seek to understand? Bion says we are trying to find the *invariants* that underpin and bind these constant conjunctions together.[8] A patient I saw when he was eight years old because of anxieties about a peanut allergy and fear of dying from a random exposure to peanuts returned to see me ten years later for help in making a decision about which university to attend. He appeared a confident young man and made a point of beginning each session by visibly placing his Epi-Pens (in case of anaphylactic shock) by his chair as if to say, "I've mastered that earlier peanut anxiety," and he was now concerned about having a concussion from a minor head bump. It felt obvious to comment about the constant conjunction between his fear of being damaged, both as a child and now as an older adolescent, but I refrained since such an interpretation would be dynamically "correct" but might well close off further exploration. I remembered him as a youngster and how he suffered then; now worrying about whether he had sustained some cognitive damage that would prevent his attending university, and I wanted to make a sweeping interpretation that would calm him and *allow me to feel helpful*. Instead I said that he wanted me to know that his peanut worries were under control but that he now was confronting a "new nemesis" that we needed to understand. The term, "new nemesis" captured my patient's anxiety, but also was sufficiently unsaturated to allow for new meanings to accrue.

Bion's ideas about invariants deal with the question of what is the essence of the "thing" that has been transformed, which, once transformed, is now a *representation*. He opens *Transformations* by speaking about an artist painting a field of poppies and suggests that any rendering of the flowers, regardless of how life-like, is always a representation of the invariants of the actual subject. *Something remains unaltered*: it may be represented, but the process of representation does not change the essential qualities of the object. I find it curious that the topic of invariants, so vital in the opening pages of *Transformations*, is mentioned only three times after page nine and never in the second half of the book. Instead, Bion introduces us to a new concept, O, that refers to the inherent nature of a thing, Kant's "thing-in-itself," which can never be known but may be represented. The introduction of O also indicates Bion's continued movement away from classical analysis since "The differentiation I wish to introduce is not between conscious and unconscious, but between finite and infinite" (p. 46).

I remain puzzled about the difference between an invariant and O: both are the essence of something being observed and cannot be directly apprehended, but only represented. In his Introduction to *Transformations* in the *Complete Works of W. R. Bion*, Mawson (2016) likens O to an invariant that is the underlying component to a representation, a statement that seems to equate an invariant and O. I think it is significant that Bion's introduction of O accompanies his exploration of the process of transformations that occur *in the clinical situation*. Indeed, Bion first introduced the term O in his (1963) paper "The Grid,"[9] in which he stated, "O must always be an emotional experience" (*CW* V, p. 119). Thus, as I try to understand the difference (if there is a difference), both an invariant and O are the unknowable essences at the core of a representation, but he appears to apply the concept of O when speaking about *the emotional essence of an experience* encountered in psychoanalytic practice.

Clinically speaking, O'Shaughnessy's critique that Bion's "late thinking becomes less boundaried . . . [that] make the texts too open, too pro- and e-vocative," is an accurate statement. His (1972) emphasis that the analyst should train his attention to what is unknowable, O (or the "Truth"), in the session is the epitome of an approach that is provocative/evocative. In his papers on "Memory and Desire," Bion (1965, 1967b, 1972) cautions the analyst that his technical recommendations may arouse significant anxiety and in following Bion's guidelines one is set firmly in the present, unmoored from comfortable illusions of being in familiar psychic territory, and without a roadmap or compass. But if our attention is to be focused on the unknown, how does one achieve this? As mentioned previously, Bion does not adhere to the notion of an instinctual drive that would push repressed and/or unrepresented material into consciousness, but he does speak of the psyche's need for *Truth* (O) in order to grow:

> Psycho-analytic procedure presupposes that the welfare of the patient demands a constant supply of truth as inevitably his physical survival demands food.
>
> (1992, p. 99)

Put another way, the mind is engaged constantly in transforming O, the Truth, and thereby providing the necessary sustenance for emotional growth. Grotstein (2004) posits a *truth drive* that seems a bridging concept between drive theory and Bion's emphasis on the phenomenology of the analytic session. He states:

> I hold that the truth drive constitutes the force behind the analysand's remaining in analysis in the face of frustration and emotional pain. The reward is truth. The truth is real and can somehow be dealt with – because it is sought.
>
> (2004, p. 1092)

Bion's (and Grotstein's) notion of the *Truth* has been criticized because it suggests that there exists an immutable truth that is beyond question; however, it is my understanding that Bion is referring to an impermanent emotional "truth" that is unique to a particular analytic couple and exclusive to the clinical hour colored by that "truth." O, or Truth, is the affective essence of what the analysand and analyst are attempting to represent and understand in the clinical hour. At times Bion uses language that seems mystical and ethereal in speaking about O, but also offers a much more prosaic definition such as "the material provided by the analytic session is significant for being the patient's view [i.e., representation] of certain facts which are the origin (O) of his representation" (p. 15). In my opinion, O is a useful concept for the practicing clinician because it requires a certain humility of us; that there are limits to what we are able to help the analysand (and ourselves) to know and that, in a peculiar way, every analysis is interminable because there is an ineffable emotional truth that may only be approached but never fully grasped. This reminds me of Freud's (1900) well known comment that even the most fully analyzed dream has at its navel an unknown part that reaches into the infinite. With regard to the analytic situation, this is always a work in progress that approaches something essentially unknowable that calls to each of us to more fully comprehend.

Types of transformations: projective, rigid motion and transformations in hallucinosis

I am grouping the types of transformations Bion described into two categories: *projective* and *rigid motion transformations* comprise one group while the other group deals with *transformations in O*. Rigid motion transformations are what Freud would call a *transference neurosis*, which "implies a model of movement of feelings and ideas from one sphere of applicability to another" (p. 19), e.g., the transfer of feelings from a parental figure to the analyst in which these feelings remain unchanged. Projective transformations relate to Klein's projective identification in which "events far removed from any relationship to the analyst are actually regarded as aspects of the analyst's personality" (p. 30) that results in a transformation of the patient's experience of the analyst – and often changes in the analyst's experience of himself – colored by the nature of what the analysand projects. It is important for us to keep in mind that for Klein projective identification was always an intrapsychic phantasy in the patient's mind and she either ignored or rejected the idea that projective identification was an avenue to better understanding the patient.

Transformation in hallucinosis is a more complex phenomenon than the rigid motion and projective transformations and seems to involve two main components. The first is the analysand's creation of his own set of perceptions, which are at odds with reality, that serve to replace an emotional situation too painful for him to experience. This construction, felt to be a perfect world, is clung to in the face of all evidence to the contrary. A second aspect of this type of transformation is that the analysand's defensive adherence to his beliefs also is an expression of rivalry with the analyst, as though he is affirming the superiority over his version of reality to that of the psychoanalyst. Consequently, transformations in hallucinosis also imply that the patient satisfies "all his needs from his own creations [and that] he is entirely independent of anyone or anything other than his own products" (p. 137).

Types of transformations: transformations in O, K and O↔K

In each session both the analyst and the patient are engaged in attempting to transform (T) or represent the essence of their emotional experience of the clinical hour. Bion uses the letter T to signify the *process of transformation*: $T\alpha$ notes the *inception* of that process and $T\beta$ as the *end product* of that transformation. Furthermore, Bion uses $Tp\alpha$ to denote the process of transformation *in the patient* and Tpβ to signify the end product of the patient's transformation. Analogously, he speaks of the process of transformation in the analyst, Taα,[10] and the end product of that transformation, Taβ. Bion wants us to direct our attention to the processes of transformation in the patient and analyst, Tpα → Tpβ and Taα → Taβ, and it is this area he considers the most important to observe and understand. He states:

> The psychoanalyst's domain is that which lies between the point where a man receives sense impressions [Taα and Tpα] and the point where he gives expression to the transformation [Taβ and Tpβ] that has taken place.
> (p. 46)

I take the phrase, "where a man receives sense impressions," to refer to the analyst's or analysand's receptivity (see Chapter 5) to raw emotional data flowing from one to the other via projective identification and/or emotions evoked within each individual as a result of these projective and introjective processes. Furthermore, the words, "where he gives expression to the transformation," refers to the representations by the analyst and analysand, Taα → Taβ and Tpα → Tpβ, of their respective unconscious emotional experiences in the session. Regarding the analyst's activity in the hour, Bion views the analyst's *interpretation* as Taβ, his transformation of the emotional facts of the session.

How are we to understand the processes by which emotional experiences unconsciously generated in an analytic session are transformed? I find it interesting that in *Transformations* Bion does not examine this aspect and leaves us with a sense of a black box into which "sense impressions" (affects) enter and from which representations emerge. What happens in that black box? Or, what needs to happen *within the analyst's* and/ or *analysand's mind* that accounts for the process of transformation: put in the language of the shorthand signifiers to characterize various transformations, what internal processes are at work in the analyst and analysand that effect Taα → Taβ and Tpα → Tpβ? My guess is that Bion assumed we are intimately familiar with the concepts of waking dream thought, reverie and alpha function he introduced in *Learning from Experience*; however, none of these great theoretical innovations are even mentioned in *Transformations*. As I discussed in Chapter 3, I see alpha function and its associated factors (container/contained, reverie, tolerated doubt, etc.) as the *engine of transformations* and so I think Bion has left it to us to apply his earlier ideas in order to explain the process of transformation and representation building.

The shared O of the session

Returning to the topic of O in the analytic situation, Bion speaks of an O of the patient (Op) and an O of the analyst (Oa) that determines each of their respective transformations in the analytic hour; consequently, the origin from which Tp and Ta emerge is different. However, this scenario is not one of isolated minds operating independently in the consulting room since the analyst's interpretation (Taβ) may serve as the initiating stimulus to the analysand's further transformations. In addition, Bion adds another dimension to the interactional complexity by introducing the notion of a *shared O of the session*, which is the *common source* of their individual transformations (Ta and Tp). *I shall signify the shared O of the session as TapO.* Bion comments that when the

> O is the same for the patient and analyst . . . the distinction has to be made between the processes by which the patient transforms his experience to achieve his representation of it and the processes by which the analyst does so.
>
> (p. 24)

Just as he did not elaborate the internal processes by which transformations occur, so Bion does not discuss the psychic mechanisms by which the shared O (TapO) is created, although he does say that "we find features of Oa and Op intersect" (p. 30) to form the TapO. Contemporary authors view this joint O, the unknown emotional essence at the core of an analytic hour, as arising from the deep unconscious engagement of analogous unrepresented and/or repressed areas in the analyst and analysand (Brown, 2007, 2011a, Chapters 2, 5, 8 this volume; Cassorla, Ogden, Levine, et al.) that await a process of mutual unconscious dreaming/transformation/representation by the analytic couple. However, the shared O is ineffable and may only be approximated through successive transformations by the analyst and analysand. Ultimately for Bion, the concept of a shared O (TapO) becomes bedrock for understanding the nature of psychoanalytic treatment as we can see in this unusually emphatic statement:

> In psycho-analysis any O *not common to analyst and analysand alike*, and not available therefore for transformations by both, *may be ignored as irrelevant to psycho-analysis. Any O not common to both* is incapable of psychoanalytic investigation; any appearance to the contrary depends on a failure to understand the nature of psycho-analytic interpretation.
>
> (pp. 48–49) [italics added]

I think the origin of Bion's idea of a shared unconscious experience between analyst and patient can be traced to his early days as psychiatrist and officer in World War II where he was exposed to Kurt Lewin's idea of *field theory* that greatly influenced the Northfield Army Hospital personnel (Harrison, 2000) at the time [discussed in the Introduction]. The shared O (TapO) of the session is conceptually similar to Bion's (1952) notion of *basic assumptions* in groups. These "assumptions" were essentially a shared unconscious phantasy that permeated work groups when their task got derailed and it is important to note that the basic assumption was experienced differently by each member of the group in accord with his unique personality. In the language of *Transformations* we can say that the basic assumption is a similar concept to the shared O (TapO) of the session: TapO of the session and the basic assumption are formed from the collective psyches of the group members (or analyst and patient) and are subsequently transformed (Tpβ) by each patient.[11] What is unique to Bion's emphasis in *Transformations* is his careful study of the process by which both analyst and analysand give representation to O in the here-and-now of the session.

Lewin's ideas about field theory, Bion's concept of group psychology and Melanie Klein's writings on unconscious phantasy were creatively combined by Madeleine and Willy Baranger (1961/2008) in Montevideo, Uruguay, in their classic paper, "The Analytic Situation as a Dynamic Field." They proposed the concept of a "shared unconscious phantasy" of the analytic couple that was partly based on their view of patient and analyst as a small group, which, like the larger groups that Bion discussed, gave rise to a shared unconscious phantasy analogous to a basic assumption. Like Bion's notion of the shared O of the session, the Barangers did not examine the process by which the shared unconscious phantasy of the analytic couple was created. These two concepts, the shared O (TapO) of the session and the shared unconscious phantasy of the couple, both derive from an intermixing of related elements in the psychic worlds of analyst and analysand that are unconsciously patched together through the "unconscious work" (Ogden, 2010) of their respective alpha functions (Brown, 2010, 2011a), resulting in a chimera about which it is impossible to say, "Whose idea was it?" (Ogden, 2003a). Thus, it seems to me that the notions of the basic assumption, the shared unconscious phantasy of the couple (Barangers), Ogden's (1994) *intersubjective analytic third* and the shared O of the session are related ideas that are rich in their intersubjective implications. All three clinical manifestations suggest the emergence of a third entity (a basic assumption, shared phantasy of the couple or TapO of the session) that is unconsciously crafted from related elements in the group members or in the analyst and patient. However, the theory of O is linked with a sense of an evolving unknown in the session and emphasizes the use of the analyst's intuition as a tool for slowly grasping that unknown.

The notion that the analyst and analysand begin each session without memory and desire, unhitched from the past and expectations for the future, introduces a sort of riddle: the analytic couple is challenged to apprehend what is essentially unknowable and to begin that quest from a point of ignorance, separated from what one believes one knows. This is an anxiety provoking situation for analyst and patient who may find some comfort by believing that one *knows* what is about to happen or what has already occurred. In *Learning from Experience* (1962b) Bion introduced the K link between patient and analysand in which the analyst is coming to know *about* the patient, but in *Transformations* he discusses the limits of the K link in the clinical situation. Bion expresses his skepticism about the K link and is critical of one model of interpretation that requires it "should be associated with a K link; the analyst is concerned to understand the associations and to communicate that understanding to the patient" (p. 129). Bion avers that this clinical approach yields *knowledge about the patient* that is an accumulation of facts that may lead the analyst into believing he *understands* the analysand. For Bion, transformations in K (TK) are an incomplete step in the process of interpretation. For example, most Bionian influenced analysts consulting on cases are less interested in extensive histories of patients, data Bion called "hearsay," since such information offers factual details that may be unrelated to the session under observation. Instead, historical material may offer insight into the model of the patient in the analyst's mind. However, TK "does not produce growth, [and] only permits accretions of knowledge about growth" (p. 156). In contrast, Bion states TO "cover the domain of [emotional] reality and *becoming* . . . and are related to growth in becoming" (p. 156).

But what does it mean to truly understand the analysand that promotes mental growth? Earlier in this chapter I mentioned that Bion considers experiencing one's emotional truth as necessary to personal growth as food is to one's corporeal self. While this statement may seem obvious, Bion observes that *becoming* one's emotional experience may evoke a certain kind of *resistance* manifest by the analysand's accepting the interpretation in order to know something (TK), yet not feel it (i.e., *become* it); what Bion terms a resistance to transform $K \rightarrow O$:

> transformations in K are feared when they threaten the emergence of transformations in O . . . Resistance to an interpretation is resistance against change from K to O.
>
> (p. 158)

While TK → O is enabled by the analyst's interpretations, this transformation also requires the analyst to achieve a state of *at-one-ment* with the O of the analysand; that is, *becoming* the patient's experience of O at that moment (either of the patient's O or of the shared O of the session). Of course, we can never entirely experience another's emotional state, but we can experience our transformation (Taβ) of the analysand's disowned (defended against) O that is projected into the analyst. Indeed, as Bion states (p. 11), the most effective interpretation is rooted in a shared O (TapO) of the session; that is, when analyst and patient are transforming a jointly created emotional experience: the affective essence that suffuses the clinical hour. However, this is not easily achieved because the analyst, too, has his resistance to transforming K → O, especially since the shared O of the session inevitably engages painful regions of his psyche that are interlaced with those of the analysand. In Chapter 9, "From ashes to ashes: the heroic struggle of an autistic boy trying to be born and stay alive," I describe how I resisted becoming the O of this boy's terror of nonexistence and the horrific nightmare I had one night after emotionally connecting with his primitive agony.

There is a tendency among some Bionian authors to minimize the role of interpretation in the clinical process, but in reading *Transformations* I was struck by the central importance Bion accorded to interpretation in the clinical situation. Grotstein (2009a), in describing his analysis with Bion, said that he (Bion) interpreted frequently and often these interventions felt typically Kleinian and hit their mark emotionally. Early in *Transformations* Bion connected the process of transformation with the activity of interpretation, which he viewed as the job of an analyst:

> I propose that the work of the psycho-analyst should be regarded as a transformation of a realization (the actual psycho-analytic experience) into an interpretation or a series of interpretations.
>
> (p. 6)

An interpretation is one point in a series of largely unconscious communications between the analyst and analysand that begins with an emotional experience, optimally the shared O of the session, that the analyst and patient each transform (Taβ and Tpβ) or represent and the clinician must be mindful that "we can only speak of what the analyst or patient *feels* happens" (p. 33) [italics in original]. However, what the analyst feels has occurred may resonate favorably with the patient's experience (Tp), then

> the interpretation given should then afford an opportunity for the analyst and analysand to contrast two sets of information . . . [which are] two transformations of the same O.
>
> (p. 72)

When the patient and analyst feel the interpretation is accurate, Bion calls this "common sense." Furthermore, though we are considering ineffable experiences, O, and how these are represented by the analyst (Oa) and patient (Op), Bion reminds us that an interpretation is also about the "truth": not some absolute incontrovertible truth but "truth in the *analyst's opinion*" (p. 37) [italics in original] that also *feels* true to the analysand. It is that truth that nurtures the emotional growth of the patient.

Bion contrasts one model of technique, "associated with a K link" (p. 129), which directs the analyst to sift through the patient's associations in order to detect the unconscious themes that are then communicated to the analysand. This is the standard analytic approach that yields *knowledge* (K) *about* the analysand that does not necessarily result in emotional growth. Instead, he considers the analyst's interpretation (Taβ) as the beginning of a process: one's interpretation is seen as a pre-conception that awaits the patient's associations, which then *saturate the interpretation with meaning*. In classical technique, the analysand's associations to the interpretation are considered to confirm, refute or amend the intervention, but here Bion is asserting that the patient's associations serve to further infuse the analyst's interpretation with meaning. Furthermore, when "the patient's response does not saturate the analyst's pre-conceptions [e.g., interpretations] . . . [it then] appears itself to require saturation" (p. 130). Interpretations, in this second model, are part of an intersubjective spiraling process by which the mutual associations of analyst and analysand broaden and deepen their unconscious elaborations of the emotional experience of the clinical hour.

Ferro's (2002, 2009b) and Civitarese and Ferro's (2013) discussion of "characters in the field" beautifully captures this unconscious give-and-take that creates and expands meaning in the subliminal dialogue between the analytic dyad in the here-and-now of the session. In their view, elements of the patient's or analyst's associations/reveries are transformational products that unconsciously depict aspects of the emotional atmosphere in the hour. In his (2009b) paper, "Transformations in dreaming and characters in the psychoanalytic field," Ferro offers a vignette about a young woman at the outset of analysis who responded to the analyst's interpretation with a memory of a trustworthy childhood friend whose grandfather molested her. There are several vertices from which the analysand's response might be considered, including reference to an actual repressed experience from childhood; however, Ferro listens to the communication from a perspective he terms a "*constantly expanding unsaturated field*" (p. 214) [italics in original] that considers the manifest characters of the "friend" and "grandfather"

> as a signal from the field of excessive closeness and depth of interpretive activity . . . [that express] her feeling that her affective world is intruded upon by tumultuous and abusive protoemotional states of her own, given that she lacks the 'equipment to contain and metabolize them' (insufficient ♀ and insufficient α-function).
>
> (p. 214)

Ferro does not ignore the patient's recollection of a childhood memory, but hears it as reactive to, and a commentary on, his initial interpretations. More important than what he actually interpreted is how the analysand imbues meaning to his interpretative action: put in the iconography of Bion we could say that Taβ (analyst's interpretation) served as an unsaturated pre-conception that the analysand saturated with her interpretation (Tpβ) of Ferro's initial remarks. Listening on this level of micro-transformations (unanticipated appearances of "characters") gives the analyst access to the unconscious building up of meaning that accrues from their communicating alpha functions.

The Grid

We have been examining Bion's theory of transformations: the transition of $\beta \rightarrow \alpha$ elements catalyzed by alpha function; rigid motion and projective transformations; transformations in hallucinosis and from K$\leftrightarrow$O; and the unconscious spiraling activity of the analyst and patient, fostered by their communicating alpha functions, around a shared emotional experience from which reveries, characters, intuitions, etc., develop. The laboratory that Bion suggests we enter in order to observe and study these processes is the individual session and he developed the concept of the Grid (1963) as a means to track the evolution of these transformational processes within the coordinates of the Grid. Bion likened its use as a kind of "homework" for the analyst "that would help him to track down after a session, in a moment of relative peace and quiet, what had happened during the session" (F. Bion, 1997; **CW**, V, p. 94). The dynamics in the development of the patient's thoughts traced by the Grid equally apply to the analyst's mental processes during the session. It is important to note that the Grid addresses the evolution of ideas and *not emotional growth* as we have been discussing earlier in this chapter; thus, the Grid is focused on K related experience. Francesca Bion (ibid) considers the Grid paper as foreshadowing *Transformations*: I would say that whereas the Grid addresses the evolution of *ideas* in the clinical hour, the focus in *Transformations* is on those processes by which *emotional growth* is nurtured in the Petri dish of the session; hence, the subtitle of *Transformations* is "Change from Learning to Growth."

	Definitory Hypotheses **1**	ψ **2**	Notation **3**	Attention **4**	Inquiry **5**	Action **6**	. . . n.
A β-elements	A1	A2				A6	
B Alpha-elements	B1	B2	B3	B4	B5	B6	. . . Bn.
C Dream Thoughts, Dreams, Myths	C1	C2	C3	C4	C5	C6	. . . Cn.
D Preconception	D1	D2	D3	D4	D5	D6	. . . Dn.
E Conception	E1	E2	E3	E4	E5	E6	. . . En.
F Concept	F1	F2	F3	F4	F5	F6	. . . Fn.
G Scientific Deductive System		G2					
H Algebraic Calculus							

Bion wrote another version of "The Grid" that offered more clinical material and a discussion of some myths (Row C constructs, see table), but soon after appeared to grow dissatisfied with it: "I can say that an early casualty in trying to use the Grid is the Grid itself" (quoted by F. Bion, CW **V**, p. 97) and later, even more skeptically, he said the Grid was "only a waste of time because it didn't really correspond with the facts I am likely to meet" (ibid, p. 98). Perhaps Bion's loss of confidence in the Grid had to do with its focus on ideas and knowledge (K) and *Transformations* represented a turning point in "the facts I am likely to meet" as his theoretical interests shifted from epistemological works toward the nature of emotional growth, O, and the importance of intuitive processes. Thus, the Grid generally tends to be seen as a more esoteric instrument, though many colleagues[12] are skilled in its use, especially as a tool in teaching.

The reader may accurately sense my skepticism about the value of the Grid, but I do not mean to be dismissive of it and there are important dimensions that I believe are useful to the practicing clinician. Some explanation is necessary at this point about the Grid: the *vertical axis* "is genetic and is divided roughly into phases of sophistication" (Bion, 1963; **CW V**, p. 101), by which Bion means stages in the growth of a thought. His delineations of various stages (e. g., $\beta \rightarrow \alpha$ elements $\rightarrow$ Dream Thoughts, Dreams and Myths $\rightarrow$ Pre-conceptions . . .) is useful in tracking the analysand's state of mind (and the analyst's as well) and how these states may fluctuate in the session. For example, the analyst may offer an interpretation that presumes the patient is in an oneiric (Row C) mindset that is capable of metaphor and instead discovers the patient, in a Row A state, responds as though being attacked by the analyst's supposed lack of understanding. In addition, I find the vertical axis to be immeasurably helpful in considering a patient's state of mind and how the analyst might phrase his interventions. Furthermore, the vertical axis offers an important metric with which to assess therapeutic change within the sessions as well as *over the course of an analysis*. With patients who are badly traumatized (Brown, 2007, 2010) and also with Asperger's children (Brown, 2016b; also Chapters 9 and 10 here), the traumatized or autistic part of their personality may at the outset of analysis register as Row A (beta) elements, but with treatment we find the emergence of more sophisticated means of registering thoughts that enable communication.

The horizontal axis proposes six "categories [which] apply to the use to which 'thoughts' may be put once they have been represented by the patient as well as analyst" (1963, p. 20) in the session. The horizontal axis follows the course during the hour of a "statement" offered in Column 1, a Definitory Hypothesis. This "statement" may be as simple as a smile or a grunt or as complex as a Concept (Row F), which is then put to certain "usage" as the clinical hour proceeds. The usage is followed along the horizontal axis, beginning with a Definitory Hypothesis (Column 1) across to Action (Column 6). (Column 2, denoted by ψ, is discussed in the next paragraph.) Column 3 (Notation) refers to statements that record a fact; Column 4 (Attention) refers to statements that have already noted but are now the focus of attention; Column 5 (Inquiry)[13] represents a use that is similar to Attention (Column 4) but refers to the analyst's curiosity about what has been brought to his attention – the challenge for the clinician here is to find a means of inquiry that is neither too incurious nor too interrogating. Finally, Column 6 (Action) signifies an action taken by either the analyst or analysand to express the original statement (Definitory Hypothesis) as it has evolved through processes of notation, attention and inquiry. For example, Bion considers the *analyst's interpretation* as a Column 6 action that expresses his perception of the status of his original statement as it has unfolded in the session. Paradoxically, regarding β elements (Row A), these may appear as Column 6 actions since such elements are acted on by projective identification aimed at unburdening the psyche of experience that has not been notated, attended to or inquired about. In each case, however, the analyst or patient has taken some action.

Each statement is further refined in terms of its placement in one of the categories that are found at the intersection of the rows and the columns, i.e., A1, C4, F5, etc. I think the Grid is most useful in helping to locate certain states of mind in the analyst and patient by their grid coordinates. For example, in *Transformations* Bion proposes that the coordinates for the ideal state of mind of the analyst and patient in the session are C3, C4, C5 and D3, D4, D5. Why does he say this? By delimiting Rows C and D, "Dream Thoughts, Dreams, Myths" and "Pre-conceptions" respectively, Bion orients the analyst toward an oneiric twilight zone between reality and phantasy and to partially conceived thoughts that await further saturation by the analyst's interpretations and the patient's elaborative associations.[14] In addition, the analyst is notating, attending to and inquiring about the ideas which come to him in this frame of mind.

Column 2 of the Grid, designated by the Greek letter ψ, denotes the "use" of a statement (α element, pre-conception, etc.) for the purpose of what is typically called *resistance*; however, Bion considers this resistance as a *lie* that aims to prevent the appearance of another statement "that would involve modification in the personality and its outlook" (1963, **CW V**, p. 103).[15] Bion comments that the Column 2 statement does not have to be true, but rather serves to avert attention away from some idea that would cause pain to the analyst and/or analysand; thus, these "lies" are related to countertransference, which may be manifest by offering interpretations about unknown turbulent experiences in the session "intended to prove to himself and the patient that this is not so" (ibid, p. 18). It is incumbent on the analyst, Bion warns, that he offers an interpretation only after he has considered whether his statement might be a Column 2 phenomenon and therefore not "ripe for interpretation" (1965, p. 167).

Bion (1965) cautioned the analyst who has a dream about the patient to be mindful of taking it as accurately representing the analysand because such dreams are often Column 2 phenomena. In an earlier paper, I (Brown, 2007, 2011a) discussed a countertransference dream about a man in analysis and how I interpreted certain elements in the dream as indicating unconscious competitive feelings that were denied by the analysand and me. This supposed realization led to interpreting his resistance to acknowledging such emotions, yet my interventions were met with a lackluster "could be" and yielded no meaningful associations. Weeks later the patient made a seemingly innocuous statement that triggered a memory of a previously overlooked element in my dream, which suddenly took on new significance for me with much associated emotion having to do with paternal longings. As I thought about this theme I realized that I had told myself a "lie" (i.e., resisted) that the analysand would not have a paternal transference since he was several years older than me. Having reached this awareness, I wondered whether this fresh "insight" was indeed meaningful or just another blind alley; however, I came to realize an aspect of my relationship with my father that had gone unnoticed and was linked to this theme. This was a process of vetting any new interpretation for its potential Column 2 qualities and I intervened from this newly discovered perspective that enlivened both the patient's and my associations to move the analysis forward.

Bion's "mystical" turn

Along with Bion's proposal of O, his alleged mystical turn towards the end of *Transformations* has contributed to the impression that he had become "less boundaried . . . [and] weakened by riddling meanings" as O'Shaughnessy has said. It seemed to many that he had crossed an unspoken border that I (Brown, 2014) have called the "separation of church and couch" by citing mystical religious texts as support for his new theory of O. However, a close reading of Bion's references to religious ideas reveals a different story in my opinion: that he discussed the concept of O from several vertices including artistic, clinical and, now, mystical/religious to help the reader grasp the meaning of O. I agree with Caper's (1998) comment that O "is a psychoanalytic model of mysticism, not a mystical model of psychoanalysis" (p. 420). Reiner (2012), in her book *Bion and Being: Passion and the Creative Mind,* similarly stated that the aim of O

> is not to bring religion to psychoanalysis. Rather, it is to clarify that psychoanalysis, as a science of the mind, is a science of spiritual proportions, and that this perspective is an essential part of analytic work.
>
> (p. 59)

These "spiritual proportions" are the analyst's recognition that, in Bion's view, there is more that remains unknown in any analysis than what is known and that our work inspires awe as we bear witness to the endless unfolding universe of meanings, unique to each analytic couple (TapO), in the analytic process.

Bion introduces the framework of religion when speaking about the individual's (TaO and TpO) transformation of O and refers to the Christian Platonistic notion of the *Godhead,* which is seen as the ultimate essence of what we call God. He refers to two medieval Christian mystics, Meister Eckhart and the Blessed John Ruysbroeck, who said "God in the Godhead is spiritual substance, so elemental that we can say nothing about it" (cited by Bion, p. 139). Meister Eckhart, a thirteenth–fourteenth-century German mystic, promulgated similar opinions that were condemned by the German Inquisition that sentenced him to death for heresy; however, he died before his sentence was carried out. Eckhart's heresy was to state that there was something more elemental, unknowable and unnamable, than God himself and of which God is a manifestation. Bion likens Kant's concept of the *thing-in-itself* – the source of a phenomenon that can only be "known" through its representation – to Eckhart's and Ruysbroeck's Godhead and says these ideas "can be represented by terms such as the *ultimate reality* or *truth*" (p. 139) [italics added].

So, had Bion gone off the rails in 1965 by bringing arcane mystical ideas into psychoanalytic thinking or was he merely using these metaphorically? As I mentioned earlier in this chapter, he had published a series of papers that dealt with making what is unknown the elusive object of analytic inquiry (introduction O in *Elements*, 1963; "Memory and Desire" lecture, 1965; "Catastrophic Change," 1966) that perhaps foreshadowed his move to Los Angeles in early 1968. I believe that Bion intentionally used the religious references metaphorically; however, I also wonder whether his thinking about the mystic and mysticism may have been a response to his ascendance to positions of importance at the British Society and the "dangers of the invitation to. . . [an] individual to become respectable" (1970, p. 78). In *Attention and Interpretation* (1970), published after his move to America, Bion wrote about the important role of the mystic in relation to the Establishment, in particular "the ruling 'caste' in psycho-analytical institutes" (ibid, p. 73). The Establishment or Institute needs a mystic who "is both creative and destructive" (p. 74): the group may destroy the mystic on whom the group's future depends and, conversely, the mystic may destroy the group. Did Bion identify with being the mystic who shook up the Establishment, threatening catastrophic change by challenging the authority of entrenched traditions?[16] There is a great deal that remains unknown about his motives for moving to California, though he commented that a person promoted to an administrative position in the Establishment might find his creative energies sapped by other pursuits, such that "He was loaded down with honours and sank without a trace" (1970, p. 78). Clearly Bion was speaking of himself: perhaps he was feeling an internal conflict about having become Establishment (President of the British Society and other responsibilities) and needed to invoke some inner mystic in order to further evolve as a psychoanalyst?

This last question about Bion's possible internal conflict between an inner Establishment and mystic relates to the clinical implications of his supposed mystical turn. I find his reference to the mystic and the Establishment to be relevant to psychoanalytic politics as well as practice. Institutes, like other organizations, need the infusion of new ideas and methodologies to avert becoming arthritic. In the book *Hate and Love in Psychoanalytic Institutes,* Jurgen Reeder (2004) detailed how insufficiently analyzed aggression in analytic candidates was manifest in their later careers as adherence to an in-group (usually training analysts) and its promotion of a group-think; that the unmetabolized aggression of the in-group was projected into an out-group of alleged apostates who were then reviled. Such calcified institutes need a jolt – whether a diminished enrollment of candidates or a sense of intellectual malaise – in order to reacquire their vitality and reignite intellectual curiosity. My impression is that until about a half-dozen years ago the American Psychoanalytic Association (of which I am a member) had a moribund sense about its annual meetings [Establishment] with many colleagues finding them unimaginative and predictable. However, more recently there has been an infusion of new ideas [the mystic] from European, South American and other analytic perspectives that have enlivened the meetings for many colleagues.

Furthermore, I find Bion's ideas about the Establishment and the mystic to be relevant clinically. As we have discussed, Bion sees real change resulting from *becoming* one's O rather than merely *knowing about* (K) oneself and he quotes Milton to give the reader one way of thinking about O:

> The rising world of waters dark and deep
> Won from the void and formless infinite.
> (*Transformations* p. 151)

This quote refers to God's creation of the world out of the "void and formless infinite" which Bion creatively links to his advice (1965, 1967, 1972) that we should begin each session without memory and desire:

> [What] is common to all developmental processes whether religious, aesthetic, scientific or psycho-analytical is a progression from the 'void and formless infinite' to a 'saturated' formulation which is finite.
> (1970, p. 170)

He goes on to say that the beginning of a session is like the notion of the Godhead, that there is an unknowable "something" (O) that will emerge from the "void and formless infinite," which I take to mean to analyst's mind emptied of memory and desire. We must wait for something to emerge – whether a thought by the patient, a reverie of the analyst, an unexpected shared emotional experience – an evolving pattern the analyst observes that "is subject to his Transformation and culminates in his interpretation Taβ" (ibid, p. 171). Each interpretation is an invitation to the analysand to "saturate" the analyst's intervention with meaning through the patient's associations, which in turn impregnate the analyst's alpha function to produce new transformations (Taβ). Through this shared fecundity some approximation of O (TpO, TaO and TpaO) is achieved that, like the future and the past, may only be glimpsed but never fully known.

Coda: Attention and Interpretation – *a deeper vision of the container/contained*

As though guided by T. S. Eliot's (1943) observation that revisiting our place of origin after a long journey permits us to know that place in a new way, Bion's (1970) next major book, *Attention and Interpretation*, revisits the container/contained relationship, the central factor of alpha function, from the perspective of his ceaseless exploration that has led him to investigate in *Transformations* what is mysterious and unknown in psychoanalytic treatment. The analytic couple – the container/contained – are charged with having to face the "Truth," which now, owing to the requirement that the analyst become the disowned O of the patient, is the "O that is common to analyst and analysand" (p. 27). Together, the analyst and analysand must "suffer," that is, bear and tolerate, the truth in order to achieve "the consolation which is drawn from the truth [which is] solid and durable" (p. 7). Given that the emotional landscape to be explored by the analytic dyad is the befogged and shadowy territory of O, then the analyst's *intuition* becomes his chief tool in probing a mental space that is unknowable. In this connection, Bion revisits his earlier (1967b) assertion that the analyst must eschew "memory and desire" to achieve a receptive state of mind, which he now relates to intuition:

> For any who have been used to remembering what patients say and to desiring their welfare, it will be hard to entertain the harm to analytic intuition that is inseparable from *any* memories and *any* desires.
>
> (1970, p. 31) [italics in original]

However, relying upon intuition instead of one's memory and desire may leave the analyst feeling off balance, which must be met with *faith*:

> faith that there is an ultimate reality and truth – the unknown, unknowable, 'formless infinite.'
>
> (p. 31)

Bion's journey in his discovery of alpha function has traveled a long distance from its initial beginnings as an inquiry into how the psyche can learn to think under fire and manage unbearable emotional experience; from there to his realization that another mind is required and, finally, to how the activity of these collaborative minds is internalized as the apparatus for thinking. What distinguishes the discussion of container/contained in *Attention and Interpretation* from previous accounts is Bion's frank depiction of the stresses on the analytic pair associated with *the transformation of O as an intersubjective process*. Bion states that patients

> experience pain but not suffering . . . The patient may say he suffers but this is only because he does not know what suffering is and mistakes pain for suffering it.
>
> (p. 19)

But the patient does not suffer alone; the analyst "can, and indeed must, suffer" (p. 19) the analysand's pain just as a mother intuitively dials into her baby's inarticulate cries, becomes that pain and through her reverie gives it a name. In my view, it is a process that goes in the opposite direction of the Biblical account of God's *word* turned into *flesh* (Jesus); instead, it is the corporeal world of sensory experience (*flesh)* that is transformed by mother's reverie into a containing *word*. It is as though genuine emotional growth occurs on a tightrope that balances between catastrophe and successful evolution of the personality, which requires the presence of a fertile connection between container and contained that itself also faces, and may present, potential danger:

> The container may squeeze everything 'out of' the contained; or the 'pressure' may be exerted by the contained so that the container disintegrates. . . [and there are] fluctuations which make the analyst at one moment ♀ and analysand ♂, and at the next reverse the roles.
>
> (pp. 107–108)

Thus, in his return to the topic of the container/contained, Bion has arrived where he has started from and the Bion who has returned is a different man, chastened by his experiences from which he has also learned much.

Notes

1 I recently attended the 2016 Regional Bion Symposium in Los Angeles, "Clinical Klein and Bion: Continuity or Caesura?" in which a colleague from Seattle mockingly said that Bion oriented analysts in LA were "in love with O," Bion's enigmatic concept in *Transformations* [discussed in this chapter]. Thus, divided opinions about "late Bion" are not restricted to any particular region.
2 The Grid (1963) is discussed in another section.
3 Later published in 1972.
4 Later published as Chapter 12, "Container and Contained Transformed," in *Attention and Interpretation* (1970).
5 George Bernard Shaw's observation that "England and America are two countries divided by a common language," also pertained to differing analytic dialects in Los Angeles and London: the Americans spoke with a primarily Ego Psychological accent that was generally hostile to the English Kleinian argot.
6 For example, he includes the "transference neurosis" under the heading of "rigid motion transformation."
7 Though he does acknowledge in several places his indebtedness to Kleinian theory.

8 Bion states, "Kleinian transformation, associated with certain Kleinian theories, would have different invariants from the invariants in a classical Freudian transformation" (p. 5).
9 Francesca Bion (2014) reports in her Introduction to this paper that it had been "lost" until Dr. Rosa Beatriz of Rio de Janeiro sent Francesca Bion a copy in 1994. Dr. Beatriz had received the paper from Dr. Hans Thorner in 1971, although Bion had given the paper to the British Society in October, 1963.
10 This denotation can be confusing since "a" for "analyst" and "α" for the "process" of transformation look very similar. In addition, many readers are familiar with the transformation of $\beta \rightarrow \alpha$ elements in *Learning from Experience*, but in *Transformations* "α" signifies the beginning transformation while "β" marks the end product of that transformation.
11 In individual psychoanalysis this is achieved through the unconscious collaboration of the analyst's and patient's alpha functions (Brown, 2010, 2011c, 2012) and Corrao (1981) has proposed a similar process, *gamma function*, in group psychoanalysis.
12 Arnaldo Chuster of Rio de Janeiro, James Gooch of Los Angeles and Rudi Vermote of Brussels are three colleagues who come to mind and are especially skilled in the use of the Grid.
13 Column 5 in the 1963 paper was titled "Oedipus" but soon was changed to Inquiry. Bion refers to Oedipus as an example of "obstinacy with which he pursues his inquiry" (p. 104) into solving the Riddle of the Sphinx; thus, Bion is cautioning the analyst about excessive curiosity such as that which "killed the cat."
14 In my view, orienting the patient and analyst to this cluster of Grid cells seems like an evolved and more detailed elaboration of Freud's (1912) concepts of *evenly hovering attention* and *free association*.
15 These "lies" may be necessary in order to bear the *truth* of the painful realities in human experience: we all need "a curtain of illusion to be a protection against truth which is essential to the survival of humanity" (Bion, 1965, p. 147). Taken from another perspective, I think Bion is saying that "lies" have an adaptive containing function in which what is too painful to endure is transformed into a bearable falsehood.
16 Perhaps we might see Bob Dylan's "going electric," also in 1965, as a musical counterpart to Bion's *mystic*? Both individuals, having established themselves at the top of their respective professions, were deemed by their peers as going too far with productions that were "too pro- and e-vocative, and weakened by riddling meanings" (O'Shaughnessy, 2005, p. 1525). Each of these highly creative men was also living in a time of cultural upheaval, which surely had some influence on their work.

CHAPTER FIVE

The analyst's receptivity

Evolution of the concept and its clinical application[1]

> [The analyst] should withhold all conscious influences to his capacity to attend and give himself over completely to his "unconscious memory."
>
> Freud, 1912, p. 112)

We have explored Bion's alpha function, "the engine of transformations," in Chapter 3 as well as the clinical implications of his *theory of transformations* in Chapter 4; however, there is another component that requires our further understanding – the *receptivity of the analyst*. In order for the clinician to submit a projection from the analysand to one's alpha function and then transform it, one must first allow it entry into the analyst's psyche; i.e., to be receptive to the patient's unconscious communication. This is easier said than done: witness Bion's (1970) caveat at the end of Chapter 4 that "the 'pressure' may be exerted by the contained so that the container disintegrates" (pp. 107–108).

My aim in this chapter is to trace the concept of the analyst's receptivity from its origins in Freud's theories, to its elaboration in the work of Theodor Reik and, finally, to Bion's contributions on this subject. My central argument is that what we call the analyst's receptivity is actually a misnomer because it does not exist in and of itself, but rather is part of a highly complex intersubjective network that is constantly operating unconsciously. I have chosen to focus on these three authors because of their seminal contributions regarding the *unconscious* aspects of the analyst's receptivity and the work of each represented a significant advance that paved the way for future elaborations. Freud introduced to us the notion of the analyst's receptive unconscious but did not elaborate it; Reik extensively described how he employed his unconscious "as an instrument of the analysis" (Freud, 1912) but did not suggest a metapsychology to account for it; and Bion's explorations of what he called *alpha function* offered valuable insights into the origin and nature of the receptive mind, whether in the analyst or the patient. I will begin with a vignette from the analysis of a man, which I will then bring to three imagined "supervisions" with Freud, Reik and Bion in order to anchor their ideas in clinical experience.

Clinical material

Mr. R., a professional in his fifties, is in the third year of analysis to deal with a sense of drudgery and anger about his life that is tied to an abiding impression that he always gets the short end of the stick. He is troubled that his wife sees him as angry, joyless and often distant. Mr. R. appears involved in the analysis, gives much thought to my interpretations and feels he is making progress, yet vigorously denies any reliance on me. He invariably rejects my mention of our relationship and that such talk feels "gay" to him, i.e., suggesting weakness and dependency. He has twice announced at the end of a session that he was leaving the treatment and was not open to returning the next day to discuss his decision. Nevertheless, he called back a few weeks later in each case to say he needed to return because his anger and depression had spiked once more. The following session occurred after I was away for one week.

Mr. R. began by saying the last three weeks had been difficult: he had been feeling tired and anxious, was sleeping poorly and that he had decided to lower his antidepressant medication. He then reported a dream: "Guys were breaking into my car, were stealing something; that's all." He initially felt anxious, and then depressed, after this dream. His thoughts turned to the graduation party for his daughter over the weekend and how "I felt like crying about her" and all her friends going off to college; feelings he quickly explained away as "sounds like it's chemical." I commented about the situations of loss he was conveying (his daughter's going away, that we hadn't met for a week, the dream of something being stolen from him) that seem to have triggered his anxious and depressed feelings. He went on to despair that he hadn't been productive last week (when I was away), worried he was not properly preparing himself for an important business meeting and that he had felt "scattered." I said, "I think coming here helps you feel grounded and perhaps your dream expressed some feelings about my not being here, like I had taken something valuable away from you." He unenthusiastically replied, "Could've been" and drifted off into silence.

During this silence a song by Linda Ronstadt, "Poor Pitiful Me," came unbidden into my mind, a tune in which she facetiously bemoans her "pitiful" state because so many men were interested in her: "bad luck" that was really an embarrassment of riches. I was brought out of my reverie when Mr. R. said he had just fallen asleep and had a brief dream of

> Two Hillbilly women; I don't know if they were actresses. They had bad teeth, were hugging, maybe kissing and laughing. I don't know if I was watching it or if they knew me.

He said it brought to mind a movie he had seen over the weekend, "Girl from Monaco," about a "Paris Hilton-type woman" who was well dressed and handsome in reality. She had perfect teeth and smile, just the opposite of the Hillbillies in his dream. I commented that it was interesting that the Hillbilly women were both laughing and happy like the rich girl and he replied that in actual life the Hillbillies are probably happier. He drifted off again and the song, "Poor Pitiful Me," came back to me once more.

I interpreted:

> I'm not sure how to say this, but I think when you're depressed and anxious you're feeling much like an impoverished Hillbilly from a poor background, but that feeling may cover over something else about you; something that may feel valuable and could be stolen from you.

Mr. R. wondered what he would have to steal and then mentioned his worries about his son getting kidnapped, email scammers who stole people's identities, another man possibly stealing his wife away and his daughter attending a university located in an unsafe area of town. He thought some more and said "I left my associate to do a bunch of stuff and I wonder if he really can," to which I offered "It's good to have an associate around you can rely on." He agreed and the session ended at this point.

"Consultation" with Freud

Within the framework of classical psychoanalysis, the analyst, having settled comfortably into his chair, places himself into a receptive state of mind that is open to communications from the analysand, which, having been received by his (the analyst's) unconscious, percolate up to the clinician's conscious awareness at which point he decodes the message to extract its unconscious meaning. This receptive state of mind was enabled by the analyst engaging

> in not directing one's notice to anything in particular and in maintaining . . . 'evenly suspended attention' . . . in the face of all that one hears . . . [and that he] should withhold all conscious influences to his capacity to attend and give himself over completely to his '*unconscious memory.*'
>
> (Freud, 1912, pp. 111–112) [italics added]

This demand on the analyst was the analogue to the patient opening himself up to *free associations* and, furthermore, the therapist was told to view his unconscious as a "receptive organ" to the "transmitting unconscious" of the patient and to "use his unconscious . . . as an instrument of the analysis" (p. 116), perspectives that I (Brown, 2011a) have called the "big bang statement from which the universe of intersubjectivity has emanated" (p. 20). Furthermore, Freud (1915a) observed that

> the *Ucs of one human being can react upon that of another,* without passing through the *Cs.* This deserves closer investigation . . . but, descriptively speaking, the fact is incontestable.
>
> (p. 194)

Thus, Freud was clearly viewing the analyst's receptivity as primarily an *unconscious* process, rooted in the "incontestable" fact of communication between a transmitting and a receiving unconscious, the activity of which was brought under analytic scrutiny through the combined handiwork of free association and evenly suspended attention. He did not develop these assertions further nor did he explain what is meant by "unconscious memory" or how to use one's unconscious "as an instrument of the analysis," thereby leaving it to future generations to expand upon. Though it would be incorrect to say Freud was introducing a "two person" model of the psychoanalytic relationship, I do believe that it is shortsighted to dismiss the scaffolding he offers us to consider how two minds communicate unconsciously.

Though this receptive stance was intended to be an "island of contemplation" (Sterba, 1934) from which the analyst carefully observed the analysand, Freud and his colleagues were well aware that the analyst's calm was often disturbed. Freud (1905a) early in his career realized that in the process of engaging with "those half-tamed demons that inhabit the human breast . . . [the analyst cannot] expect to come through the struggle unscathed" (p. 109). This realization led him (Freud, 1910) to propose the concept of *counter-transference*, that is, the analyst's *neurotic* reaction to the patient's transference that *was implicitly an intersubjective idea because of the linkage between an aspect of the* analysand's psyche with an equivalent region in the analyst (Brown, 2011a, 2011b). Accordingly, since "no psychoanalyst goes further than his own complexes and internal resistances permit" (Freud, 1910, p. 145), it became necessary that the analyst was receptive to, and aware of, his unconscious reactions to the transference. In this regard, the "material" of analysis was not simply the patient's free associations but also included the analyst's subjective experience. Freud has often been criticized for advocating a dispassionate stance similar to a surgeon, but in my view

> Freud appears most concerned about the heat of the analyst's unconscious affecting the analysis negatively; hence, his advocacy of 'emotional coldness' is meant to help the clinician keep his 'cool' rather than to promote an air of aloofness.
>
> (Brown, 2011b, p. 81; Chapter 2)

I did not know what to expect in my "supervision" with Freud since virtually nothing has been written about it, though Eduardo Weiss (1970) reported an exchange of letters with him in which he sought out consultations on some of his patients. Freud's responses were always very direct and his comments were not offered as opinions, but rather as the truth. Thus, I find Freud friendly and confident in his assessments, but also usually on target. He was quick to point out that I began the hour with an agenda of which I was unaware at first: to show my patient that he *did* rely on me and to "prove" this by evidence gleaned from his associations. I found Mr. R.'s resistance to his dependency frustrating and his dismissal of the genuine sadness he expressed about his daughter's graduation by saying "it's chemical" felt devaluing and provocative to me. When I made a general interpretation about the themes of loss, including reference to me, he went on to describe his unproductive week and how he felt scattered. Feeling that I had an opening to be more direct about the transference, I intervened and made a direct transference interpretation, a kind of Hail Mary pass, in an attempt to drive home his defense against relying on me and the analysis. His response was to drift off and to fall asleep. Freud observed that I should remember to follow his advice about "not directing one's notice to anything in particular" and he said it appeared I had cherry picked through my patient's associations to bolster my agenda of showing Mr. R. that he had trouble relying on me. In other words, explained Freud, I had neither given myself over to my receptivity nor allowed my "unconscious memory" to work on my behalf.

Freud reminded me that "no psychoanalyst goes further than his own complexes and internal resistances permit" and that I ought to do some self-analysis or consult with my analyst about what unresolved childhood complexes in me were stirred by Mr. R.'s transference. Freud continued and pointed out that he thought I was unwittingly assisting my patient via my counter-transference to repeat his infantile conflicts rather than remember them (Freud, 1914). Resolution of the patient's resistance, therefore, depended upon awareness of my forgotten infantile memories in order to help Mr. R. remember his repressed past so he could stop repeating it and instead work it through.

It is fascinating that in the silence following my direct transference interpretation both Mr. R. and I fell into a dreamy state: he literally dreamed of the two Hillbilly women and I was awash in Linda Ronstadt's song, "Poor Pitiful Me." I asked Freud what he thought of this and I find that he is of two minds about this phenomenon: first, that Mr. R. went to sleep to resist becoming awakened to a repressed memory that my interpretation aroused and that my distraction by the song was a countertransference-based resistance borne of my own conflicts. Freud also stated that he viewed the dream image of the two women frolicking together as a wish-fulfillment of Mr. R.'s transference desire for some homo-erotic encounter with me that was disguised by picturing the analytic couple as two Hillbilly women. Freud might also remind me of his statement from the Wolfman case that "dreaming is another kind of remembering" (1918, p. 51), which is to say that Mr. R.'s infantile neurosis was being expressed both through the transference and through the unconscious content of his dream, each of which were silently voicing repressed childhood conflicts.

But there was a second line of reasoning that Freud brought to explain the coincidence of Mr. R.'s dream and the appearance of "Poor Pitiful Me" in my mind, which has to do with the notion of the transmitting and receiving unconscious. Though he spoke with greater conviction about the resistance aspects of Mr. R.'s falling asleep, Freud was much more speculative about the unconscious communication occurring since this was a less well-developed part of his theory. Now, in a more tentative voice, Freud referenced an earlier statement that "everyone possesses in his own unconscious an instrument with which he can interpret the utterances of the unconscious in other people" (1913c, p. 320) and said that the nature of this "instrument" remains a mystery to him. Finally, with skepticism and some embarrassment, he quoted from his paper on *telepathy* in which he opined that, if it did occur, "that sleep creates favorable conditions for telepathy" (1922, p. 220) and perhaps the dreamy state that Mr. R. and I shared could account for this telepathic-like unconscious to unconscious communication.

It was clear to me that the forced hiatus in the session brought on by Mr. R.'s falling asleep in which each of us had our private experiences opened up a fresh line of associations that threaded back to his initial complaint of having been depressed and anxious. He talked about the "Girl from Monaco" who was carefree and fun-loving like the two Hillbillies who were probably even happier and for some reason the song, "Poor Pitiful Me," returned to my mind. My association to the song was about an embarrassment of riches that was denied and hidden, which reminded me of his first dream of someone stealing something from his car, and so I offered the interpretation, more of a hunch actually, about his depression being linked to a sense that something valuable of his could be stolen. My conjecture appeared to pay off and he was able to speak with greater feeling about his anxieties of having what is valuable to him stolen. As I shared this "interpretation," and my thoughts about it, with Freud he congratulated me for giving up my efforts to demonstrate Mr. R.'s reliance on me and instead to reinstitute my evenly suspended attention.

Before moving on, some important questions remain about Freud's view of the analyst's receptivity. First, how does the analyst use his unconscious as "an instrument of the analysis?" Second, Freud's (1913) enigmatic remark that "everyone possesses in his own unconscious an instrument with which he can interpret the utterances of the unconscious in other people" (p. 320) raises the question about the nature of this receptive "instrument," the answer to which we shall have to wait nearly 40 years to learn from Bion in his theory of alpha function. The third question about Freud's views on the analyst's receptivity is, "What does the analyst's unconscious receive?" For Freud, the harvest of the clinician's receptivity, whether emanating from the patient's unconscious or from sources within himself, was always a repressed memory: either one from the patient that was encased in the transference or one of the analyst's embedded in his countertransference. To assume a repressed memory that was unlocked from either the patient's or analyst's psyche is to say that the receptive unconscious has received a fully formed message, the meaning of which simply needs to be uncovered. The possibility that one's unconscious might be the recipient of a cacophony of formless noise that communicated unarticulated affects and required formulation had not yet been considered by psychoanalysis. We will see as we move forward a gradual shift from regarding the analyst's receptivity as central to decoding an organized repressed memory to considering it as a partner, with its counterpart in the patient, in giving meaning to undifferentiated emotional experience.

"Consultation" with Theodor Reik

Theodor Reik and Freud met in 1910 at the suggestion of Freud after having received Reik's doctoral dissertation, a psychoanalytic study of Flaubert, a meeting which for the 22-year-old Reik was "love at first sight" (Sherman, 1965). Freud dissuaded the young man from pursuing a medical education and instead encouraged him to continue with his interests in applied psychoanalysis. Seeing Reik's innate gift for psychoanalysis, Freud sent him to Karl Abraham for a personal analysis and he went on to become a renowned clinical analyst as well as insightful critic of culture and society. However, I want to underscore Reik's devotion to one of Freud's therapeutic principles that most analysts left unexplored: the recommendation that the analyst use his unconscious as an instrument of the analysis. In following this suggestion, Reik came to learn this rule required that the analyst must be receptive to any and all subjective experiences he encountered since these were how his mind registered communications from the analysand's transmitting unconscious. The chief payoff to this stance of openness was an experience of *surprise*, an affect that was a centerpiece of Reik's thinking for much of his career.

As early as 1926, Reik began to identify in the patient a "peculiar series of shocks . . . [that] is essentially a surprise" (Reik, 1933, p. 322) in response to the emergence of repressed memories. Though disarming to the analysand, the presence of these jolts determined "whether anyone merely passes through an analysis or whether it is a living experience to him" (p. 322). This necessity that analysis must be a "living experience" *applies equally to the patient and to the analyst* and Reik cautions the therapist to adopt an "openness of mind" (p. 327) that eschews seduction into the orderliness of theory and instead to find his "bearings again in the chaos of the living psychic processes" (p. 327). Thus, he moves us away from simply considering the analyst's receptivity and instead views it as one half of an analytic pair who are equally open to unconscious experience. He repeatedly urges the analyst

> to trust ourselves to the unconscious . . . [and] allow ourselves to be surprised . . . and to surrender . . . without resistance to the guidance of the unconscious.
>
> (p. 328)

The primary approach of the analyst, therefore, is the same as for the analysand: to be receptive to whatever comes to mind "even though their ideas seem futile, illogical, meaningless, irrelevant, or of no importance" (p. 330). Reik acknowledges that his technical suggestions may be difficult to follow and they require the analyst to be inwardly truthful, emotionally courageous and to use his *intuition* as a guide.

Reik's (1937) book, *Surprise and the Psycho-Analyst: On the Conjecture and Comprehension of Unconscious Processes*, continued his investigation of the role of surprise and intuition in analysis but *from the perspective of the analyst's experience. Intuition* (and hunches and conjectures) was the analyst's primary tool because "intellect is a completely unsuitable instrument for the investigation of the unconscious mental processes" (1933, p. 331). He emphasizes that surprise appears as a reaction to the emergence from repression "of a part of the ego formerly known to us but lost to knowledge" (p. 51). This view mirrors Freud's archeological model: that once defenses and resistances have been cleared the underlying fully formed memory, like a buried ancient artifact, is revealed. Just as Plato thought that all learning was a recollection of knowledge that was lost at birth, so Freud and Reik believed that beyond the repressive barrier lay forgotten knowledge, fully formed and awaiting entry into consciousness. Furthermore, although what arises from the analyst's unconscious appears to materialize from the void, it feels that way because of the alien sense which accompanies contact with unconscious phenomena. In addition, the analyst's experience of his own unconscious productions may also feel foreign because these are products of his unconscious reaction to encountering the analysand's unconscious:

> Where the analyst's idea penetrates to the profoundest depths of the other's [patient] inner life, it may be recognized as the offspring of what is repressed in the analyst and appears to him as something alien.
>
> (p. 59)

Reik's (1948) magnum opus, *Listening with the Third Ear: The Inner Experiences of a Psychoanalyst*, is "eminently an autobiography" (Grotjahn, 1950, p. 56) that delivers on its title and gives the reader a behind-the-scenes glimpse of the workings of the mind of an analyst who has a bond of ambivalent friendship with his own unconscious. This unconscious is sometimes a messenger of painful truths and, at other moments, an invaluable oracle bearing important news that must be deciphered. Borrowing the term "third ear" from Nietzsche (1886), Reik deploys it to mean using one's *intuition,* which is the analyst's awareness that his unconscious has been affected by subliminal cues from the patient's transmitting unconscious. Writing at a time when ego psychology claimed greater "scientific" status (Lothane, 2006) than plumbing the murky depths of unconscious processes aided only by one's intuition, Reik instead embraced the more aesthetic dimensions of analytic work. Together, the patient and analyst, receptive to the unconscious transmissions from each other and/or from within themselves, entered a dreamy ego state which the "analyst shares with the patient . . . [a] realm between reality and fantasy" (p. 109) with the only tools for this exploration being their intuitions, hunches and conjectures.

Prior to meeting with Reik, I contacted some people who had been supervised by him and was told that "his style was free floating and loose" (Kahn, 2012) and that "he depended on his own associations" (Sherman, 2012) as an important source of his supervisory comments. In my "consultation" I find that much of what Reik has to say echoes Freud's comments: that the analyst's task is to help the patient recover repressed childhood conflicts and that an important dimension to the work is for the clinician to be aware of his own unconscious processes. I experience Reik as much more at ease than Freud in asking about my subjective reactions to Mr. R. and he is also genuinely interested in my need to "prove" my patient's reliance on me. We talk some about my childhood conflicts around needing to feel important, which is made easier because the emphasis is not on my "resistance" but rather on using my unconscious "as an instrument of the analysis." I find that I am learning something new about my repressed problems as they have surfaced in response to Mr. R.'s provocation, insights I share with Reik, to which he replies by informing me of his concept (1937) of the "reciprocal illumination of unconscious happenings" in the analyst and patient. The idea of "counter-transference" is beginning to feel less a burdensome mistake and more a vital, though mercurial, companion.

Reik told me that Freud's idea of evenly suspended attention is the one rule to which he always rigorously adheres and he observed that I strayed from the prescription to "not directing one's notice to anything in particular" (Freud, 1912) when I pushed my agenda to show Mr. R. he needed me. Instead of being receptive to surprise, Reik commented that I was guided by my intellect, which is "a completely unsuitable instrument for the investigation of the unconscious mental processes" (1933, p. 331). Consequently, the session initially failed to develop into a spontaneous, emotionally alive experience, which Mr. R., paradoxically, had to invigorate by falling asleep and dreaming. From one point of view, his somnolence might be viewed as resistance; however, Reik said he regards the sleep, and especially the dreaming, as an effort by the analysand's transmitting unconscious to re-establish connection with my mine. Indeed, the fact that Mr. R. and I had slipped into a mutually dreamy position indicates to Reik that my patient and I had entered into the "chaos of the living psychic processes" from which true emotional growth may occur.

Although Reik did not have a metapsychological explanation for the shared oneiric state Mr. R. and I had entered, he nevertheless was delighted to hear about our emergence into this "realm between reality and fantasy." The session had suddenly evolved into a fertile exchange between one unconscious and another; however, as the analyst only I was privy both to Mr. R.'s dream of the Hillbilly women *and* to Linda Ronstadt's tune playing in my mind. Having been chastened by my earlier attempt to impose the theme of Mr. R. supposedly defending against needing me, I decided to give myself over to my unconscious and not pre-emptively assign meaning to our respective reveries – a strategy advocated by Freud and robustly endorsed by Reik. Reik added to Freud's original recommendation by highlighting the analyst's *intuition* as a beacon in this foreign, incomprehensible territory and Reik encouraged me to stay the course in facing this void, which is an indicator that Mr. R. and I each had achieved contact with repressed memories. My patience was repaid with an intuition of what our subjective experiences *might* mean, and I tentatively shared this conjecture with my patient: the hunch yielded his heartfelt string of associations about fears of having the important people in his life being taken away. Though my "interpretation" was helpful to him, he ended the session with some doubt about whether his "associate" (the analyst) could truly be relied on.

In summary, "it would seem that Freud was interested in the forces *within the patient* that prevented recall, whereas Reik is concerned with powers *within the analyst* which facilitate recall" (Sherman, 1965, p. 20, italics added). Reik was perhaps the greatest expositor of Freud's notion of the transmitting and receptive aspects of unconscious communication and he elaborated these in creative and new ways. At first he set his sights on the patient's receptivity and the surprise/shock that followed from the emergence of repressed memories, though he later realized that the analyst, through his evenly suspended attention, was also susceptible to the same experiences. Indeed, such shocks were necessary for a meaningful analysis that was a "living experience," an aim that was advanced by the analyst abandoning "the idea of a preconceived goal" (1933, p. 331). He artfully demonstrated how one may use his unconscious as an instrument of the analysis at a time when most analysts avoided dealing with the subject at all and I believe he set the stage for later developments. Reik also described the intertwining of unconscious processes in the patient and analyst but lacked a theory to account for this phenomenon and also did not formulate a theory to explain how "everyone possesses in his own unconscious an instrument with which he can interpret the utterances of the unconscious in other people" (Freud, 1913, p. 320). In addition, he viewed the surprises that awaited the analyst and patient as fully formed repressed memories in each of them and thought that the experience of a void reflected the "foreignness" of unconscious experience rather than the possible existence of a formless inner territory devoid of meaning. But the time had not yet arrived for the kinds of insights he realized to be fully appreciated and the unanswered questions to be given further thought.

"Consultation" with Bion

I do not see Bion's contributions to our understanding of the analyst's receptivity as merely an extension of Freud's and Reik's positions, but it is important to recognize continuity in their views that advance and deepen our comprehension of this territory. Interestingly, when Bion (1980) lectured in New York City in 1977 the only American work he cited, and spoke highly of, was Theodor Reik's (1937) book, *Surprise and the Psychoanalyst*. Where Freud and Reik advocated that the analyst engage in evenly suspended attention without "directing one's notice to anything in particular" (Freud, 1912, p. 111), Bion (1967b) takes this advice a step further by saying the analyst ought to begin each session without *memory* and *desire* and that "Every session attended by the psychoanalyst must have no history and no future" (p. 17). This statement echoes Freud's (1912) recommendation that the analyst "should withhold all conscious influences to his capacity to attend" (p. 111), but also seems to critique both Freud and Reik's strategy of seeking to unearth repressed memories by instead squarely directing the analyst's attention to what is happening in the here-and-now in order to "cultivate a watchful avoidance of memory" (Bion, 1967b, p. 18). By reorienting the analyst to the present situation Bion radically reconceived the analyst's receptive stance and he was aware that this advice will increase the clinician's anxiety, which seems parallel to Reik's appreciation that an analysis can only be an emotionally alive experience if the analyst is open to being shocked and surprised by what registers in his unconscious receptivity.

Bion (1959) extended Klein's (1946) description of projective identification to include the unconscious communication of one psyche to another. In this connection, the analyst's unconscious receptivity was the beneficiary not only of jettisoned unbearable experience from the patient but may also be registering a communication from the analysand whose aim was to inform the analyst, in the emotional immediacy of the moment, how the patient was feeling unconsciously. Thus, projective identification generally, and its communicative version more specifically, describes how one unconscious transmits to another; thereby accounting for unconscious transmission and reception that Freud and Reik could not explain.

Bion's theory of the container and contained (Chapter 3) offers the clinician a veritable treasure chest of insights into the nature and function of the analyst's receptivity. Owing to his traumatic World War I experiences, his work with schizophrenics in the 1950s and personal struggles with many losses (Brown, 2012; Chapter 3), Bion began to investigate the nature of some aspect of the personality responsible for processing and giving meaning to affect, what Bion (1962b) calls *alpha function*, which addresses how the receiving unconscious processes emotional messages from the transmitting unconscious. Bion's further researches led him to propose the *container/contained* relationship as the central factor of alpha function (Brown, 2012). The notion of the "contained" was not new and it referred to that which was projected into the object, but the existence of the container and the operations it performed on the contained represented a significant advance. Simply put, by proposing the presence of a container, Bion shone a revealing light into an unexplored region of the mind to disclose the nature of that "receptive organ" (Freud, 1912) into which the analysand's transmitting unconscious projects.

Bion (1962b) believes that the container is an internalization of the relationship between the infant and its mother who is able to take in her baby's projective identifications and tolerate bearing these disowned experiences. This is accomplished through her capacity for reverie, which is

> the *receptor organ* for the infant's harvest of self-sensation gained by its conscious.
>
> (1962b, p. 116) [italics in the original]

I think it is important that Bion has used Freud's term of a "receptive organ," surely not by accident; thereby, in effect, linking Freud's idea of the receiving unconscious to a structure established in earlier infancy (the container) that makes sense of the infant's (or patient's) projections (the contained). Through its reverie function, the container (receiving unconscious) *transforms* the unconscious communications into emotionally meaningful narratives, like an editorial writer who sifts through the "raw" data of the news to attribute significance to these events. Bion connects the reverie function to the *capacity for dreaming* by which the container transforms raw emotional experience into meaningful psychic events, a process that happens when we are awake and also asleep. Thus, when Freud counsels the analyst to give himself over to our "unconscious memory" and Reik urges us to "trust ourselves to the unconscious," both have sensed the existence of some psychic entity which "everyone possesses in his own unconscious [as] an instrument with which he can interpret the utterances of the unconscious in other people" (Freud, 1913, p. 320), what Bion (1962b) called alpha function.

Bion also widens the bandwidth of frequencies to which the analyst must attend because one's receptive unconscious is inherently attuned to multiple channels of information: Freud was exquisitely attentive to the subliminal messages in the patient's verbalizations; Reik, in addition, was gifted in analyzing his private reactions to the patient as these reflected "reciprocal illuminations of unconscious happenings" in the analytic pair; and Bion extended further the reach of possible new wavelengths carrying important unconscious transmissions. Thus, the analyst must be at the ready for psychic networks that convey "rhythmical communications" or come to us "in frames of mind with which we are not familiar whether we are awake or asleep" (Bion, 1997b, p. 34). Like Reik, Bion asserts we must use our intuition and "speculative imagination" (Bion, ibid, p. 40) to grab hold of unconscious communications that may, at first glance, seem ridiculous or incomprehensible; however, and this is where Bion moves into new territory: he considers these "wild" and "stray" thoughts as indicating that *the analyst's mind (alpha function) is in the process of transforming the unconscious communication*. It is this process of giving meaning to what the receptive unconscious takes in that separates Bion's views from Freud and Reik, who believed that the meaning was established *a priori* and required "unwrapping" whereas for Bion the analyst's reveries were the procedure by which meaning was attributed *in statu nascendi*. Put another way, in Bion's (1965) view the payload launched by the transmitting unconscious consisted of "thoughts without a thinker," i.e., ideas that were too unsettling for the transmitting mind to fully realize and required another mind to finish that transformation.

Before moving on to my "consultation" with Bion, I want to mention two related concepts regarding one's receptivity that are derived from Bion's thinking. The first is Ferro's (2009) idea of *transformational receptivity*, which refers to the specific function of the containing/receptive mind that aims at transforming the received "raw" material into a dream image, reverie or some other form that enables the capacity to think. The second is the notion of *altruistic identification* (Brown, 2011a) "that is initiated by a compassionate concern for the individual with whom one is identifying" (p. 227). Here the analyst accepts the patient's "transfer of pain" (Meltzer, 1986) knowing that we may be burdened and suffer our own version of that pain (the analysand's projected pain linked with analogous regions in the analyst). An altruistic identification is at variance with Grinberg's (1990) concept of *projective counteridentification* in which the clinician is invaded by disowned parts of the patient. In contrast, altruistic identification grows out of a compassionate willingness to bear the pain of taking on the patient's "illness" and through that identification to serve as a witness to vouchsafe the analysand's experience.

In preparing for my "consultation" with Bion, I learned that he did not like the term "supervision" and preferred to think of offering a "second opinion" (Grotstein, 2007), believing that the analyst was much better acquainted with the patient than the supervisor or consultant. Indeed, Bion (1997b) encouraged his "supervisees" to trust their "speculative imaginations" and that the candidate "should dare to use his imagination and dare to try to articulate it in supervision" (p. 45). He was most curious about the "model" of the patient in the analyst's mind and the mental model the analysand held of the analyst (Aguayo, 2012); thus, he was uninterested in so-called "process notes" and he dissuaded candidates from presenting these in consultations (Barrows, 2008). In other words, Bion placed a premium on the analyst's receptivity to the analysand's unconscious communications and how his receptive mind, through the work of his reverie/alpha function, transformed the received messages into a model of the patient's psyche, a process that has been described as "dreaming the patient into existence" (Brown, 2007; Ogden, 2005).

Although I eschewed bringing notes into the consultation, by now I had the session memorized. Bion questioned why I introduced Mr. R. as a "professional man in his fifties" and what importance I attached to being in the third year of analysis. I quickly replied that I knew Bion was commenting on the possibility that I might foreclose other sides of my patient from emerging to which he said I was being too Bionian, what did *I* really think? What came to mind is that I wanted to present Mr. R. as an "established" man in an "established" analysis, which actually was not how I truly felt about him. In fact, I went on, I found him somewhat pathetic and that reminded me that later in the session the Linda Ronstadt song, "Poor Pitiful Me," had come to my mind unbidden. Bion offered his opinion that that tune must have been my way of giving voice to some unnamed feeling. When I attempted to recall the moment in the clinical hour when the song came to me, Bion said he meant that it had come up just *now* as he and I were conversing and I immediately felt I was mocking my patient through the song as though he were a little boy with a minor injury about which he was overly alarmed. Bion said it may be that I "preferred" seeing this "established" professional man than allowing myself to be receptive to the injured and frightened boy who was with us. Bion reminded me that my patient needed me, like an infant needs its mother, to absorb and *become* this feeling – to know it through my own experience – so I could speak with an insider's knowledge[2] of Mr. R.'s pain. I then realized that Mr. R.'s falling asleep made me feel pathetic as an analyst, which Bion thought reflected my unconscious receptivity of my analysand's projective identification that was a "gift" from Mr. R. aimed at helping me understand him better.

I said to Bion that his comment about identifying with Mr. R.'s pain brought to mind a sequence in the hour that I was trying to understand: that there was a sudden halt in the session following my interpretation that Mr. R. might have felt my vacation was taking something valuable away from him. It was in the midst of this break in the hour that the song came to my mind at the same time that Mr. R. had fallen asleep and had a dream, which I then related to Bion. He commented that there was a sudden stop, an impressive *caesura,* in the hour in which my patient and I had our respective, but simultaneous, dreams. When I asked what he meant by "caesura," Bion explained that it was a seeming break from one way of relating to an apparently completely different mode as though no continuity existed between the two, like the supposed divide between intrauterine life and early infancy that Freud has described (Bion, 1977). Defensively, I said that my interpretation was too direct and pushed him into escaping through sleep, but Bion offered a different "model" of that exchange and instead reminded me that "the patient is our best ally." Mr. R., he said, had "decided" to speak to me through the language of dreams since I was not receptive to what he was telling me when he spoke in English about how he experienced himself as an injured and pathetic boy.

He went on to suggest that Mr. R. and I had entered a shared reflective state demarcated by his dream and my reverie; that in those dreamy moments each of us were bringing meaning to an undefined, shared emotional state about which we were unable to consciously think and which required us to dream it together. I asked Bion what he made of the content: the two female Hillbillies in Mr. R.'s dream and the song in my head, "Poor Pitiful Me," and he speculated that these were commentaries on what was happening in the here-and-now of the analysis though we were unsure of what was going on. Regarding the meaning of such content, Bion suggested consulting the theories of Freud and Klein, that the shared dreaming process in which Mr. R. and I were engaged interested him most, which seemed to reflect our mutual receptivity to a shared emotional experience of which each of us were equally unconscious. He went on to say that there was an emerging unknown in the session, what he calls "O," the emotional unconscious *truth* permeating the hour that my patient and I were gradually coming to understand through the synchronous dreaming activity of our alpha functions transforming that emotional "truth."

My "supervision" with Bion left me somewhat off balance: I had arrived with a fairly comfortable feeling from consultations with Freud and Reik that I knew what was transpiring in Mr. R.'s analysis. Like Freud and Reik, Bion placed great emphasis on the analyst's evenly suspended attention, though Reik and Bion gave greater credence to one's subjective experience and listening intuitively with the "third ear" (Reik, 1948) or through "speculative imagination" (Bion, 1997b). Both Bion and Reik investigated the yield of subjective experience that accumulated in the analyst's receptivity when he turned himself over to his "unconscious memory" (Freud, 1912). Bion and Reik also believed that in order for analysis to be a "lived" experience, the therapist and analysand were obliged to feel "turbulence" (Bion, 1977b) and the "chaos of the living psychic processes" (Reik, 1933, p. 327). However, whereas Freud and Reik always considered that the harvest of this unconscious memory would lead back to repressed childhood conflicts in the patient or analyst, Bion was primarily concerned with how the analyst and patient together transformed the unrepresented emotions alive in the here-and-now of the session. All of these similarities and differences notwithstanding, Bion's greatest advancement in our grasping the nature of the analyst's receptivity was his discovery of alpha function (Brown, 2012; Chapters 3, 4) and its constituent factors of containment, reverie and dreaming upon which we rely when the analyst gives "himself over completely to his 'unconscious memory'" (Freud, 1912, p. 112).

Conclusion

One evening a few years ago, the scientific community waited with baited breath to hear if the so-called "God particle," the Higgs boson that holds all matter together, had finally been revealed. However, no sooner had the announcement of its discovery been made, than Laurence Krauss, the theoretical physicist, noted that even with this astounding breakthrough we must "allow room for even more exotic revelations that may be just around the corner" (Krauss, 2012). Knowledge, including psychoanalytic understanding, is always in the process of "becoming," approximating some great mysterious truth that seductively beckons the explorer to press further on. Freud (1900) reminded us that even in the most thoroughly analyzed dream there is a part that remains unknown and Reik taught us that we, analyst and patient, must be receptive to, and tolerate immersion in, the void of the repressed unconscious in order for an analysis to be a living experience. Bion viewed analysis as an undertaking that aims at apprehending the unknown and evolving shared emotional truth, O, that emerges from the interacting psyches of patient and analyst in the immediacy of the analytic encounter. As I was leaving his office at the end of my "consultation," I turned to Bion and said I was reminded of line from a Bob Dylan (1966) song, "Inside the Museum, Infinity Goes Up on Trial." Bion looked up and said, "Yes, in the consulting room too."

Notes

1 Published as Brown (2016a) The analyst's receptivity: Evolution of the concept and its clinical application. *Rivista di Psicoanalisi*, LXII: 29–49.
2 What Bion (1965) calls a "transformation in O" (Chapter 4).

CHAPTER SIX

Ruptures in the analytic setting and disturbances in the transformational field of dreams[1]

In the movie *Field of Dreams*, Kevin Costner plays a man estranged since adolescence from his father, an avid baseball fan. One day Costner hears a voice say, "If you build it he will come," which compels him to carve out a baseball playing field in the midst of a corn pasture in rural Iowa. His neighbors think he is crazy to undertake such folly; nevertheless, he perseveres and creates a diamond-shaped sports ground bordered by tall spires of ripening corn that becomes the setting of the film's denouement: a dreamy sequence of long deceased Hall of Fame baseball players emerging like heroes through corn stalk curtains onto this field of dreams and, finally, an oneiric reunion and longed-for game of catch with his father. The pastoral setting, meticulously cleared from the thick rows of corn, had to be built first in order for there to be a setting in which Costner's beloved baseball players could make their appearance, dreamed once again back into existence. However, these athletes could only endure as long as they remained within the boundaries of this field of dreams: once they stepped out of the baseline they vanished.

In this paper, I explore and expand upon Jose Bleger's (1967/2013) classic paper, "Psycho-Analysis of the Psycho-Analytic Frame," recently retranslated from Spanish, and examine the interaction between the analytic setting or frame and the psychoanalytic process that occurs within that setting. In going forward, it is important to keep in mind three primary concepts of Bleger: the *psychoanalytic situation* is the overarching concept that is comprised of two elements; the first is the *analytic setting* or *frame*[2] as the enclosure in which the second element, the *psychoanalytic process*, may unfold. Just as Costner first had to construct the baseball field in order for the field of dreams to come alive, so the clinician must establish the analytic frame as the space in which the process of analysis may flourish. And just as Costner's fabled players could only exist within the confines of this field of dreams, so disruptions to the analytic setting or frame can bring a halt to the development of the analytic process. I will examine the essential importance of the setting as described in the writings of Bleger, Winnicott and Andre Green and the effects that disturbances in the frame have upon the analytic process that occurs within the structure of that setting. Furthermore, I offer a view of the *analytic process* as an "incessant process of transformation" (Green, 2005, p. 34) arising from the mutual intersubjective dreaming that unfolds in the treatment dyad as described by Cassorla, Ogden and myself. When inevitable disturbances occur causing a "crack" (Bleger, 2013, p. 235) in the frame, a "phantom world" (p. 230) of archaic emotions is released that shakes the stability in the analytic (process) field of dreams; yet, paradoxically, the capacity for mutual dreaming must be restored in order to work through these primitive apparitions. Finally, I present a clinical vignette to illustrate a disruption in the analytic setting, stirred by contributions from the analysand and myself, and how a rejuvenated capacity for our mutual dreaming provided a medium through which the setting was repaired. This vignette continues the discussion of Mr. R. from the last chapter, but through a different lens – his attacks on the analytic setting and the transformational field of dreams.

Bleger's paper is densely written and challenging to comprehend, even for analysts familiar with the contributions of the River Plate region:[3] his use of terms such as *agglutinated objects* and the *glischro-caric position* can give the reader a sense of impenetrable thickets in a foreign terrain. Another source of ambiguity is that Bleger appears to use the "setting" in two different ways: first, to denote the actual formal elements (fees, frequency, etc.); and second, as a virtual space into which the patient and analyst project unbearable aspects of their respective psyches. Therefore, the first usage refers to concrete factors which are relative invariants and the latter addresses metaphorical aspects of the setting that are unique to each individual couple. Regardless of the difficulty of the paper, I believe there is much of value to be discovered here that is clinically relevant.

"Nonhuman" aspects of the analytic setting

I suggest that we think of the setting as comprised of "nonhuman" factors, discussed in this segment, "object relational" aspects, considered in the next section and, finally, aspects of the analyst's "person" (including his mental functioning). Freud (1912, 1913c) originally described the importance of establishing the ground rules for psychoanalysis (abstinence, neutrality, free association, etc.) that aimed at *safeguarding the transference* so that it may flourish free of intrusions from the analyst. Winnicott (1949) creatively introduced the notion that the formal setting of the analysis, i.e., the ground rules, is not simply an inert background but itself carries important unconscious meaning, especially in the treatment of more troubled patients:

> For the neurotic the couch and warmth and comfort can be *symbolical* of mother's love; for the psychotic it would be more true to say that these things *are* the analyst's physical expression of love. The couch *is* the analyst's lap or womb, and the warmth *is* the live warmth of the analyst's body.
> (p. 72) [italics in original]

But perhaps these concrete elements of the analytic frame also carry a meaning that has not yet been transformed into an object relationship as Winnicott asserts? Searles (1960), in his book *The Nonhuman Environment in Normal Development and in Schizophrenia*, suggests a developmental phase in which the infant is not only undifferentiated from its human (maternal) environment but also from the nonhuman milieu and is "unable to be aware of the fact that he is living rather than inanimate" (p. 36). Furthermore, Searles states

> at unconscious levels of concept formation, subjective oneness with that [nonhuman] sector of the environment persists long after differentiation on a purely perceptual and conscious level has been effected.
> (p. 37)

Thus, in addition to Winnicott's emphasis on the relationship to the human (maternal) environment from which the infant must differentiate itself, Searles highlights the more elemental task of separating from the nonhuman environment and also asserts that traces persist in the psyche of that earlier state of oneness. Searles does not connect his ideas about the nonhuman environment to our understanding of the analytic setting, but his thoughts seem to me to link with the importance of the inanimate "pragmatic" aspects of the frame such as fees, the analyst's office, schedule, etc. His emphasis on the undifferentiated state between the infant and the nonhuman environment appears to anticipate Bleger's exploration of a *symbiosis* between split off parts of the analyst and patient that are "deposited" in the non-human aspects of the analytic setting.

Bleger (2013) further develops the model of the setting and speaks of an "ideally normal setting" (p. 229) that, when maintained, is almost invisible; not consciously perceived but always there, providing the boundary in which psychic growth evolves. Bleger adds, and I think this is his major contribution beyond Winnicott's original idea, that the setting holds in abeyance a "'phantom world' of the most primitive and undifferentiated organization"[4] (p. 230). This phantom world is "deposited" in the setting through projective identification of unbearable parts of the patient *and* analyst and "in such a way that a large part of the subject's ego is estranged in the other" (p. 33). However, Bleger asserts, there is a "symbiotic link" between parts of the analyst and/or patient deposited in the setting and the individual (analyst or analysand) who has projected those parts. This symbiosis permits the analytic process to move forward because the dangerously destabilizing experiences have been incarcerated in the frame.

Bleger often uses language that suggests the frame is a nonhuman enclosure, which he compares to an "institution": the psychotic part of the personality (Bion, 1957) is "deposited in the setting" (p. 231) and its phantoms are released through "cracks" in that frame, infiltrating the psychoanalytic process in an avalanche of elemental anxieties that have been placed into the setting in order to protect the analytic process from experiences too powerful to be managed.[5]

Bleger, importantly, uses the term "immobilized" to refer to the status of parts of the personality evacuated into the setting. This immobilization essentially freeze dries the psychotic part of the personality that is rendered as *non-process* (Baranger, Baranger & Mom, 1983; Bleger, 1967/2013) and remains lodged in the frame in a state of suspended animation, separated out from the evolving analytic process. It is important to note that *those parts of the analyst and analysand "estranged" in the setting are not transformed* while the contents of the psychoanalytic process undergo ever-evolving transformations (Bion, 1965). Thus, in terms of Bionian (1962b) language, it would be incorrect to say that the psychotic part of the personality deposited in the setting is "contained" there, since containment always implies that the contained is transformed, processed, digested, etc.

Object relational aspects of the analytic setting

This phantom world arrested as non-process originates in the deepest recesses of both the patient's *and* the analyst's mind. Bleger asserts that the patient and analyst come to analysis with their own *internal settings*: each bring with them their own fears and anguish as well as environmental requirements to keep such anxieties at bay. In addition, from the perspective of intersubjective unconscious processes (Brown, 2010, 2011a), I believe that the idiosyncratic internal settings the patient and analyst bring to the psychoanalytic situation may combine along shared areas of conflict and overlapping needs for safety. The deepest regions of primal fears in each become a fused chimera that is projected into the frame, immobilized there as non-process[6] until the psychoanalytic process is capable of tolerating and transforming these experiences. Both members of the dyad unconsciously look to the frame to house and freeze their deepest fears (each individual's as well as the "third" area of their interconnected pain), the nature of which may be considered from various developmental perspectives. In Bleger's view, these primitive agonies are about undifferentiation (agglutinated objects), including the loss of psyche-soma discrimination, and predate Melanie Klein's description of the paranoid-schizoid and depressive positions. I think that Frances Tustin's (1986) observations about autistic anxieties of dissolving and falling out of oneself are also relevant here.

I have been addressing the characteristics of the "phantom world" encased in the frame and now turn to considering the "ideally normal setting" from an object relational perspective. Winnicott (1949) spoke of how the physical qualities of the frame are concretely experienced by the very disturbed patient as *equivalent* to the mother, but the situation is significantly different in less troubled neurotic patients and/or when experienced by the non-psychotic part of the mind. When potentially destabilizing psychotic elements have been cordoned off in the setting to safeguard the analytic process, the frame is then experienced unconsciously as an invisible secure state of primordial oneness with the mother, which is referred to by many authors using different terminology.[7] Winnicott (1955) associates Freud's concepts of *primary narcissism* and *primary identification* with what he (Winnicott) calls the *holding environment*:

> In primary narcissism the environment is holding the individual, and *at the same time* the individual knows of no environment and is at one with it.
>
> (p. 19) [italics in original]

Sandler (1960) refers to a feeling state that he calls the *background of safety*, which is defined as the experience of sensory integration that protects the infant from traumatic sensory overload "that we take for granted as a background to our everyday experience" (p. 352). Other related concepts are Tustin's (1994) *rhythm of safety* and Grotstein's (1977) description of the *background object of primary identification*, both of which are internalizations of the earliest maternal experiences of oneness that promote sensory-/self-integration and live on as an unseen source of protection.

The analyst's "person" (and mental functioning) and the analytic setting

In addition to the nonhuman and object relational aspects of the analytic setting, characteristics of the analyst's mental functioning and physical presence have received increasing attention. Andre Green (2005) emphasizes the vital role played by the *fundamental rule* as an essential factor of the analytic setting. In doing so, Green elevates the analyst's *free floating attention* (Freud, 1912) to a central position as part of the frame. The fundamental rule, for Green, "encourages a mode of waking reveries during the session" (p. 33) and a view of the analytic pair as a "*dialogical* couple in which analysis is rooted" (p. 33) [italics in original]. By adopting a benevolent attitude of "understanding receptivity,"[8] the analyst opens himself to the flow of unconscious transmissions emanating from the patient and from within himself. In an earlier paper, Green (1975) likened the analytic setting to the body that is silently present when healthy, but demands our attention when disturbed by illness. Green's metaphor of the analytic setting as a body dovetails with Bleger's (1967/2013) original observation that "the patient's setting is his most primitive fusion with the mother's body" (p. 240). Lemma (2014) has extended this to include the body of the analyst as an integral constituent of the analytic setting, which she has termed the "embodied setting" (p. 225). This concept refers to aspects of the analyst's appearance that remain relatively constant such as one's typical attire, consistent health, hairstyle, etc., and that

> When the analyst's body reaches the patient's awareness *because* of a more obvious change (e.g., pregnancy, weight fluctuations, a visible injury, change in hairstyle), it mobilizes primitive phantasies and related anxieties in the patient.
>
> (p. 228)

However, Green (2005) later considered the model of the dream, rather than the metaphor of maternal care, to best describe the analytic frame; indeed, he sees a direct parallel between the "conditions of the setting and those of the dream" (p. 57). In this regard, any failures of the dream function adversely affect the capacity of the analytic setting to be a generative haven for a creative analytic process: what should have been a field of dreams becomes an arena for the "phantom world" of nightmares, night terrors and the "white terror"[9] of what Green terms "blank dreams."[10]

Bion's (1962b, 1965, 1970, 1992) theory of dreaming has had a profound effect on contemporary psychoanalytic theory and has given us new ways to conceptualize the nature of the interactive psychoanalytic process that occurs within the analytic setting.[11] The *dream-work* Freud (1900) introduced accounted for how unconscious impulses were disguised so that they may pass by the censor unnoticed into consciousness; however, Bion (1992) subsumed dreaming under *alpha function* and in doing so stated that dreaming operated constantly, while we are awake and asleep, to transform *affects* into thinkable thoughts. In other writings, I (Brown, 2012, 2013; Chapter 3) have termed alpha function as the "engine of transformations," which is achieved through the unconscious work done by the linked alpha functions of patient and analyst constantly at work to transform the affects arising from the encounter between their respective psyches. Indeed, Bion has single-handedly expanded our appreciation of the complexity of what occurs between patient and analyst: the archeological model has been *supplemented* by a view of the analytic process as mutual intersubjective dreaming (see Chapter 4), which, as Green states, produces "an incessant process of transformation" (p. 34). To say that this incessant mutual dreaming is operating is to say that the analytic process is at work.

When treatment is progressing smoothly, as Bleger has said, the setting is an almost invisible factor in which the analytic process may proceed. In this situation, the analyst and patient are engaged in a constant unconscious dialogue enabled by subliminal communications, achieved by projective and introjective processes, between their alpha functions. This is a situation Cassorla (2008) has called "dreams-for-two," which creates a shared emotional experience that each partner represents in his own idiosyncratic manner, a concept related to Ogden's (1994) notion of the "intersubjective analytic third" in which a third subjectivity is unconsciously created from the individual psyches of patient and analyst. However, when there is a disruption of the frame the crevasse that forms unleashes the previously interred bogeymen that invade the analytic process. In the best of situations, small perturbations affect the analytic couple who are able to dream/transform their shared turbulence.

On the other hand, when the disruption to the frame is severe, the primitive forces released flood the setting with a devastating blow to the psychoanalytic process: anxieties of a psychotic and autistic nature overload the connected alpha functions of analyst and analysand, thereby completely arresting the process of dyadic dreaming/transformation. The analytic couple is thus faced with a situation that Ogden (2003b, 2004a) likens to a night terror: the individual, or in this case the analytic couple, is confronted with such awesome fears that the capacity of the mind to dream is entirely overrun. The equivalent for the analytic couple is what Cassorla (2012, 2013) calls "non-dreams-for-two," which can result in chronic enactments of that which cannot be transformed by the patient and analyst dreaming together. This presents the analyst with a seemingly impossible dilemma: how to rescue the analytic process, which depends on shared dreaming, when the capacity for dreaming itself is disabled?

Relationship between the setting and the psychoanalytic process

In summary, the setting is the "depositary" (Bleger, 1967/2013) for the deepest anxieties of the patient, the analyst and, I add, the shared intersubjective terrors that arise from the intersection of their respective psyches. The analyst and patient maintain a symbiotic link between themselves and the disowned terrors each has projected into the setting, which protects the analytic process from being destabilized by the contents of the frame. These agonies are deposited in the frame through projective identification and are immobilized in a state of suspended animation, thereby allowing the analytic process to develop without being overwhelmed by the terrors encased in the setting as *non-process*. Thus, *the contents of the setting remain unchanged and do not evolve,* which is in contrast to *the material of the analytic process that is constantly being transformed* through the mutual unconscious dreaming of the analytic pair and *apres coup* in the here-and-now of the session. But is this contrast between the non-process contents of the setting that do not evolve and the contents of the analytic process that undergo transformation as sharp as Bleger asserts? For example, when an intersubjective amalgam is formed from similar fears in the analyst and patient, is this combination assembled in the analytic process or in the frame? Although Bleger does not refer to "trauma," it seems to me that his view of what has been deposited in the setting remains separated from the on-going analytic process and exists similarly to that of a trauma that may not be transformed until gaining access to that analytic process.

Like so many analytic concepts, Bleger's notion of the setting appears similar to other related ideas such as the Barangers' (1961/2008) conception of a *bastion* and Cassorla's (2012, 2013) *non-dreams-for-two*. In my opinion, Bleger's concept differs from these because the mental experiences that have been exiled to the setting remain distinct from, and viewed as having no impact on, the analytic process. In contrast, the shared unconscious phantasy of the analytic couple that the Barangers describe and the arrest of mutual dreaming in the dyad detailed by Cassorla *reflect an analytic process that has become stalled because the couple are unable to process the affects that are active in their relationship*. Rather than being absent from the analytic process and encased in the setting, these emotional experiences delineated by the Barangers and Cassorla are alive in the process and have a stranglehold on it. It seems probable that the formation of a bastion or halt to dreams-for-two *is a consequence* of the analytic process being flooded by powerful emotions that have been prematurely freed from the setting.

But how do the fears enclosed in the setting enter the analytic process without derailing the analytic work? As noted previously, there may be major tears in the setting that let loose its contents in a flood of primitive emotions to upend the analytic process with a catastrophic effect. Optimally there is a succession of small fractures that release doses of the encased fears that shake the analytic process, but are not ruinous to its functioning. However, the nature of what has been kept apart in the setting is defined by each member of the analytic dyad and the "thirdness" of what is constructed by their unconscious intersubjective connection. For some analytic couples, aggression may be so terrifying that it is projected into the frame and kept there indefinitely by an unconscious collusion. In other analyses, a shared unconscious phantasy that loss/separation is literally "unthinkable" may lead to the disappearance of such themes from the analytic process that have been deposited in the frame (as in the clinical vignette in this chapter). Thus, predictable breaks in the frame such as weekends, change in fees, etc.,[12] are unavoidable and necessary as a means to slowly introduce manageable bits of deposited fears into the analytic process for "gradual and controlled re-introjection" (Bleger, 2013, p. 35). In this manner, the re-absorption of elements previously frozen in the setting becomes one source of material for the analytic couple to dream/transform in the analytic process, in addition to unconscious themes that arise spontaneously from their interacting psyches.

Clinical vignette

I wish to return to the analysis of Mr. R., whom I presented to Freud, Reik and Bion in the imagined "consultations" in Chapter 5, to look at the material from a different vertex – his attacks on the analytic frame. In that chapter, I mainly addressed how my agenda to convince him that his trouble relying on me kept me from being adequately receptive to the deep feelings of sadness, weakness (expressed in disdain for gay men) and fears of loss with which Mr. R. struggled. On two occasions, he abruptly terminated the analysis, only to return because of his anxiety about losing his wife. Mr. R.'s sudden decisions to immediately end the analysis occurred without any apparent warning: he simply and calmly said he was not returning and thanked me for my help. The manner in which he abruptly ended our work understandably left me feeling blindsided, weak and helpless. As I reflected on Mr. R.'s mode of ending, it seemed clear that his feelings of weakness and dependency had been projected into me and now had become my burden with which to struggle, leaving me feeling puny and impotent. After his return, I brought up his leaving suddenly as a means by which he got rid of feeling weak and "gay" and instead sought to evoke those emotions in me, i.e., "giving" them to me as my problem to handle. He paid lip service to my interpretation, but it did not seem to affect him and I interpreted how painful it must be for him to experience such feelings. He agreed and went on, with much emotion, to speak about his shame that his business was dropping off and it had become a struggle to afford analysis. I said that the expense of his analysis had become difficult financially and that there was also an emotional "cost" in facing how impoverished, weak and dependent it made him feel. The analysis appeared to take on a fresh aliveness until some months later when he again unexpectedly and without warning terminated treatment at the end of a session, leaving me feeling not only helpless but also incredibly angry.

This vignette begins at a point when the analytic situation was intact and within which a good analytic process was underway produced by the intertwining of our dreaming/alpha functions: his anger, feelings of weakness and dependency were expressed in dreams, associations and my related reveries. In retrospect, I believe that Mr. R. simultaneously attacked me as well as the setting when he abruptly terminated analysis. The attack on me as analyst was expressed by the forceful projective identification of his feelings of weakness and dependency into me, perhaps to show me the true force of these emotions to which I may not have been adequately receptive. Simultaneously, his attack on the setting by stopping treatment unleashed a deeper experience of helplessness that had been cordoned off in the frame that exceeded our ability to transform-/dream at that time. However, when he resumed treatment the second time, we were able to repair the damage to the setting and reestablish a fresh aliveness to the analytic process that permitted a deeper elaboration of his feelings of impoverishment and helplessness. However, it seems that deeper terrors of loss, shared by each of us in the context of our own histories and unconsciously sensed as too unbearable for the analytic process, were projected into the analytic setting and thereby rendered non-process, awaiting expression at some future point. Nevertheless, Mr. R. again suddenly ended the analysis, once more leaving me feeling impotent and angry and also seriously mangling the frame.

When he called to resume analysis for the third time, I was reluctant to restart working together. Mr. R. was apologetic for acting like a "jerk" and promised never to suddenly end treatment. I said that I appreciated his apology, but that we needed to understand what this was about and he said that his wife had threatened to leave him because of his constant anger and unabating depressed moods. Over a period of many sessions Mr. R. spoke movingly about his anger toward his wife when she had a woman friend staying at their home, which made him furious because he felt abandoned. His rage took on an Oedipal cast: he was excluded from the special, intimate time his wife and her friend enjoyed and this was an unbearable loss for Mr. R. As we explored his rage and feelings of being dismissed, I was mindful that he had previously ended treatment suddenly around feeling dependent and that I had a three-week vacation coming up soon. I grew anxious that he would end treatment once again and, in my desire to prevent this, I began to over-interpret his fears of realizing his dependency on me and his feeling abandoned by my upcoming vacation. On reflection, I was attempting to treat *my* anxiety of loss, which was likely magnified by Mr. R.'s projection into me of his similar fears. Thus, Mr. R. and I seem to have been caught in a morass of loss, anger and abandonment – an intersubjective analytic third or non-dream-for-two – which defied our capacity to collectively dream and transform.

In meeting again to discuss resuming analysis for the third time, Mr. R.'s apology for stopping treatment without warning and his admission that he had acted like a "jerk" felt genuine. When I said this was an action we needed to understand he quickly reiterated his previous fear that his wife would leave him because of his anger, something he did not want, and so he hoped we could resume. After further discussion, I agreed to resume the analysis, but was aware of not being able to fully relax into a receptive state of mind; thus, my capacity for free floating attention, which is an element of the setting (Green, 2005), had only been partly repaired. I found myself on the alert for early signs of his possibly leaving again and so my receptivity was compromised as I interpreted his fears of depending on me and his resentment about that. In retrospect, I can see that the emotional field became permeated with strong feelings of loss, anger and abandonment that Mr. R. needed me to dream and help transform for him, but instead I was on a mission to keep him from leaving once more. The fears of loss were already alive and powerful in me (my elderly father's health was fading), but I failed to reflect sufficiently on my experience to realize the massive projective identification that was also in operation; thus, the analytic process had been overtaken by my fears of an actual loss and had ceased to be a field of dreams.

However, with this awareness I was able to recover my receptivity to the sadness and loss that entered the analytic process in a more manageable way: powerful emotions that previously swept into the analytic process that overwhelmed Mr. R. and were projected into me, were now more manageable. Mr. R. said he felt more "alive" and was pleased that his business picked up as well, and he and his wife entertained buying some vacation property. He and I, too, were now a fertile analytic couple – the analytic process now restored and the "phantoms" too difficult for us to countenance now de-activated and reposing in the setting. On a Monday session, he appeared troubled and said that he and his wife had looked at some property to buy, a lovely spot that excited him until he noticed a small nest along the perimeter of the planned home. "If we bought that property and built on that spot it would mean an end to that family of little critters, chipmunks, or whatever they were; I'd be killing them, the helpless little animals." I said it was ironic that building a new structure and the lively feeling that gave him should bring about the death of these small, helpless creatures and he nodded a silent agreement.

The murderous implications of building a vacation home unleashed a new attack on our work: maybe he should quit again right now, he said; mocking himself that the thought of killing a "few rodents" should evince such powerful feelings of guilt and sadness. For some reason, the death of his younger brother in a motorcycle accident many years earlier came to my mind. It was something he had mentioned in a casually factual manner once or twice during the analysis, but he and I passed it over as if was a story about someone distant from him that held little importance.[13] As I thought about why this came to my mind, I believe the word "rodents" was linked to his disdain for his brother and how Mr. R., then in his twenties, did not attend the funeral. I then said that "You're surprised that causing the death of a few 'rodents' would upset you so much and I find myself thinking about your brother's death in the accident and how you don't remember feeling anything about it." He replied that "It wasn't much of a loss for me. We weren't close and he was a 'bad boy' in town. I sort of expected that accident would happen anyway. Those little mice in the nest, I can feel something for them, but not him. . ." A long pause followed and he spoke softly about a time when they were much younger, went for a walk in the woods, and his brother got lost. Mr. R. frantically searched for him and remembered crying, then burst into tears in the session. In subsequent weeks, he visited his brother's and both parents' graves and cried a cry of deep release of sadness.

Discussion

In a paper delivered at the 1975 International Psychoanalytic Association congress, Andre Green (1975) noted three trends in the development of psychoanalytic theory and practice. The *first* is characterized by the search for the "historical reality of the patient" (p. 9), which aims to discover repressed remnants of the actual past as these are revealed in the transference. The *second* tendency is represented by the movement towards object relations theory in which the transference is considered as the externalization of the analysand's inner object world into the psychoanalytic process occurring between patient and analyst. The *third* development focuses on the mental processes of the patient and analyst with an appreciation of the role of the analytic setting, which, however, Green does *not* see as a precondition to the establishment of the analytic process. Though he does not explicitly speak of a *fourth* trend, in this paper Green implicitly offers an additional perspective that speaks of the necessity of a setting that "allows the birth and development of an object relation [and psychoanalytic process]" (p. 11).

At this point, I want to remind the reader of the model I proposed of the analytic process in Chapter 1 and we can now appreciate the vital role the setting plays in it:

> The active here-and-now process of continuous transformations of affects arising in the intersubjective field to create new meaning which is achieved through a perpetual unconscious joint process of dreaming and Nachtraglichkeit (apres coup) made possible through the linked alpha functions of the patient and analyst, all of which is enabled by, and depends upon, a stable analytic setting/frame.

Related to establishing and maintaining the setting, Fromm (1989) writes that the analyst must also function as a *medium* who sustains the analytic frame as a preserve of illusion in which the transference and countertransference are viewed as dream-like rather than factual. However, just as Costner's long deceased baseball players could only come to life within the limits of the playing field, so serious disruption of the setting results in an arrest of the analytic couple's capacity "to dream the analysis as it is taking place" (Bion, 1992, p. 216). Such disturbances to the frame "release" the primordial affects deposited there, which overwhelm the dyad's mutual dreaming made possible through their linked alpha functions; thus, the capacity to digest and give meaning to emotions is curtailed and what ought to have been a field of dreams collapses into a constricted arena of unmetabolized and concrete experience.

When analysis was resumed for the third time, I was reluctant to begin once more. As Green (1975, 2005) suggests, the fundamental rule, including the analyst's free floating attention, should be considered as part of the analytic setting/frame. In this connection, I seriously questioned whether that component of the setting, that is, my capacity to be comfortably receptive to Mr. R.'s unconscious communications, had been so ruined that the framework for treatment was irreparably damaged. Bion (1992) has emphasized the attack on the analyst's alpha function in which

> The analyst is to be so treated that he cannot stay awake, and so interrupted and importuned that he cannot go to sleep,
>
> (p. 217)

which was the effect Mr. R. had on my ability to think clearly and to be empathically accessible to him. Additionally, Ogden (2004a) states the analyst

> must possess the capacity for reverie, that is, the capacity to sustain over long periods of time a psychological state of receptivity . . . The analyst's

> reveries are central to the analytic process in that they constitute a critical avenue through which the analyst participates in dreaming the dreams that the patient is unable to dream on his own.
>
> (p. 862)

However, when I considered resumption of the analysis my feeling of being an enraged and impotent analyst *felt real and without metaphorical (transference) value*; thus, my cognitive functioning had slipped into a concrete mode and the analytic process had become a place of facts rather than a field of dreams. I questioned whether I could work through these emotions in order to be a receptive dreaming partner with Mr. R.

Mr. R.'s reply to my interpretation and subsequent associations about fears of losing family members, whom he greatly valued, surprised him and made him question his long-held sense of poverty. The session became more animated as he puzzled about this conflict and the reasons why he diminished the importance of his family. His fears of loss and abandonment took on new meaning as he was able to slowly absorb into himself the terror of loss that was previously deposited in the setting and, once that setting had been trampled on, flooded Mr. R. who then projected these experiences into me. These projections readily found company in worries about my father's failing health, which would have left me an abandoned "orphan," and I became aware of my wish to see anguished fears of loss as solely Mr. R.'s problem to own. Thus, I believe that Mr. R. and I had developed an unconscious pact to consign our overlapping fears of loss to the metaphorical realm of the setting where they were kept immobilized out of the analytic process. My earlier interpretations about his anxiety of depending on analysis missed the mark and it was not until the capacity for mutual dreaming was restored (his dream in the session coincident with my reverie) that the setting was repaired, which had been damaged by the loss of my free floating attention (Green, 2005) due to the repeated terminations. In subsequent months he was able to deal with the death of his younger brother, killed in a motorcycle accident when Mr. R. was in his twenties: this was a fact that he briefly mentioned at the beginning of analysis but had been "forgotten" by both of us and placed into the analytic setting where it remained cordoned off from the analytic field of dreams as non-process. When I presented my work with Mr. R. to a study group a few years ago, I spontaneously remembered one of the few times I rode a motorcycle and on one occasion came close to a possibly deadly accident. Thus, Mr. R. and I had our own reasons for blotting out the affective portions of the memory of deadly motorcycle accidents and, in Bleger's model, these "phantom" memories/emotions were freeze-dried and relegated to the setting. In retrospect, the suddenness of his terminations appeared to convey something about the unforeseen and startling loss of his brother; an experience projected into me when I had to endure the realization of an analysis that was suddenly and unexpectedly wrecked.

Conclusion

Gabriel Garcia Marquez's (1995) statement that "It is not true that people stop pursuing dreams because they grow old, they grow old because they stop pursuing dreams," can be paraphrased to apply to psychoanalysis: analyses grow old and stale because the capacity for mutual dreaming between patient and analyst becomes arrested. Like dreams themselves, mutual dreaming depends on certain conditions without which transformations of emotional experience will not occur. I have focused on the necessity for the analyst to establish and maintain the analytic setting or frame that becomes the protective enclosure in which the process of analysis may proceed. The setting holds the more primitive internal objects and associated affects as "non-process" (Bleger, 1967), meaning that they remain separated from the analytic process occurring *within* the frame. However, with more deeply disturbed patients who seek to dismember the setting and with less troubled analysands who attack the frame (as Mr. R. did by twice stopping analysis abruptly), insult to the setting opens up a fissure through which the split off or repressed phantoms held there invade and hijack the analytic process.

When this occurs, the analyst and analysand are confronted with new "material" to dream/transform; however, successful transformation of the emotional effects of ruptures to the setting that have taken over the analytic process depends on the capacity for mutual intersubjective dreaming. In the best of situations, the analytic couple are able to manage the disturbance to the process: an intersubjective analytic third is created from the unconscious operation of combined projective and introjective identifications; the alpha function, which is the "engine of transformations," of each partner kicks into gear to assign characters to represent the affects permeating the field of the analytic process; and the analyst formulates some interpretation to the patient that optimally evokes further associations to widen the web of meanings. In the case of Mr. R., his unannounced terminations ruptured the setting and the analytic process devolved into what Cassorla calls non-dreams for two and chronic enactments characterized by his provocations and my anxiety of treatment unexpectedly ending again. Our capacity to engage in a mode of mutual intersubjective dreaming was brought to a halt until I was able to recover a proper analytic attitude of receptivity, thus allowing me to gain a reflective distance from my contribution to the stalemate, repair the setting and restart a fertile analytic process.

Notes

1 Published as Brown (2015b) Ruptures in the analytic setting and disturbances in the transformational field of dreams. *Psa Q*, 84: 841–865.
2 Written in Spanish, the paper was translated into English and published in the *International Journal for Psychoanalysis* in 1967 under the title "Psycho-Analysis of the Psycho-Analytic Frame." It was subsequently retranslated and published in 2013 as "Psychoanalysis of the Psychoanalytic Setting," a chapter in a collection of Bleger's papers, *Symbiosis and Ambiguity*. This new version is nearly identical to the former except that the Spanish word *encaudre*, translated as "frame" in the earlier paper, is now termed the "setting," which I believe has contributed to some of the confusion about Bleger's ideas; thus, many analysts use the terms "frame" and "setting" interchangeably, which I will do.
3 The River Plate forms the boundary between northern Argentina and Uruguay and a rich psychoanalytic tradition developed there, including Jose Bleger (Brown, 2010).
4 Bleger refers to these most primitive "phantoms" that inhabit the analytic setting as *agglutinated objects*.
5 Robert Langs wrote extensively about the therapeutic value of maintaining a consistent frame and that "alterations in the frame create a bipersonal field in which action, discharge, and evacuation, predominate" (1978, p. 111).
6 The means by which affective experiences are "immobilized" remains mysterious to me. It's a process that seems analogous to "the cloud" in the computer world by which a piece of information is "de-activated" and deposited in the cloud where it remains until being "re-activated." However, what I am suggesting is more of a metaphor than an explanation.
7 It is also important to note Faimberg's (2014) recent discussion of Winnicott's (1955) lesser known view about the symbolic role of the father as another factor of the frame. Winnicott asserts that maintenance of the setting is the analyst's responsibility and that, in ending the session, Faimberg asserts he is functioning as a paternal figure who is "acting to separate the patient from the 'analysis-mother'" (p. 634).

8 Compare with Aguayo's (2014) recent characterization of Bion's recommended technical stance as "disciplined receptivity." Issues of the analyst's receptivity are the subject of Chapter 5.

9 A term used by one of my patients to describe a dream that was terrifying but with no content.

10 Put another way, "It is not true that people stop pursuing dreams because they grow old, they grow old because they stop pursuing dreams" (Marquez, 1995).

11 This may seem somewhat blurred to the reader. The *capacity* for dreaming is an aspect of the mental functioning of the analyst that is a central component of the analytic setting, while the *activity* of dreaming/transformation is necessary for the analytic process to proceed.

12 Also including changes in the analyst's physical appearance; see Lemma (2014).

CHAPTER SEVEN

The unbearable glare of living

The Sublime, Bion's theory of "O" and J. M. W. Turner, "Painter of Light"[1]

> In the beginning God created the heaven and the earth. And the earth *was* without form, and void; and darkness was upon the face of the deep. And the Spirit of God moved upon the face of the waters. And God said, Let there be light: and there was light. And God called the light Day, and the darkness he called Night. And the evening and the morning were the first day.
>
> (Genesis *King James Bible*)

Thus far we have been investigating the process of transformation within the narrow focus of the psychoanalytic session; however, the arc of one's life is a story of transforming certain themes – both conscious and unconscious – over the course of one's existence in an unending process to give personal meaning to our experiences. When a patient comes to us for psychoanalysis or analytic psychotherapy the work typically reveals a few major motifs that occupy much of the therapy that over time give shape and form to our lives. During the analytic encounter, each of these themes surface and command our attention for a while; then, having been addressed, their affective origins traced and enacted in the transference, the theme leaves the analytic field of attention. Not forever, as we know, but reappears at some other time to give the analytic couple the opportunity to discover another aspect of the theme that had eluded the original encounter. Each major "issue" in an analysand's life is not a singular event to be addressed once; indeed "working through" may take so long because each theme is a multifaceted composite that does not emerge until the conditions are "right" in the field to enable its appearance. For example, as we saw in Chapters 5 and 6 in the analysis of Mr. R., the analyst must be sufficiently receptive, the analytic frame needs to be established and respected, and there needs to be an on-going unconscious exchange between the patient and analyst, i.e., an analytic process.

If we apply Bion's theory of transformations to the overall course of an analysis we may ask, "What are the unconscious invariants – the emotional essences or O of one's life – which the patient is attempting to transform or represent to bring meaning to his or her life?" I believe that each of us struggles to come to terms with, make sense of, represent and create a narrative of a few central emotional situations that, while potentially very painful, once mastered create a life worth living. This pursuit can take a lifetime and may, at best, only be glimpsed and never fully realized, but that is the essence of O: it is at the intersection of one's individual psyche and the river of humanity's essence, where we each scoop a handful of clay and dream ourselves into being.

In this chapter we will examine some aspects of the life of J. M. W. Turner (1775–1851), who many consider the greatest landscape painter ever to have lived, and in this short biographical study identify two invariants in his life that seem to have fueled his creative talents in order to transform these powerful affective experiences through his art. In identifying these emotional trends in Turner, I do not wish to "reduce" his life and incredible creativity to a symptom-like status and it is naïve to link specific events from one's early years with later complex development such as producing magnificent works of art. As I discussed in the Introduction, the work of *Nachträglichkeit* goes on constantly, always re-narrating unconscious perception. The two strands of emotional significance in Turner's life that I want to address are the numerous losses he endured, especially early in childhood, and, second, his relationship to light. Perhaps as an attempted antidote to the darkness of loss, *Turner seemed to focus his impressive artistic skills as though he were on a mission to discover the essence of light*. In the last 20 or so years of his highly productive career many of his paintings became increasingly impressionistic,[2] emphasizing a bold use of color over form that seemed to probe the nature of color and light itself. However, before looking into these issues further, I want to say something about the notion of the *Sublime* that was a central concept in the Romantic period and relates to Turner's artistic exploration of light.

The Sublime

Whether we reference the ancient wisdom of the Bible or consider the Big Bang theory of the universe's origin, we are speaking of a great cosmic flash that ultimately brought substance to what lacked form and eventually life growing from the goodness of that light. In the Book of Exodus (3:2), God appears to Moses from within a burning bush that was not consumed by the fire and later (Exodus 19:16–25) the Almighty, speaking from within a burning bush, reveals the Ten Commandments. God also tells Moses (Exodus 33:20), "Thou canst not see my face: for there shall no man see me, and live," implying that it is unbearable to countenance the unfiltered essence of the Lord. One can only approach that essence indirectly through a *theophany*, such as the burning bush, which represents God but is not the deity himself. It is through such a theophany that the ineffable and unbearable essence is made known, but by its representative and is not the "thing itself" (Bion, 1965; Kant, 1799).

The quality of *an experience that is simultaneously terrifying and joyful* has been discussed in the literature on aesthetics as the source of the *Sublime*. The notion of the Sublime has been with us since antiquity (Shaw, 2006),[3] e.g., the mixture of awe, beauty and terror of the burning bush and also captured in Turner's painting, *Mt Vesuvius in Eruption* (1817), painted in menacing dark red and orange tones that overshadow the onlookers depicted at a safe distance from the erupting mountain. Interest in the Sublime became prominent in the Romantic (1750–1850) period, an aesthetic movement that influenced the work of artists, musicians, philosophers and literature. In particular, the British Empiricist, Edmund Burke (1729–1797), wrote a long essay on the nature of the Sublime, "A Philosophical Enquiry into the Origin of Our Ideas of the Sublime and Beautiful" (1756), in which he stated the experience of the Sublime arose from objects that evoke an emotional mixture of terror and delight and that the Sublime is

> the strongest emotion which the mind is capable of feeling . . . [but] when danger presses too nearly, they are incapable of giving any delight and are simply terrible . . . [but that] at *certain distances*, and with certain modifications, they may be, and they are delightful, as we every day experience.
> (pp. 36–37) [italics added]

As an Empiricist, Burke argued that our knowledge of the Sublime could only be accrued through the senses, which are the origins of all our ideas. With respect to the arts, he believed that painting clearly captured the heart of its subject because it so accurately represented, in a *sensory way*, the object; however, Burke asserted that words were superior to painting to best capture the essence of the subject.

Immanuel Kant (1724–1804) came at his study of the Sublime from a different angle and emphasized the importance of *the subjective experience of the Sublime*. Where Burke believed that the origin of the Sublime lay in its sensory qualities that evoked powerful feelings, Kant stated that the perception of the Sublime depended on the viewer's inner processes and imagination. In his book (Kant, 1764, German original; 1799, English version) *Of the Distinct Objects of the Feeling of the Beautiful and Sublime*, Kant describes the differences between the Beautiful and the Sublime: that beauty "is connected with *the form of the object*" [italics added] and is bounded by that form, while the sublime "is to be found *in a formless object*" [italics added] and is instead associated with an infinite "boundlessness." Unlike Burke's empiricist perspective, Kant held that the Sublime "shows a faculty of the mind surpassing every standard of Sense," while Beauty, on the other hand, relates to understanding. Where Beauty creates deep emotions of admiration and perfection, the Sublime creates fearfulness "without being afraid of it." For Kant, a person unable to be impressed by the sublime destructiveness of a volcanic explosion (Turner's painting, referenced earlier) is an individual whose imagination fails to register the awesomeness of that experience. I would temper Kant's assertion with Burke's emphasis on maintaining proper distance from the terrifying event: from a distance, a volcanic eruption may be a thing of beauty and awesome power, but for those in its immediate path it is deadly, like God's warning to Moses from within a burning bush: "Thou canst not see my face: for there shall no man see me, and live." However, what joined Burke's and Kant's views was a shared emphasis on the Sublime emerging out of darkness, vastness and the boundless infinite.

The notion of the Sublime as an emotional experience that mixed awe and fear began to lose favor after the middle of the nineteenth century. Indeed, current dictionary definitions of "sublime" do not include this meaning and one must comb through the obscure listings in order to reach this particular denotation. Changes in aesthetic and cultural values shifted the view of what is sublime to an emphasis on beauty. With the ascent of the Industrial Revolution at the end of the nineteenth century, and scientific values in general, artistic works eschewed study of the Sublime and instead focused exclusively on beauty and realism. However, though the thematic admixture of fear and awe in painting is less prevalent, it remains central to religious beliefs (Elkins, 2011), science fiction films (e.g., Spielberg's *Close Encounters of the Third Kind*) and especially scientific discovery that reinforces our sense of vulnerability and smallness in the infinite universe. The Hubble telescope's awe-inspiring pictures of galaxies thousands of light years away are hauntingly beautiful, yet the realization that the light which reaches us began its journey across the heavens thousands of years ago underscores our insignificance in the vastness of space.

Wilfred Bion, O and the Sublime

Whyte (2011) speaks of a paradox in the concept of the Sublime:

> we can know the ocean through our senses and dip our toes into the briny, but the vastness of the ocean is an idea that cannot be an object of sense experience, because it lacks contours and boundaries.
>
> (p. 5)

Bion was acutely aware of the apparent divide between knowledge that accrues by knowing a thing through sense experience (transformations in K) and experiencing that aspect of the object which "lacks contours and boundaries" (transformations in O). He (1965/2013) frequently refers to Kant, especially when introducing the concept of "O" (1963), which he likens to Kant's notion of the "thing itself." However, though O is described as sharing many qualities that both Burke and Kant attribute to the Sublime, the essence of O and the Sublime is emotional experience that may be too powerful to be known directly, requiring that they be viewed from "certain distances, and with certain modifications" (Burke, 1756, p. 36) in order to be grasped. In Bionian terms, this necessary "distance" and "modification" is achieved by forming a *representation* of the emotional experience in question, i.e., transforming that experience.[4] However, Bion (1970) believed that the true essence of O could not be grasped through the senses, but rather through one's intuitions and, in this regard, comes closer to Kant's rather than Burke's perspective on the Sublime. For Burke the Sublime could be known through the senses and rational thought (ideas) whereas Kant emphasized accessing the Sublime through one's subjective emotional reactions to the sublime object. And just as Burke emphasized the "terrible" nature of the Sublime, which must be viewed from a "certain distance" and Kant stressed the importance of the one's imagination to appreciate the fearfulness of the Sublime, so Bion recognized that the psychoanalyst, like the painter, is always transforming the glare of O through various internal lenses: "For my purpose it is convenient to regard psycho-analysis as belonging to the group of transformations" (1965, p 4).

Bion does not specifically refer to the Sublime but Civitarese (2014) convincingly argues that the work of Romantic authors and thinkers show "the aesthetic concept of the sublime is a fundamental theoretical operator in Bion's thought" (p. 1060). I concur with this conclusion and in reading *Transformations* and *Attention and Interpretation* (1970) the influence of Romantic period thinking is abundantly evident. In this discussion, however, I will keep the focus on the concept of O and its relations to the Sublime. *Like O, the Sublime may be evoked but not achieved.* For example, in speaking about his view of psychoanalysis Bion states that "The differentiation I wish to introduce is not between conscious and unconscious, but between finite and infinite" (1965, p. 46). Analogously, the works of many Romantic painters conveyed a sense of the awesome and dangerous beauty of nature that evoked feelings of vulnerable smallness in the face of the infinite power of natural forces. This apposition of conflicting emotions is frightfully captured in Turner's painting of *Hannibal and His Army Crossing the Alps* (1812), in which we see his troops overpowered by, and cowering before, the charcoal stormy skies and the lashing of snow. The blackness of the storm appears like a huge mouth about to devour the dispersed soldiers. We might also view this painting as a depiction of Bion's (1965) *catastrophic change*: the once formidable army having been transformed by the elements into a scattered group of frightened men. Hannibal is nowhere to be found and they are left without a leader to contain and transform their fear.

J. M. W. Turner, "Painter of Light"

J. M. W. Turner (1775–1851), perhaps the most famous of all British painters, was greatly influenced by the concept of the Sublime and his landscape paintings excelled as the greatest expression of this trend among Romantic period artists. British artists prior to this era were especially keen on painting landscapes that aimed at achieving a near photographic rendition of their subject "with a degree of detail worthy of a legal document" (Meslay, 2005). Having mastered the necessary fine skills this approach required,[5] Turner very early in his career injected his watercolors and oil paintings with a strong sense of the Sublime that evoked powerful emotions of joyous fear amid the grandeur of nature's wondrously infinite and destructive power. His work is distinctive for the use of light, captured in bright yellows, reds and related hues, to convey what is awesome and beyond words, earning him the unofficial title of "Painter of Light." Thus, though influenced by Burke, Turner's paintings challenged the philosopher's statement that "it is in my power to raise a stronger *emotion* by the description [in words] than I can do by the best painting" (1799, p. 55). Perhaps, also, this is a false argument since both writing and painting are pathways to the transformation of emotional experiences.

To say that an artist is fascinated by light is to state the obvious; however, there was some sort of magnetic pull drawing Turner's attention to try to comprehend the essence of light that he sought to discover in his work, which evolved toward progressively abstract studies of the nature of light itself.[6] Turner spent much of his youth near the Thames: he was especially enthralled by the reflection of light on the water and as it peered out from the clouds. He was once observed by a friend:

> The way in which he studied clouds was by taking a boat which he anchored in some stream, and then lay on his back in it, gazing at the heavens for hours and even days, till he had grasped some effect of light which he desired to transpose to canvas.
>
> (E. Ruskin quoted in Bailey, 1997, p. 104)

Several years before his death he exhibited *The Angel Standing in the Sun* (1846), which received mixed critical reviews and depicted another side to Turner's fascination with light: "the merciless light of this solar furnace that blazes behind the Angel" (Bailey, 1997, p. 388). Turner himself amplifies this particularly maudlin transformation of light when he added two lines from a poem to the painting:

> The morning march that flashes to the sun;
> The feast of vultures when the day is done.
>
> (*The Voyage of Columbus*, Samuel Rogers, 1810, in Latane, 1983)

Listening as a child psychoanalyst, it strikes me that the poem's lines capture and express a terrifying view of sunset – that the day has been torn apart and chewed up by nightfall – reminiscent of a child's fear of going to sleep and darkness. Turner experienced some significant losses and dislocations early in his life. His mother suffered from melancholia, was frequently hospitalized, and was described as "a person of ungovernable temper, and to have led her husband a sad life" (Bailey, 1997, p. 8). Turner had a younger sister who died at four years old when he was eight, which exacerbated his mother's depression and, due to her infirmed state, he went to live with a maternal uncle at age ten at which time it is likely that he started to draw his first sketches (Meslay, 2005).[7] Turner's father, with whom he enjoyed a lifelong warm and close relationship, was a barber and wig-dresser who had a small shop in Covent Gardens, London, and was proud to display his son's sketches in the window of his establishment. The stay with his maternal uncle was not long and the next year Turner returned home; however, he was sent the following year (age 11) to live with another maternal relative in Margate in Kent, which was on the seashore, where he attended school. It was at Margate that his love for the sea was nourished and his passion grew for capturing the play of light on the waves and poking through the clouds. One of his first surviving drawings stems from this time and shows a Margate street with the masts of ships and the sea in the background.

Upon returning to London, Turner's father proudly displayed his son's work, selling them at a reasonable price, and announced, when asked about his 12-year-old son's future, "William is going to be a painter" (Bailey, 1997, p. 16). Indeed, Turner's painting (and engraving) skills rapidly grew in sophistication under the tutelage of older and esteemed artists and his reputation as a talented young artist spread, earning him entrance to the Royal Academy of Art at the unheard of age of 14 years. When he was in his early twenties he moved out of his parents' home to his own apartment and studio: "His mother's mental disorder may have been a crucial factor" (Bailey, 1997, p. 35). Her hospitalizations for depression had become more frequent after 1790 (when Turner was 15 years old) and she was eventually declared incurable, dying in 1804 at a private asylum. Thus, her psychiatric condition worsened during the years when Turner's reputation as a painter was growing: his relationship with his mother is unknown, but we can imagine that witnessing her melancholic episodes from early in his life and onward must have affected him deeply. Did his later (1846) painting, *The Angel Standing in the Sun*, depict his mother as suffering a living torment among the shades of a burning hell?

In addition to these early separations and his mother's relentless melancholia, Turner in his early twenties fell in love with a young woman and they exchanged vows to remain true to each other. Turner went on a tour to paint in the countryside and never wrote to her, discovering upon his return that she had given her affections to another man, a painful experience that "soured him for life" (Bailey, 1997, p. 41). Turner never married but lived with two different women at various times; once, not long after his mother died, he lived with Sarah Danby, eight years his senior, and they had two daughters with whom Turner had distant relationships. The relationship ended when Sarah gave birth at age 43 to their second child, perhaps overwhelming him with responsibilities. Later, in his mid-fifties, Turner took up with a 30-year-old woman, Sophia Booth, first as a lodger in her home and later as a bed mate. He was very secretive about this relationship and introduced himself as Mr. Booth when they were seen in public and they remained together until his death. Turner seemed unable to give himself fully to the women in his life, a mistrust rooted in him from his younger days when he wrote in one of his sketchbooks, "Woman Is Doubtful Love" (Bailey, 1997, p. 120).

Turner's early experiences with loss and separation occurred when he was beginning to show artistic abilities and his fascination with light, which suggests to me that his great capacity for artistic expression was initially brought to bear in order to cope with these separations and that he was specifically drawn to a study of light as an avenue to transform his darker experiences of childhood. Although a woman's affection was "Doubtful Love," he could always count on the sun to rise each morning and fill his heart with light. A great many of his paintings were backlit with either the sun or moon illuminating an impressionistic scene – could these represent the wished-for "light" of a mother's face that was ordinarily mournful? However, are these factors sufficient to help us understand this artist's unique relationship to light: it is not as though he was simply "looking on the bright side" (he was known to be taciturn), rather he aimed to explore and dissect light in his paintings as Isaac Newton refracted light through a prism. I think that Turner's use of light, especially later in his career, signaled a movement from using color to depict the Sublime to experimenting with color to plumb the infinite.

The death of Turner's father in 1829 was a great loss and "he felt as if *he* had lost an only child" (Bailey, 1997, p. 261). Turner told friends two years earlier that he had begun to think he would be truly alone in the world when his father died. The painting *Death on a Pale Horse* is said to

> have been in response to the death of Turner's father in 1829, suggested by the unusual treatment which is both tender and menacing. Death appears, not as a triumphant, upright figure astride his horse, but as a phantom

> emerging from a turbulent mist: his skeletal form, arms outstretched, and draped submissively over the horse's pale back. Such disturbing visions were considered to embody the very concept of the sublime.
>
> (Llewellyn, 2013)

The Sublime in this work is a "gloomy grandeur" (Bailey, 1997, p. 48): this bleak painting is imbued with deep sadness and Death himself seems depleted and directionless as though riding between hell (the red) and oblivion (the yellow), weakly reaching out toward some unknown horizon. Turner's statement that he felt *he* had lost an only child conveys a sense that he was both the one who was lost as well as the one who had endured the loss.

One of Turner's earliest watercolors was of an actual fire that had a significant effect on his painting over the years. At 16 years old Turner was hired to help paint the backcloths of a stage production at the Pantheon, a famed theatre/opera house in London, which burned down one morning in 1792. He painted a watercolor of the scene, *The Pantheon, the Morning after the Fire,* which was much appreciated by the Royal Academy and was included in an exhibition that year. Bailey asserts that the fire had a lasting impression on Turner:

> It was to be demonstrated in paintings in the following decades in which he indulged his fondness for bright lights and flaring colors.
>
> (p. 39)

He traveled to Italy for the first time in the early 1820s[8] and encountered the splendid "Southern Light" that had enchanted previous artists. Following his Italian travels, Turner's use of colors grew bolder and yellow featured significantly in his subsequent paintings, especially *chrome yellow,*[9] a new pigment that was introduced in the second decade of the nineteenth century. This was a brilliantly luminescent color considered by some critics as gaudy and uncomfortably bright; his having been captivated by this color was lampooned in a newspaper cartoon. The hypnotic beauty and terror of great fires were often the subject of painters of the Sublime,[10] but few were as awesome and horribly destructive as the conflagration that burned down the Houses of Parliament in October, 1834. Over the course of one night these icons of British history burned, witnessed by mesmerized and helpless crowds of thousands of Londoners. Turner, now exceedingly skilled in the use of yellow and reds, perched himself on the Thames in a rented boat to capture this national loss for generations to come.

Some authors have suggested that the explosion of Mount Tambora on Sumbawa Island (Indonesia) in 1815, the greatest volcanic eruption since the Ice Age, had an impact on landscape painters of the time. Within weeks,

> Tambora's stratospheric ash cloud had circled the planet at the equator, from where it embarked on a slow-moving sabotage of the global climate system at all latitudes.
>
> (D'arcy Wood, 2014, p. 2)

The catastrophic effect on the world's climate from China to Europe and the Eastern United States led to 1816 being dubbed as the "Year without Summer" in which temperatures dramatically dropped, crops failed and snow fell in New England[11] in August. At times, the sunsets were more brilliant with reds and some blue colors, yet at most other times the skies were dark and overcast from Tambora's sulfate cloud of "140 billion tonnes of ash and debris" (Moyle, 2016, p. 285). It has been suggested that Mary Shelley's *Frankenstein*, and Lord Byron's poem *Darkness*, were both written on the shores of Lake Geneva in the benighted summer of 1816 while they were trapped indoors by the sublimely dreary days. Lord Byron's poem begins with "I had a dream, which was not all a dream. The bright sun was extinguish'd." Although Turner painted *Mt. Vesuvius in Eruption* in 1817, there does not appear to be a connection to the Tambora explosion since Vesuvius had erupted several times in the previous century and was a frequent subject for Romantic paintings. D'Arcy Wood (2014) cites some Turner paintings of colorful sunsets, such as *Chichester Canal*, as evidence of the effects of Tambora; however, that painting is from 1828 and he had been painting bright sunsets well before the eruption. Turner in 1816 was braving the horrid weather *brought on* by Tambora as he traveled through the rain-soaked countryside of Yorkshire on a commission to make 120 drawings of the landscape (Moyle, 2016). Thus, it seems to me that more evidence is needed to bolster the hypothesis that Tambora's climatic effects were a factor in Turner's use of color.

Together with his love of the sea, Turner's fascination with bright colors and the sun and moon reflecting on waters was expressed in many later paintings and in a particularly brilliant way in the renowned *The Fighting Temeraire Tugged to Her Last Berth to Be Broken Up*. The mood is somber here: the sun setting on the great warship, the Temeraire, which played a significant role in the victory of the Battle of Trafalgar, now being put to rest. Like his watercolor 47 years earlier of the fire at the Pantheon theater and the 1834 painting *The Burning of the Houses of Parliament*, Turner is channeling the loss of a cultural icon. The brightness of the yellow and red hues[12] belies the mournful scene of the great warship, noted for her audacity in battle, pulled by a rather faceless tugboat in an almost ignominious scene. Turner rescues this mood somewhat by adding the masts, which had already been removed, to the painting. The sun is literally setting on this ship, but the painting may also be seen as an elegy for the Age of Sail (Bragg, 2016); the steam powered tugboat anticipating a new era of propulsion and a vessel no longer constructed from wood.[13] Meslay (2005) comments:

> Rarely has a work illustrated with such poignancy and simplicity the sense of time passing, and the vanishing of former glories, alongside the relentless activity of men and the brutal invasion of modernity.
>
> (p. 103)

The painting seemed to speak to some deeply felt experience at the core of the British character that eluded words to describe, but nevertheless gave representation to, in this precious work of art.[14] Turner refused all offers to purchase *Temeraire*, even a blank check from an interested American, to which he replied in a note, "no considerations of money or favour can induce me to lend my Darling again" (Bailey, 1997, p. 347). The painting was bequeathed to the British nation.

Turner's paintings became progressively more experimental following *Temeraire* (Bragg, 2016) and the emotions these evinced were more complex, puzzling and even frightening. Where *Temeraire* dealt with loss, ageing and more clearly defined emotions, these later creations were often disorienting and disturbing. In contrast to the universal praise and adulation he had won with *Temeraire*, his new works in the 1840s were met with criticism: these were seen as "too hazy, too poetic, too imprecise, too romantic and too subjective" (Bailey, 1997, p. 362). A year after *Temeraire*, Turner painted *Slavers Throwing Overboard the Dead and Dying – Typhoon Coming On* (1840),[15] also known as *Slave Ship*. Although slavery had been abolished in the British Empire in 1833, some of Britain's trading partners – notably the United States – continued with this "tragic obscenity" (Moyle, 2016). It is likely that Turner began *Slave Ship* in 1839, the same year that the British and Foreign Anti-Slavery Society had its initial meeting aimed at eradicating slavery worldwide. If *Temeraire* was Turner's "Darling," *Slave Ship* was an angry and turbulent mistress: the sea in *Temeraire* a gentle bed of calm welcoming a hero into its port, but in *Slave Ship* it is roiling and enraged, swallowing the poor victims of bondage and the greed of men.[16] In my view, the painting captures the essence of the horrors of slavery the backlit sun mercilessly exposed and may partially account for the negative reviews this work received. John Ruskin, Turner's champion and advocate, claimed that *Slave Ship* was "the noblest certainly ever painted by man" and purchased it, keeping the painting for 28 years, "but finally he found it too painful to live with" (Bailey, 1997, p. 363).

Turner's paintings continued to become more abstract and the images lacked discernible form. His work, *Rain, Steam and Speed* (1844), "is a painting that both represents and transcends its time" (Meslay, 2005, p. 104). Just as *Temeraire* expressed the evolution away from the Age of Sail in the somber rendering of the ship being towed to her last berth, so *Rain, Steam and Speed* heralded the newfound force of the steam locomotive racing across the countryside at 50 miles per hour. Turner, now 69 years old but still the Professor of Perspective, employs this technique along with light and color to convey the feeling of speed. He pointed out a small hare on the tracks to a friend who was watching him paint and suggested that the animal, a symbol of speed, could not match this manmade creation; thus broadening the notion of the Sublime beyond nature's wonders to now include mankind's miraculous inventions.

In 1843 Turner submitted two works to the annual Royal Academy exhibition in which depictions of the biblical deluge were employed to illustrate Goethe's theory of light: *Shade and Darkness – The Evening of the Deluge* and *Light and Color (Goethe's Theory) – The Morning after the Deluge – Moses Writing the Book of Genesis.* Turner had obviously been reading Goethe's treatise, which discussed the distinction between "warm" and "cool" colors and also emphasized that the eye was not a passive receiver of light simply recording color but had an active role in the *perception* of color. These paintings offered a new "visual category (Meslay, 2005, p. 108), which

> provided new insights into the shifting nature of visual perception, in which the familiar features of traditional landscape painting — horizontal line, single-point perspective, the illusion of depth, the scenery itself – dissolve into a painterly mist.
>
> (Pfeffer, 2004, p. 4)

Both *Light and Color* and *Shade and Darkness* mix these cool and warm colors together to suggest different emotional experiences.

These companion pieces seem to pick up on the two main themes I have been addressing in Turner's work: the subject of loss and his explorations to penetrate into the essence of light itself. With respect to loss, these paintings portray the impending extinction of life and its rebirth afterwards as depicted in the shadowy figure of Moses in the center of the picture composing the Book of Genesis. The title, *Light and Color,* also implies the return of the sun's life-giving warmth and color the morning after the deluge. The circular globe occupying most of the painting *is* the sun (Pfeffer, 2004), signifying creation (the round fullness of the image also suggests a life-giving breast) and the timeless generation of light that transforms the "*Shade and Darkness*" of night into the *Light and Color* of the day. Furthermore, just below the blurred image of Moses is a faint curlicue that could imply an umbilicus, yet another symbol of the birth of life.

It seems to me that Turner's later works were a search to represent the infinite, a frequent subject of more religious art. Indeed, the subject matter of the Sublime touched on territory – awe, reverence, the infinite – which religious paintings explored more deeply prior to the Romantic period when these emotions were represented without reference to God. Elkins (2011), writing about our contemporary views of the Sublime, offers a perspective that could well capture attitudes in Turner's day:

> In past centuries, some of the ideas now contested under the name "sublime" were known more directly as religious truth or revelation. Today, writers in the humanities mostly shy away from open talk about religion . . . [and] the sublime has come to be the place where thoughts about religious truth, revelation . . . have congregated.
>
> (p. 84)

Though he worshipped the brilliance of natural wonders, Turner was not formally a religious person and, like Bion, both sought to explore the essence or the immutable Truth of their respective subjects: for Turner the nature of light itself and for Bion the Ultimate emotional Truth upon which our representational worlds depend. His paintings in the later years of his life suggested a spiritual quest in which "The significance of light was to Turner the emanation of God's spirit" (Turner website) and he was able to evoke a sense of pure light through techniques[17] that produced luminous, ephemeral colors and atmospheric effects. These may be viewed as "evidence of Turner's search for the numinous" (Prodger, 2012) in a private religion of his own design: an adoration of nature's glory and the light that revealed that glory. He died in December, 1851, when the sky had been cloudy for some time and said, knowing his death was imminent, "I would like to see the sun again." A few days prior to his death he was discovered on the floor as he crept to the window to glimpse at his two great loves – the sun and the river. Turner "did not profess to be a member of any visible Church" (Hamerton, 1879, p. 367) and his truest religious feelings were perhaps expressed on his deathbed when he uttered his last words,[18] "The sun is God."

Conclusion

When I was a young boy, I rushed home one day after school to watch live on our black and white television a detonation of the hydrogen bomb. I recall my excitement as the countdown proceeded and witnessed the explosion; beginning first as a constantly enlarging fiery donut of glaring light, which released a darker, more ominous black cloud that climbed skyward. The power of the eruption was awesome and beautiful in a frightening way, but soon my feeling shifted when, as I recall, one of the newscasters uttered some statement that conveyed great fear followed by a silence mixed with awe and regret. I can imagine now that the reporter, overcome by shock and vulnerability, said in disbelief, "What have we done?" I can still feel those emotions many years later; feelings that were rekindled when I read a recent *New York Times* article[19] about a reporter present at the first atomic explosion who said, "One felt as though one were present at the moment of creation when God said, 'Let there be light.'" These are experiences, when encountered too closely, are terrifying; but when witnessed from a "certain distance" (Burke, 1756) are the essence of the Sublime. Turner, like any great explorer of the unknown, dared to probe the essence of that light – manifest sometimes as a fiery inferno and other times as the giver of life – and enriched mankind's artistic heritage through his wondrous creations.

Notes

1 The reader is encouraged to view the paintings referenced in this chapter online to enrich one's reading experience.
2 I do not mean to suggest that he was an Impressionist, though it has been argued that his later work was a bridge from the Romantic period to the Impressionist artists of the late nineteenth century.
3 The origin of this perspective on the Sublime is typically traced to Longinus, a first-century author, who wrote a treatise on the aesthetics of good writing that emphasized evoking strong emotions in the reader. Longinus' essay was translated into English in 1739 by William Smith (Rosenblum, 1961/2005) and subsequently influenced both Burke and Kant in their reflections on the nature of the Sublime. Though Longinus is credited with originating the

notion of the Sublime, I would offer that the Biblical image of the burning bush and of God's presence as wondrous and fearful preceded Longinus.

4 Civitarese (2014) concurs, "In the end, what does 'represent' mean if not placing oneself at a safe distance from a real that is experienced as threatening" (p. 1065).

5 He was given the official title of Professor of Perspective, a technique important in Sublime paintings by which the artist conveyed a juxtaposition of smallness and grandeur; ordinary and infinite.

6 He also studied Goethe's (1810) treatise on the nature of light, which emphasized the subjective experience of light in the viewer. Goethe had taken issue with Newton's (1672) more "scientific" approach, which was the prevailing theory of light at the time.

7 Though it is rumored that "he first showed his talent by drawing with his finger in milk spilt on a teatray" (Bailey, p. 9).

8 He had hoped to visit there much sooner but the Napoleonic Wars and other political upheavals kept him away.

9 Mixture of lead and chromium.

10 Indeed, fires are an enduring source of Sublime fascination. The comic, George Carlin (1992) said: "I watch television news for only one thing – entertainment. My favorite thing is accidents and fires. I'm not interested in the budget. You show me a hospital on fire and I'm a happy guy."

11 In New England, the summer of 1816 was sometimes nicknamed "Eighteen-Hundred-and-Froze-to-Death" (D'arcy Wood, 2016, p. 9).

12 Turner used two new red pigments in this painting that had only recently been introduced.

13 Reports vary, but the Temeraire was constructed from between 2,000 and 5,000 oak trees.

14 Can there be an emotional essence at the heart of a nation – a national O of sorts – that may be represented but never fully grasped? The *Temeraire*, like other national symbols, evinced something vital about the heart of the British nation, just as the Eiffel Tower, the Statue of Liberty, Mt. Fuji, etc., give expression to some essence of each respective culture.

15 On display at the Museum of Fine Arts, Boston.

16 Bailey (2016) believes this painting may have been based on a book that described a captain throwing sick slaves into the sea because he could claim insurance payment only if the slaves had died from drowning.

17 He employed brush techniques used in watercolors for some of his oil paintings that gave a luminous shine to the colors.

18 Bailey (1997) states that Turner's actual last words were a suggestion to a friend, "Go downstairs and have a glass of sherry."

19 "Witnessing the A-Bomb, but Forbidden to File," *New York Times*, 8/8/15.

CHAPTER EIGHT

Three unconscious pathways to representing the analyst's experience

Reverie, countertransference dreams and joke-work

Deep into my training analysis as I struggled with longstanding conflicts around ambition that had not yielded to numerous attempts to understand the dynamics from a variety of angles, my analyst told me the following joke:

> Two cavemen were talking and one asked the other, 'Have you seen Oop lately?' 'No,' he answered, 'do you mean Oop, the one who discovered fire?' 'Yes, that's the one,' said the first one. 'Isn't he the one who invented the wheel?' said the second one. 'Yes, that's the Oop I'm talking about.' 'Right,' said the second caveman, 'but what's he done lately?'

I was surprised that he shared a joke, something he had never done before, which had a deep resonance in me that seemed to tap into the essence of what I was struggling with, though I could not say why. However, over the years, I have repeatedly returned to that joke and each time appreciated its value in having addressed the various layers of conflict that were unpacked in subsequent treatment and self-analysis. In retrospect, the joke was one of the most memorable interventions my analyst had made in terms of its direct and lasting impact and it served the same function similar to an interpretation, but actually more comprehensive in its reach. In preparing to write this paper I contacted my analyst and asked if he recalled telling me the joke and whether it had spontaneously arisen in the moment that he told it. He replied that it had crossed his mind before but in that particular session it arose spontaneously and he said it as it came to him.

In this paper I examine three pathways to representing the *analyst's unconscious experience of the analytic hour*: reverie, countertransference dreams and joke-work, and I will discuss the similarities and differences between these modes of representation. I emphasize that each of these phenomena occur spontaneously in the analyst's mind either in the immediacy of the clinical hour (reveries and jokes) or occurring serendipitously while asleep (dreams); thus, I see each of these as related occurrences I term *spontaneous unconscious constructions* that are formed by a similar process. Briefly put, each are created by a preconscious thought that initiates an unconscious process from which the dream, joke or reverie emerges unbidden in the analyst's mind. The "end product" (joke, dream, reverie) of this development is an unconscious depiction, as the clinician experiences it, of what is occurring in the analytic field of the moment. In addition to rendering an unconscious "snapshot" of the momentary analytic engagement, I also see these modes of representation as potential markers and important elements of *working through*. Clinical material from the analysis of an adult man will be offered to illustrate these three forms of representing the analyst's unconscious experience in the analytic session.

In *The Interpretation of Dreams*, Freud (1900) detailed the process of dream formation. He observed that a *preconscious thought*[1] that evoked an emotion during the day became linked during sleep with a forbidden *unconscious wish*[2] and that this formation (preconscious thought infused with the unconscious wish) was subjected to a process of *dream-work* to disguise the unconscious wish so that it might pass through the censor that kept it from appearing in consciousness. Dream-work, therefore, engaged in an operation of *representation* by which one thing (unconscious wish mated with preconscious thought) was represented by another (dream symbol). The dream-work accomplished its camouflaging mission through the mechanisms of condensation, displacement, faulty reasoning, turning into the opposite and absurdity.[3]

In *Jokes and Their Relation to the Unconscious*, Freud (1905b) introduced the notion of *joke-work*, which is a mental process closely allied with *dream-work* and that "nonsense in jokes is made to serve the same aims of representation [as in dreams]" (p. 175). Freud pays most attention to jokes that appear involuntarily in the joke-teller's mind: this process is launched by a barely recognized preconscious thought that "plunges into the unconscious" (p. 170) where it is linked with words and then effortlessly emerges as the joke "as a rule ready-clothed in words" (p. 167). In my view (Brown, 2016b), the true joke is a temporary structure that appears unbidden in the joke-teller's mind, like a dream or a reverie, and is one pathway to representing unconscious (or unrepresented) psychic material (Brown, 2016a). Like a reverie and the countertransference dream, joke-work creates a *selected fact* (Bion, 1962b) that unconsciously and instantaneously organizes the affects permeating the intersubjective field, which through the process of evoking laughter binds the meaning conveyed in the joke as a kind of *interpretation*.

Each of these three *spontaneous unconscious constructions* demonstrates the mind's way of representing the range of unconscious emotions active in the analytic hour by compacting these into a highly condensed, multiple layered and detailed construction. I use the word "construction" deliberately to suggest an active process of transforming the affects of the intersubjective field that yields a more or less "finished" product – a dream about one's patient, a reverie or a joke. In Freud's (1937) usage, a *construction* was a consciously formulated idea in the analyst's mind[4] about what could have happened in the analysand's early life to explain his symptoms; however, I am emphasizing an unconscious process that forms instantaneously to depict the manifold levels of emotional meaning activated in the here-and-now clinical situation. These interwoven affective layers that are compressed into the spontaneous unconscious constructions are comprised of the patient's affective pain of the moment, its associations in his inner object world, the analyst's unconscious reactions to the patient's "transfer of suffering" (Meltzer, 1986) via projective identification and the analyst's inner objects that resonate with the patient's projections.

Freud's theory describes how a dream forms within an individual's psyche and I want to focus now on the mutual unconscious process of shared dreaming that defines the analytic field. The concept of the field derives from Bion's work on groups in which he hypothesized three kinds of unconscious *basic assumptions* that appeared in work groups when the task of the group was derailed, such as the shared phantasy that a savior will appear to rescue the group and reinstate the earlier calm. In the early 1960s, Willy and Madeleine Baranger (1962/2008) in Uruguay extended Bion's concept of basic assumptions and viewed the analytic couple as a two-person group in which a *shared unconscious phantasy of the couple*, analogous to a basic assumption, may emerge. In this regard, taken from a field theory point of view, it is not important to ask, "Who's thought was it?" as Ogden (2003a) has posed, but rather the shared phantasy is created through the intersection of the analysand's and analyst's unconscious experience in the hour. Each member of the dyad may transform that phantasy or dream in his own way, but the source of their respective transformations is a jointly constructed shared unconscious phantasy.[5]

I cannot overemphasize the centrality of *condensation* in the formation of the spontaneous unconscious constructions I am describing. In *The Interpretation of Dreams*, Freud (1900) included condensation as one of the elements in dream-work and I think it is one of the least understood components of dream creation. Freud, of course, approached the dream's formation from an exclusively intrapsychic perspective and through the activity of condensation the preconscious thoughts (day residue) alloyed with unconscious wishes were mixed, matched and assembled together, as it were, to create the dream's narrative through the dream-work. Interestingly, he adds a fascinating twist to this process of combining different unconscious wishes and notes that the act of condensation is preceded by a *destructive process*:

> When the whole mass of these dream-thoughts [unconscious wishes] is brought under the pressure of dream-work, and its elements are turned about, broken into fragments and jammed together – almost like pack-ice.[6]
> (p. 312)

This evocative metaphor captures the image of fragments of ice massing together and conveys an important aspect of the dream's construction: that the dream is not built from whole unconscious wishes (combined with preconscious thoughts) pieced together like a jigsaw puzzle, then disguised and assembled into a narrative; rather, each unconscious wish is violently dismantled as though sledge-hammered into shards and these fragments are reassembled into the manifest dream content. Thus, Freud asserts, in the formation of a dream "a work of *condensation* on a large scale has been carried out" (p. 279) [italics in original]; therefore, the fragments from which the dream is built derive from many sources. For example, one may have a dream of a threatening man, which analysis shows is a composite of the sneer of a High School teacher, the hair color of a favorite uncle, the tie one's father wore at a funeral, the perceived impatience of one's analyst, etc. Thus, the relationship between the latent and manifest content is not veridical, which accounts for the frequent impression that a dream may never be fully understood because of the seemingly endless array of unconscious wish shards from which the dream is built.

Freud (1900) wonders, "How is that condensation brought about?" (p. 281) and goes on to detail how unconscious wishes cluster around a "nodal point" (p. 283) but leaves this idea unexamined. In the *Jokes* book he observed that the *day residue,*[7] defined as a "tissue of thoughts . . . which has been built up during the day and has not been completely dealt with . . . joins with an unconscious wish to provide[s] a fulcrum for the dream-work" (pp. 160–161). This nodal point initiates the dream-work that through the activity of condensation compacts ("pack-ices") the fragmented unconscious wishes coupled with preconscious thoughts and binds them to each other. Where Freud sees the role of dream-work to disguise the unconscious wish, Bion asserts (1992) that the origin of a dream, while asleep or awake, is an affective experience that has not yet been represented; that is, not having been transformed into what he calls an "emotional thought" (transformation from $\beta \rightarrow \alpha$ elements) upon which *the capacity to dream* rests. In my opinion, *it is the emotional event that is yet to be represented which both calls forth the associated unconscious wishes and also binds these together into the dream's narrative.* If the individual unconscious wishes are the bricks from which the dream is built, then the mortar holding these together is the affective experience that resides at the center of the dream.

However, we may wonder if it is sufficient to explain the formation of the dream solely by an emotional event that pulls the shattered unconscious wishes to its core, thereby creating the dream's highly condensed narrative, like an impersonal magnet draws iron filings together? Or, perhaps, is there a psychic agency at work that conscientiously chooses those elements (alpha elements) that best signify the emotional experience in order to represent it, like a painter who carefully chooses the best color to capture a particular mood? If so, the handiwork of such an agency would also be evident in the creation of a joke or reverie. James Grotstein (2000) has thought about this question from an anthropomorphic perspective and proposes the existence of an internal presence[8] when he asks, "Who is the dreamer who dreams the dream?" He suggests that we replace "dream-work" with the notion of a "dreaming couple," an heir to the earliest exchanges between the infant and the mother whose containing reveries give meaning to the baby's painful experiences. Italian colleagues have viewed this activity as a sort of stagecraft (Civitarese, 2005) with an internal "casting agent" (Civitarese & Ferro, 2013) who picks the best inner object, or creates it anew (a "character"), to represent the emotions that suffuse the field.

In my view, the same process of condensation is at work in the architecture of jokes, reveries and countertransference dreams that appear spontaneously in the analyst's mind during the session, though these constructions are even more complex than the creation of an individual's dream. In the analytic situation, these unbidden psychic events arise from strands of emotional meaning that flow from the unconscious activation of the analyst and patient in the immediacy of the clinical hour: analogous regions in each of their minds are mobilized and bits and pieces of their respective psyches are instantaneously condensed to forge the shared unconscious phantasy of the couple that represents the mood of the session. This shared phantasy, which seems akin to Ogden's (1994) *intersubjective analytic third,* is a highly complex network that flows spontaneously from the unconscious interaction between the analytic couple. An unconscious jointly constructed affective mood takes hold of the hour and is subsequently transformed through each member's personal metaphors.

From an intersubjective perspective, the same question may be raised: by what process and through which psychic agency is the shared unconscious phantasy of the hour organized? In the immediacy of the analytic hour affects arise as the internal worlds of the patient and analyst unconsciously communicate and a shared unconscious phantasy of the couple evolves to narrate/dream the emotional situation of which the analytic couple remains unaware. This shared phantasy is constructed from experiences in the psyches of analyst and patient that resonate with the emotional core of their mutual unconscious experience and represents their respective transformation/dream of the field's emotional hue from within each of their respective representational worlds; thus, particular internal objects in the analyst's and patient's psyches are identified as best suited to represent the emotional coloring of the field. Just as Freud described how unconscious wishes in an individual's dream have been deconstructed, so these inner objects of the analysand and analyst are subsequently broken apart and then reassembled as the images populating the dream, the reverie or the joke. These oneiric images are composite figures assembled from aspects of each member of the analytic pair that have been quarried from various levels of their individual emotional lives, resulting in an infinite number of potential chimeras to represent the shared unconscious phantasy.

I will now turn to discuss how the unbidden appearance of a joke, a reverie and a countertransference dream occurred to me at various points in the analytic work with a patient and how these spontaneous unconscious structures served to represent the emotional climate of the hours in which these appeared. These manifestations prompted self-analytic work that enabled me to grab hold of sadistic themes that hovered at the edge of our respective awareness, yet which both the patient and I defended against. I also address how a working through process was evident in the emergence of first a joke, then a reverie and, finally, a countertransference dream.

Clinical Material – "Mr. 72"

Mr. B., a man in his mid-sixties, has lived alone his entire adult life although he has had many relationships with women, some lasting several years. He has enjoyed significant success in his career that has enabled him to fashion a life in which he needs little from others. His lively imagination and sense of irony is very engaging and he is proud of a particular aesthetic characterized by simplicity: he appears to wear the same casual clothes every day, though in reality he has a large number of identical slacks, shirts and shoes. The interior of his home is nearly monochromatic, with some splashes of color, and he has a picturesque summer residence that is quiet and bucolic. In his analysis we have understood this need for sameness as offering a buffer zone against various impingements from sounds that are too loud, colors too bright, an unpredictably rageful father, a painful experience with a woman who "dropped" him, and latency age friends who would unsuspectedly physically attack him. I commented that his nickname could be Mr. 72 degrees, which he has subsequently adopted for himself, since he committed much of his life to maintaining an unwavering physical and emotional climate.

Not long into Mr. B.'s analysis, he was buffeted by numerous losses of important family members which broadsided him with unexpected waves of sadness. However, what unnerved him the most was the stormy relationship and his intense rage with R., a beautiful woman much younger than he, who embodied "aesthetic perfection." In one session, Mr. B. expressed his fear of getting openly angry towards R. and I commented that he seemed anxious about his anger invading the quietly peaceful time with her and that it was also difficult to bring his rage into the sessions, which he preferred to keep tranquil. He went on to talk about the order of things getting disrupted, his fears of overreacting and that he easily feels overwhelmed; that "it's a less than easy way to be."[9] I said that the phrase, "a less than easy way to be," and took the fire out of his rage, which he acknowledged as his typical defense of smoothing things out.

At this point in the session, the following joke spontaneously came to my mind:

> It is the mid-1930s in Berlin and two Jewish men, fearing that Hitler was going to be very bad for the Jews, hatched a plot to assassinate him. They followed his routine travels around the city and discovered that every Tuesday at 11 AM he passed a certain corner. They got a gun and waited for him to appear. They wait 15 minutes, no Hitler; then one-half hour and still no Hitler. Finally, after an hour, one man turns to the other and says, "Gee, I hope he's OK."

I assumed that this was a product of my unconscious joke-work giving representation to emotions in the intersubjective field and that the appearance of the character, Hitler, pointed to powerfully destructive affects permeating that field (Ferro, 2009a). In addition, to paraphrase Ogden (2003a), who's joke was this? I thought of the joke as a tragic-comic story arising in *my mind* but sponsored by linked unconscious processes operating out of the awareness of Mr. B. and me. Furthermore, given Freud's observation that joke-work, like dream-work, is partly created through the mechanism of condensation, I immediately detected multiple themes active in the hour, and also tied to our respective histories, tightly compacted into this joke. On one level, the two Jewish men out to assassinate Hitler were Mr. B. and me, with Hitler representing my patient's, and I believe my, feared destructiveness. The humor disguises the terrible reality of the Holocaust, which, despite the manic feeling of being able to prevent it in the joke, nevertheless wrought its annihilating slaughter. Was I representing a feeling that Mr. B. and I were equally incapable of managing powerful hostile emotions should they arise in our relationship? Unbeknownst to Mr. B., he and I were born in the same part of New York City several years after World War II and, though neither of our families had been directly touched by the Holocaust, knowledge of its horrors permeated the emotional atmosphere of our early childhoods. For example, my mother, who was an identical twin, talked about Mengele's inhuman twin experiments, which brought the barbarism of Auschwitz too close to home. From the angle of Mr. B.'s inner object world, we can see how his internal persecutors (his father and childhood bullies) were also folded into the Hitler figure. Thus, from a Freudian perspective, this joke expressed a shared wish that we could avert sadistic aggression from invading the analysis; from a Bionian vertex, the joke represented the immediate unconscious anxiety of the session, i.e, our shared fear that a cruel aggression might spiral out of control.

I had the sense that this joke contained a preliminary sort of interpretation and noticed that the joke came to mind immediately after Mr. B. diminished feeling overwhelmed by saying, "it's a less than easy way to be." It felt important to offer some statement about what I thought was going on in the moment though I was unable to extract something cogent from the joke to say and thus I decided to let the joke speak for itself. I said that when he stated "it's a less than easy way to be" a joke came to mind that I thought had something important to say about what was happening in the session at the moment. He said it reminded him of the story of the *Golem* (a Frankenstein-like figure created out of earth) who came to life to save the Jews of Prague from ruin. I said that the Golem prevented a catastrophe and Mr. B. continued by talking about his pleasure in creating something good that made him feel things were under his control. I interpreted:

> Putting together what you are telling me about the Golem saving everything from ruin and the joke about trying to kill Hitler, I think there's something about preventing a devastating catastrophe that we're talking about.

Mr. B. replied:

> I have a fear that equilibrium, that existence could be knocked over – there's a scared little boy in there, he exists within me. When I'm in my element everything's OK, but often I'm not. I set the bar of a 72 degree room to keep from feeling vulnerable, but maybe it's too high and I'm making myself even more vulnerable because of that.

If we pay close attention to Freud's view of how jokes are unconsciously constructed, we can place their spontaneous appearance in the analyst's (or patient's) mind on equal footing with the importance accorded to dreams and reveries. Like reveries, jokes that appear unbidden in the analytic hour are instigated by a preconscious thought that "plunges into the unconscious" and is associated with powerful affective experiences that magnetically draw associated memories and internal objects together, molding these into the reverie or dream that then appears in conscious thinking as a visual/auditory reverie or as a spontaneous joke already "fully clothed in words." Both may express a wish and also offer a "commentary" on what is happening in the unconscious intersubjective field of the moment. I want to underline once more that we cannot overemphasize *the essential role that condensation plays in the formation of a reverie, joke or dream* and reflects the incredible capacity of the mind, in barely a moment, to fashion a multi-layered composite that symbolically registers unconscious and/or unrepresented affects.

Reverie and a countertransference dream

I will now present material from Mr. B.'s analysis several weeks after the "joke" session to illustrate the use of reverie and a countertransference dream as pathways to representing the analyst's unconscious experience in the analytic hour. In a Thursday session, the last of the four sessions of the week, I returned a minute late from an appointment out of my office to be greeted by Mr. B. in my waiting room who said somewhat sarcastically, "Welcome home, you're cutting it close!" On the couch he spoke anxiously about an angry argument with R. and that she was not returning his calls. I commented that perhaps it feels that both R. and I are "cutting it too close," leaving him in an uncertain situation. He went on to speak about things being out of his control, which inevitably brought up memories of childhood friends who unexpectedly bullied him. I said that he needs to feel in control of situations in order to avoid being thrown into an unsafe and unprotected place, to which Mr. B. responded by speaking about feeling trapped doing things he did not want to do and having feelings he did not want to have. He continued, "I don't like being that angry, I end up not feeling like a *player* anymore."

I think Freud's observation that a joke is initiated by a preconscious thought that is pushed into the unconscious and then resurfaces as a joke also applies to the formation of a reverie. When Mr. B. spoke of "not feeling like a player" the word "player" triggered the following reverie for me: a scene from the film, *The Pope of Greenwich Village*, in which three small time hoodlums, one of whom is an older man probably in his sixties, steal money from a Mafia boss and are found out. One of the younger men has his thumb cut off and the older thief, realizing that he would be killed, moves out of town in haste leaving behind his wife and child. The central part of my reverie is the look of having been beaten down in the older man's face, which evokes a sense of humiliation in me. I was distracted by my evocative reverie and then "rejoined" Mr. B. as he said he would like a t-shirt with "just leave me alone" printed on it. He continued by expressing a wish for a Fortress of Solitude, Superman's private place for rest and reflection and that, "I have no breathing room, no place to go; it would be an important place to go to for my survival." I replied, "I think being here feels like a place of solitude and my being a minute or two late today seems to have punctured that, threatened your survival." As the hour came to a close, I felt that my interventions had emphasized Mr. B.'s need for safety to the exclusion of sadistic themes of being beaten down, castrated and his survival threatened.

Over the weekend I had the following dream:

> He and I are in a bathroom and he is on his knees washing out the tub, cleaning it. I notice that he has stacked some items, perhaps on the sink nearby, that look like they could be from my desk. I have a feeling of being intruded upon: that he has gone into *my* bathroom, moved *my* things and placed them somewhere they don't belong and that he is cleaning *my* bathtub.

The dream brought to mind that even though Mr. B. is respectful of my boundaries, doesn't ask where I go or other personal questions, that he enters the office *like he owns the place*: he puts his keys and cell phone on my desk and drapes his jacket on the desk chair in a friendly manner while asking me how I am, so that I have not been aware of feeling intruded on. Nevertheless, the dream evokes emotions of being controlled by and encroached on through his apparent kindness, like his scrubbing the tub as though it belonged to him. There is also something pathetic and devalued about the dream image of him on his knees cleaning the bathtub and this brings to mind the defeated and humiliated older man from my reverie in the last session. Finally, the phrase, "like he owns the place," is an idiom my mother used and, together with the image of scrubbing the tub, brings her intrusiveness to mind.

I (Brown, 2007) view the countertransference dream as revealing the deep unconscious way the patient is being dreamed *into existence* (Ogden, 2005) in the analyst's mind. This is an unconscious mental activity by which the analysand gradually comes emotionally alive for the analyst through the linkage of aspects of the patient with analogous sectors in the analyst's mind. In addition, affects that arise within a session that exceed the capacity of the analyst and patient to represent in the hour may serve as preconscious day residues that stimulate the countertransference dream. In the session in which my *Pope of Greenwich Village* reverie occurred, Mr. B. began with a sarcastic comment when I was late for a minute and went on to speak about his fear of losing control of his anger, feeling bullied and needing to be in charge of situations. I interpreted that being in control was a means of feeling safe and he replied that when he is not in charge he no longer feels like a "player," which triggered my reverie and associated emotions of being beaten down and humiliated. Thus, my reverie picked up on and represented Mr. B.'s fear that survival was at stake and his need for safety; however, by emphasizing the need for protection I unconsciously sidestepped the aggression in the hour: "*cutting* things too closely," being beaten down and the sadistic Mafioso cutting off a thumb.

I believe that the theme of sadistic control that was not directly addressed in the session sponsored my countertransference dream three days later that depicted these emotions on several levels. My initial feeling in the dream was that Mr. B. was being helpful in cleaning my tub, but this quickly changed to feeling invaded by him, which brought to mind his controlling behavior in the sessions, masked by chatty friendliness, and acting "like he owned the place." In addition, casting Mr. B. as cleaning the tub on his knees made me aware of my sadistic wish to control, diminish and humiliate him, which reminded me of the beaten down older thief in my reverie, a representation that condensed my empathy for Mr. B. with a sadistic wish to dominate him. Furthermore, the connection to memories of my mother amplified the theme of invasiveness and control and added another layer of meaning that transformed the shared emotional field into one colored by sadism, dominance and humiliation. Thus, my countertransference dream appeared to give representation to a conflict active at that moment in the analysis: two men in their sixties engaged in an unconscious struggle for dominance, hidden by friendly feelings and apparent helpfulness, and both struggling to stay oblivious to these emotions.

Discussion

In this chapter, I have focused on three pathways by which the analyst represents his unconscious experience in the immediacy of the clinical hour: reverie, joke-work and the countertransference dream. There is much that these transformational processes have in common and important ways in which they differ. *All three are formed by a similar process: an emotional experience that must be represented for unconscious communication to occur through the evocation of analogous affects in the receiver,* what E. L. and E. M. da Rocha Barros (in press) call the "expressive function of the mind." I want to emphasize that joke-work, reveries and dream-work in the countertransference dream are not only pathways to representation, but also offer a window into seeing the expressive function of the mind at work in the moment of the session. Thus, we can posit the same general mechanism by which all three phenomena form: an emotional event (preconscious thought/day residue) occurs that is not represented at the moment it is experienced, which then "plunges into the unconscious" (Freud, 1905a) where it is instantly condensed with a network of associations through dream-work or joke-work and then reappears in conscious thought as a reverie, joke or countertransference dream.

However, there are also differences between these psychic events. Reveries and jokes are formed in the here-and-now of the analytic hour while countertransference dreams are constructed perhaps days after the initiating emotional stimulus. Put another way, the reverie and the joke are more experienced near to the instigating emotional event and are more clearly tied to the affects alive during the session in the intersubjective field. On the one hand, since there are many interceding events occurring between the clinical hour and the subsequent countertransference dream, it is much more difficult to trace the dream images back to the original emotional residue of the session. However, on the other hand, the countertransference dream offers us insight into how these affects have been transformed by dream-work/alpha function and folded into the dreamer's unconscious associative networks. Consequently, we see how my countertransference dream gave vivid representation to the sadistic feelings that were embedded in my joke and in my reverie, but were defended against in the here-and-now of the sessions and avoided in my interpretations.

I would like to offer some comments about interpretation. As Bion (1965) has taught us (Chapter 4), an interpretation is the analyst's transformation of the affects active in the here-and-now of the session. How does the clinician use such data in formulating an interpretation, that is, developing an hypothesis about what is occurring in the moment? It is here that I believe the joke differs from the reverie and countertransference dream. We will recall that Freud (1905a) stated the joke emerges from the unconscious "as a rule ready-clothed in words" (p. 167), which immediately distinguishes it from the countertransference dream and reverie that are primarily visual and/or auditory in nature. The joke is a more organized structure that has already been encoded verbally at the time of its appearance in consciousness, having condensed various levels of meaning through the process of joke-work. Thus, in many instances, such as my joke about Hitler, the joke is also a sophisticated interpretation that may yield an image of the momentary emotional field, thereby evoking further associations in the patient and analyst. However, due to the fact that the joke has been created unconsciously and comprises many condensed levels of meaning, the analyst may remain unaware of what he is fully communicating to the patient, as in the joke that my analyst told me. Thus, in relating a joke to the patient, the analyst may be offering an *inadvertent interpretation*. Similarly, David Lieberman, the Argentine psychoanalyst, would occasionally tell a joke to a patient that he considered an *interpretive action* (Pistiner de Cortiñas, 2015).

In contrast, the reverie and countertransference dream also offer potential insights into the therapeutic relationship, but these require the analyst to first ferret out meanings that are less clear and have yet to be registered verbally. Thus, the *Pope of Greenwich Village* reverie was at first enigmatic until I was moved by the feelings of humiliation and being beaten down as well as the need for safety that the reverie induced in me. I was swayed by these anxieties to ignore the implicit sadistic trends in the joke as well as in the reverie. However, away from the pressure of the session in which sadistic control was mutually defended against by Mr. B. and me, the countertransference dream absorbed and gave expression to the affects too threatening for this analytic pair to face in the hour. In this manner, the three pathways to representing the analyst's unconscious experience of the hour worked in tandem; each providing a unique vertex by which the patient, and the relationship between the analyst and analysand, come to life in the analyst's mind.

What I have been describing is how reverie, joke-work and countertransference dreams have a role in *working through*. Although Freud's (1914) focus in working through was on repetition of the repressed past as encrypted in the transference neurosis, he also stated that the analysand *acts out* his neurosis "not [as] an event of the past, but as a present day force" (p. 151). When Bion (1967b) gave his first lecture in Los Angeles recommending that the analyst forgo "memory and desire," he introduced his talk by saying he really had nothing new to say. In another publication I commented that

> What is most evident to me in "Notes on Memory and Desire" is Bion's unequivocal emphasis on the here-and-now of the session that is implicit in Freud's (1914) notion of the transference neurosis as a "present day force" (p. 151), but which Bion brings into bold relief as the centerpiece of his technical recommendations.
>
> (Brown, 2015a, p. 334; Chapter 11)

In addition, just as Freud (1912) recommended that the analyst "give himself over completely to his 'unconscious memory'" (p. 112), so Bion urged the analyst to be patiently receptive to "some idea or pictorial impression [which] floats into the mind unbidden as a whole" (p. 279). Thus, the spontaneous unconscious constructions of reverie, joke-work and countertransference dreams are the equivalent of Freud's "present day force" that represent the emotions alive in the moment of the session; however, unlike Freud's view that these are crafted from repressed memories, these constructions are highly condensed creations assembled from facets of internal objects in both the analyst and analysand adhered together by the unconscious affects permeating the hour.

Brenman Pick (1985) has written about working through in the countertransference by which she means how the analyst manages the inevitable disturbing effect of the patient's projective identifications. She importantly asserts that the clinician must internally work through the evoked emotional disruption, what she calls "catch the illness" of the patient, in order to be able to give the analysand a "truly deep versus superficial interpretation" (p. 158). Her focus remains on the analyst achieving a clarity between what the patient projects and the analyst's reaction to the projection in order to enhance interpretive accuracy. With regard to contemporary analytic field theory, Ferro (2009b) broadens Brenman Pick's notion of the analyst catching the illness of the patient and comments that the intersubjective field itself may fall ill, contaminated by the shared "illness" of the analytic couple. However, for Ferro, the "cure" for this malady is the restoration of a capacity for dreaming (in the Bionian sense) in order to resume transformation of emotional experience that has been arrested by the "illness" of the field. In this regard, once transformative dreaming returns the analytic couple recover their fertility and spontaneous unconscious constructions reappear as though out of hibernation.

What, then, is the role that reverie, joke-work and countertransference dreams play in working through? As Ogden (2004a) has said, patients come to us for help with dreaming their psychotic dreams too painful to dream (night terrors) or their interrupted non-psychotic dreams (nightmares). In assisting the analysand to dream split off or inaccessible experience the analyst is helping the patient symbolize and "it is through the process of building up of symbols in the dream work that part of the process of *working through* takes place" (Rocha Barros, 2002, p. 1085). The process of transformation from a raw emotion into a symbol, what Bion terms an "emotional thought," is a beginning stage in working through since one cannot work through anything unless it is first represented. Unrepresented experience is evacuated from the psyche by acting out or as psychosomatic difficulties, drug addiction, etc. The analyst's capacity to transform affective experience through his reverie, joke-work or countertransference dreams is therefore a vital step that leads to the capacity for working through.

Notes

1 In *The Interpretation of Dreams* he called used the term *day residue* but later replaced this with *preconscious thought*. I will use the latter term for purposes of clarity.
2 Again, Freud (1900) appears to use the terms *latent dream thoughts* and *unconscious wishes* interchangeably, but I will use unconscious wishes for purposes of clarity.
3 With regard to "absurdity" as one of the mechanisms of dream-work, in Strachey's Introduction to *The Interpretation of Dreams* he notes that the original draft of the book included many jokes as examples of dream-work. However, Wilhelm Fleiss advised him to remove most of them and Freud resolved to write an entire book dealing with that subject, which he did in the (1905) *Jokes and Their Relation to the Unconscious.*
4 Even though the construction is a consciously deliberative act by the analyst, I (Brown, 2009) suggest that it is the end product of an unconscious process within the analyst's mind that is partly sponsored by the analysand's projective identifications and the analyst's transformation of these.
5 In Bionian terms, the Barangers' "shared unconscious phantasy of the couple" corresponds to his notion of the "shared O of the session" (what I labelled as TapO) in Chapter 4.
6 "A large area of floating ice, usually occurring in polar seas, consisting of separate pieces that have become massed together," Collins English Dictionary.
7 Freud (1922) later considered the day residue to be a *preconscious thought*.
8 Indeed, the subtitle of Grotstein's (2000) book is, "A Study of Psychic Presences . . ."
9 This comment is reminiscent of a joke Freud recounted in his *Jokes* book: a man is about to get hanged on a Monday morning and his last words are, "Well, this week isn't turning out too well."

CHAPTER NINE

Autistic transformations I

From ashes to ashes: the heroic struggle of an autistic boy trying to be born and stay alive

Well into the third year of his analysis, one day Mr. B. (from the previous chapter) entered my office pale and shaken, looking terrified, and melted into the couch. He had a dream the previous night that was the most frightening one ever; he could not describe it since it had no characters, color or form:

> it was just blackness, no up, no down, left or right; like floating, but there was nothing there to float on or in; just blackness, emptiness . . . like that movie, *Gravity*, about the two astronauts and George Clooney's character floated away into oblivion. Like I disappeared, vanished, no trace of me. I kept trying to wake up, but I couldn't.

It felt like we were suddenly in a completely new terrain and I asked him what this experience brought to mind, but he could only utter words like "nothingness, weightless," etc. Regaining his composure, he said "I never want to feel that again; what the hell was that?" He had no other associations and I thought about a joke an Asperger's Syndrome boy (discussed in Chapter 10) told me: "Did you hear about the guy who lived in a house so small that when he went into the front door he was going out the back door?" Mr. B.'s experience is one of suddenly finding himself in an unboundaried and *dysdimentionalized* (Grotstein, 1977) world with a horrific feeling of falling into a black hole and no gravity that would give him a sense of physical being.

We may ask the same question, "What the hell was that?" The short answer is that Mr. B. was experiencing an *autistic transformation* (Korbivcher, 2005, 2014) in which

> the emotional experience is that of emptiness, an absence of emotions . . . [leading to an] *autistic universe* . . . [which] organizes itself under the aegis of sensation and is, thus, ruled by laws of its own, different from those found in the realm of neurosis and psychosis.
>
> (2014, p. xxii) [italics added]

In Korbivcher's opinion, the autistic transformation is yet another type in addition to the other categories described by Bion (1965; Chapter 4) and is a universe with unique qualities, chiefly organized around sensory experience. Emotional life is flattened out, like the small house with no depth, with an accompanying terror of falling into nothingness and an innermost sense of emptiness, different from the depressed patient who has a diminished and tormented self; rather, a feeling of not existing at all. However, it is important to note that an autistic transformation is not autism proper, but refers to a cordoned off part of oneself in which *autistic phenomena* prevail.[1] These may be hidden in an "enclave" of the self and appear as neurotic manifestations that seem impervious to change. I had been thinking of Mr. B's need for sameness, anxieties about impingements by strong affect and fear of losing control of sadistic feelings as obsessional in nature; however, these features were like a palimpsest that revealed a subtext of autistic anxieties that had eluded me. However, now in hindsight, the joke about Hitler, Mr. B.'s statement that "I have a fear that equilibrium, that existence could be knocked over," the Golem preventing annihilation, and his search for a "fortress of solitude" cluster around autistic-like terrors that occupied a darkened corner of his psyche.

This brief vignette from Mr. B.'s analysis is a segue into the next two chapters in which we survey the nature and dynamics of autistic phenomena. In this chapter, I present my analytic work with a boy who was diagnosed with significant autism at 20 months, yet when I first saw him at three and a half years old there was little sign of his being autistic. Thus, I raise the question, "What happened to his autism?" The focus in the next Chapter (10) is on the nature of the internal representations, developmental challenges and difficulties with empathy in Asperger's Syndrome (high functioning Autistic Spectrum Disorder). These questions are explored through the lens of "the capacity to tell a joke" that is generally impaired in these children and is linked to the nature of Asperger's pathology. Extensive material from the long psychoanalysis of an Asperger's boy is offered to illustrate these points.

A life teetering on the brink of oblivion

Periodically our planet has been subjected to geologic upheavals that have nearly destroyed all life on earth. The most recent of these, the huge meteor that crashed into the Yucatan peninsula, caused the extinction of 70 percent of all life and brought about the demise of the age of dinosaurs some 60 million years ago. Records of this cataclysm abound: fossils unearthed through the detailed work of archeologists and paleontologists provide us with ample evidence that ties this catastrophe to the disaster in the Yucatan. The names of the dinosaurs, which ones were plant eaters and which ate flesh, are the stuff of myth that both entertain and terrify in nightmares school-age children and adults alike. But we have names for these creatures and a more or less coherent narrative about their fate that has enabled us to imagine this disappeared world as represented in books, films and individual fantasy.

However, nearly 200 million years earlier, an apocalypse occurred during the Permian epoch that destroyed all but 5 percent of the species on earth. While it is not entirely clear what brought on this immense extinction, current thinking (Benton, 2005) is that massive volcanic eruptions lasting a half million years choked the atmosphere and "life itself teetered on the brink of oblivion" (Benton, 2003, p. 38). Millions of years of evolution were dramatically reversed by this Permian extinction and the only surviving species were simple creatures like shell-encased mollusks that required very little food and could swim in the shallow, deoxygenated mudflats. There is no existing narrative for this barely described era; only a handful of nameless primordial survivors dragging themselves along in an endless trek through the most unimaginable hostile environment. The deep layers of sedimentary rock in which the history of life on earth is recorded in fossil remains and climactic readings show a sudden lifeless level of material and low levels of atmospheric oxygen during the Permian era.

In this paper, I discuss the psychoanalytic treatment of a boy with *psychogenic autism* whose beginning development was shut down due to extreme parental neglect, resulting in a picture of classic autism diagnosed at 20 months. By the time he came to see me at three and a half years old because of temper tantrums and aggressive behavior, there were few traces of his autistic history. It was as though he had endured a psychological version of a Permian extinction: an initial period of development that was snuffed out by a deoxygenated "facilitating environment" (Winnicott, 1965) and survived only through encapsulation in a protective autistic shell (Klein, 1980). He appeared to come alive again through intensive behavioral treatment, but where were the traces of his former autism? Were these worked through or transformed into newly evolved modes of being or, perhaps, lying fallow in some split off autistic pocket (Mitrani, 2001, 2011)? I will address these questions through an in-depth examination of my analytic work with Sean.

Frances Tustin (1986) has described *psychogenic autism* as

> a reaction to a traumatic awareness of separateness from the sensation-giving suckling mother. Autistic reactions divert attention away from this mother who is spurned in favor of self-generated sensations which are always available and predictable, and so do not bring shocks.
>
> (p. 27)

Implicit here is that the infant is in the earliest stage of psychic development in which a *skin envelope* (Anzieu, 1979) must first form in order that a developing "core sense of self" (Stern, 1986) has a boundaried and safe wrapper in which to grow. According to Meltzer (1975), this container for the emerging self is formed through a process of "adhesive identification" by which the infant adheres as great an area as possible of its skin surface to that of the mother's. In this manner, the boundaries of the nascent self begin to be demarcated; however, when a traumatic early awareness of separateness occurs the result is an experience of a porous "skin boundary frontier" (Grotstein, 1980, 1984) with accompanying terrifying fears of dissolving, spilling and leaking out of oneself. Without a psychic "home," i.e., a skin envelope in which to grow, the emerging self will fail to flourish. Furthermore, in order to shore up this defective "skin envelope" the psyche resorts to primitive defenses, perhaps actually closer to inborn *tropisms* (Bion, 1992; Korbivcher, 2014), that are maneuvers aimed at plugging the psychic holes created by premature separateness from the mother. In the absence of a mother to adhere to in order to gain a fortified boundary, the infant relies on *autistic objects* (Tustin, 1980, 1984), which are always available and under its complete control. In higher functioning autistic patients, the purpose of autistic objects to bind the terror of fragmentation may also be served by metaphorically leaning up against the analyst's voice (Power, 2016) or perhaps a ruminative state (Ogden, 1989).

The patient's reliance on autistic objects to forestall terrors of atomizing or falling into a black hole of nonexistence makes such objects addictive and therefore relinquishing these may be felt as horrifying. Tustin (1986) cautions us to keep in mind the patient's profound need for these objects and that "It is a serious responsibility to deprive such patients of their autistic protections" (p. 46). Speaking of the analyst's approach she says

> The emphasis in this type of psychotherapy is not on our attempting to make up for what we infer may have been the deficiencies of their infancy . . . The emphasis is on helping them to go through primitive processes of mourning, which will heal the wound of their too-early sense of loss, and relax the tension associated with the trauma, so that they can begin to use the capacities with which they are usually well endowed.

Korbivcher (2014) notes that the autistic shell in which the patient is encased is a "peculiar universe" (p. 91) governed by its own unique rules and which requires the analyst to "speak another language; a sensory language that is a two dimensional world of surfaces (Rhode, 2011), and to adopt more active techniques to draw patients out of their cocoons

> and then to try and help them turn sensations into emotions while favoring their development of alpha function and their ability to think.
>
> (p. 91)

Korbivcher's (2014) notion of the "peculiar" universe of autism builds on her (2005) earlier work in which she proposed the idea of *autistic transformations* that she views as an extension of Bion's (1965) theory of transformations. For Bion, the analytic relationship and the minds of the patient and analyst are always in flux: there is a constant process of unconscious exchange between, and within, their minds that transforms raw emotional experience into representational thought. In contrast, autistic transformations imply a movement away from the world of feelings and

> The emotional experience of the analyst in autistic transformations is one of emptiness, lack of emotion . . . 'Absence of affective life' . . . and auto-sensual activities.
>
> (Korbivcher, 2005, p. 1601)

Autistic transformations are not synonymous with autism proper, but are characteristic of an "autistic part of the personality" (Tustin, 1981) that may be cloistered away from either the neurotic or psychotic parts of the personality. Inasmuch as the concept of transformations usually implies change of form and a constant process of emotional evolution, autistic transformations involve a flattening of emotions into a two-dimensional sensory experience of feelings that drains the patient's affective life and deadens the analyst's countertransference.

Autistic protections, therefore, suffocate further psychic development: the mollusk-like shell that is formed insures a minimal level of survival from the shock of premature separateness. The autistic child is thus faced with an impossible dilemma: to live without an adequate skin boundary that leaves him vulnerable to the onslaught of an overwhelming sensory implosion or, on the other hand, to be shielded in an impregnable carapace. In both situations, the "semi-transparent envelope" of which Virginia Woolf spoke is absent and there is no dialogue between inner experience and the outer world. In the clinical material to follow, I address the question of the fate of autistic phenomena once the patient has begun to leave, or has already left, this protective stranglehold. Tustin says the patient must "go through primitive processes of mourning," but how is this working through to be achieved and what are the methods of transformation by which this is accomplished?

Sean: being born and staying alive

A psychoanalyst's and a behaviorist's world don't often intersect, so I was surprised to receive a telephone message from a behavioral therapist asking if I had time to see a three and a half year old boy in play therapy. The therapist explained that the patient, Sean, had been diagnosed with autism at 20 months and had been receiving intensive behavioral therapy 25 hours a week, which had been very successful. She said Sean was now able to invite another child over to his house to play, but had no idea of what it meant to play, and so she thought it would be useful for Sean to receive play therapy. I told her that I did not have experience with severely autistic children per se though I had treated many with Asperger's. The therapist said Sean had made excellent progress and was now more accessible, so I decided to see him in consultation.

I initially met with Sean's paternal grandparents with whom he lived and who had custody of their grandson. They were decent, goodhearted people deeply involved in Sean's life, providing the majority of emotional support. They explained that they had been involved in Sean's life from the outset, visiting frequently although he lived in another part of the country with his parents. They reported that Sean appeared to be developing normally in the first few months of his life, then regressed. Sean's mother had been addicted to crystal meth and heroin since she was 16 years old and his father, who had been diagnosed with schizo-affective illness, also heavily used drugs. The grandparents became alarmed on a visit when Sean was 18 months old that he was nearly non-responsive and they found him in his playpen self-stimulating while his parents were asleep in a drug stupor. The grandparents then arranged for Sean to come to Boston for an evaluation at Children's Hospital where he was diagnosed with autism. He had no speech at 20 months old and no eye contact with others. The findings from that evaluation observed that

> He did not walk until 17 months of age and now walks on his toes. He does not play with toys appropriately and tends to turn over things like cars and spin the wheels . . . He is fascinated by watching lights and fans. He does not respond to his name . . . and will turn the lights off and on continually and recently has started examining his shadow.

Sean was seen in an early intervention program and intensive applied behavioral therapy (up to 25 hours a week) was initiated, mainly in his home, where he lived with his grandparents, father and a nanny who was with him 10 hours a day, five days a week. His mother moved to the area, but rarely saw Sean because she was so disorganized that she couldn't make appointments; however, when she did see him, she sat next to him and was unable to interact with Sean. The grandparents described this as deeply sad for Sean. I also met two times with Sean's mother, who was like a vacuumed out ghost with obvious cognitive limitations. Thus, on the level of reality, she has had little to do with him though, in his play, the mother figure assumes a central role.

In my first meeting with Sean, I was surprised to see this robust three and a half year old come right into my office, make good eye contact with me, and start to play interactively. I had the thought, "This is the wrong boy, where's the nearly obliterated boy I was expecting?" There were only a few remnants of his "autism": he occasionally walked on his toes and carried with him a small wooden object in the palm of his hand. I asked about it and he shrugged off my question, saying he liked to carry it with him. I asked if he had a name for it and he said "mom," to which I questioned, "You mean "mom" like "*your* mom?" Sean replied, "No, it's not my mom, I just call it that." This seemed to be a *hard object* (Tustin, 1980, 1984) that did not *represent* his mother but instead was an object that gave him the sensory experience of leaning up against a smooth and substantial surface. At times in this first session, he interrupted the play and lay parallel on one of the arms of an office chair, hugging it while in a near fetal position. I said, "It looks like a good feeling to hold onto the arm of the chair" and, surprisingly, Sean responded, "It makes me feel strong."

However, these vestiges of autism were in the background in the consultation visits and more prominent was Sean's symbolic play that had to do with feeling injured and broken. A variety of play characters endured broken limbs, falls, accidents, etc., so that the ambulance was kept very busy shuttling these patients to the hospital and back. He introduced a character, "Mr. Fixit," played by one of the toy figures I enacted with instructions and dialogue provided by Sean. Also, in these first couple of visits, Sean played out a mother putting a baby to bed in its crib and forcing it to stay there despite the infant's pleas for her. I said the baby must be very scared and needs its mother and asked if Mr. Fixit might be able to help but Sean said he couldn't help with this problem. I thought that Sean was telling me that the damage to his infantile self could not be repaired, even by the uniquely talented Mr. Fixit. I subsequently met with the grandparents and recommended analysis, but they lived nearly an hour away and questioned whether he could tolerate spending so much time in a car travelling to sessions. Thus, we agreed to three sessions a week and, in addition, that I would meet every two weeks with the grandparents. Not surprisingly, Sean is eager to come to all his sessions and the car rides with his nanny are generally pleasant; however, we continued at three sessions a week because of time considerations.

Over time, Mr. Fixit has disappeared from our play as well as the remnants of Sean's autism, except for occasional moments of wrapping himself around the arm of a chair when especially distressed. For roughly the last year and a half (we have recently started the fourth year of analytic work), the play has been completely dominated by the story of "Little Sean," a boy figure from the dollhouse who day after day endures the worst imaginable treatment (e.g., eaten by wild animals and dinosaurs, set aflame by dragons, thrown into lava pits and turned into ash) while desperately seeking some security from a protective defender. Each session during this long period began in an identical way: Sean, speaking with his own voice, would call to Little Sean "Sean, do you want to see something?" thus beckoning him to leave the dollhouse. Sean's (the patient) voice in inviting his little avatar out to play was a mixture of friendship as well as a taunt because Little Sean was inevitably mauled.

At first Little Sean called for his mother for protection when leaving the house, but she either was unavailable or proved to be entirely feckless. I admired his wishful determination to establish within himself an internal experience of a competent mother who, unfortunately, predictably failed him. I said that Little Sean really wanted to have his mother there to protect him, but it was very sad and scary that she could not.[2] Over time Little Sean stopped calling for his mother and replaced her with a toy bird that he called "second mother," which sometimes kept him safe and, at other moments, attacked him. She, too, faded from the play stories and Little Sean turned to other figures to safeguard him, such as Batman and Wolverine, who always did their best to fend off the myriad of attackers; however, in each session he was inescapably torn away from his guardians to be chewed up, burned, etc., and then to be left for dead. It was at this point that Sean (the patient) told me to call for "Doc." Doc was actually the Freud figure from the toy box who always brought Little Sean back to life with some magical injection or soothing salve to his burnt skin.

I have seen this sort of intensely violent play with many other children, though Sean's was especially unrelenting, and realized that I had been treating this as paranoid-schizoid phenomena; thus, the question arose again of where are the vicissitudes of Sean's earlier autism? Were these issues being worked through *apres coup* in Sean's powerful persecutory anxieties? Two experiences led me to think about these seeming persecutory anxieties as also reflecting more primordial fears. The first was reading Tustin's (1984b) paper, "The Growth of Understanding," in which she spoke about the "fear of predators,"[3] that is

> in evidence in psycho-analytic work with children who have suffered psychological separation from their mothers in early infancy. *Their fear of predators does not seem to come from active projection of their own predatory impulses.* Rather, these passive children seem to feel at the mercy of terrors of which they are the helpless victims.
>
> (p. 145) [italics added]

My attention thus shifted from Sean's anxiety of being constantly attacked to the theme of being repeatedly destroyed and reborn and my interpretations were directed at Little Sean's efforts to stay alive in a scary world with little protection.

This refocusing from Little Sean's fear of constant attack to his terror of dying helped me to see the analytic work in new light but also evoked primitive fears in me that became the second experience (in addition to the quote from Tustin) that convinced me Sean was not simply dealing with paranoid-schizoid anxieties. As the focus in the sessions turned to the fear of no longer existing, I found it difficult to be with Sean. The hours felt endless and I couldn't wait for him to leave. In one session, Little Sean was being mauled and chewed up by a huge bear, which made me think, "My God, this is Sean's inner world, how horrible and sickening this is." That night I had a terrible nightmare:

> I am trying to escape someone who is after me. I see an old car, like a 1940s car that has high ceilings and lots of inner space. I hide in there and feel momentarily safe. I'm in the back seat, but it opens up into the trunk like a dark cave. Suddenly a huge bear enters the car and comes to the back, as though after me, and I can feel it pushing me into the "cave" in the back and have the sinking horrible feeling that "this is the end of me."

My first thought was of Sean being clawed and chewed by a huge bear and that I was now in a state of at-one-ment (Bion, 1970) with his inner house of horrors: a life of feeling only "momentarily safe" before one's existence will be negated, i.e, "this is the end of me." I also think that seeking refuge in the old car with "lots of inner space" reflected my experience of feeling my "inner [mental] space" invaded by Sean's terrors. We were now two people dreaming a shared nightmare of coming face to face with a horrible death and the threat of nonexistence. However, analyzing my nightmare helped me to more deeply understand the emotional landscape that permeated our shared field; thus, having dreamed and named the terror I felt better equipped to deal with it in myself and in Sean.

Sean's struggle to be psychologically born and to stay alive was graphically depicted in one session after two weeks of intermittent meetings because of his illness and a snow storm. He had been worried about fire since there had been a power outage during the storm and candles were lit at home.

Sean: [Entering the office with a toy torch he brought] "Look out the chair's on fire!"

Me: "We'd better be careful with that; there have been some dangerous fires here."

Sean: [Calling out to Little Sean] "Do you want to go to the zoo and see some bears?"

Me: [As little Sean] "I love bears, but sometimes they're scary and try to hurt me."

Sean: [Assuring tone] "These are friendly bears, come and see them. You can get Batman and take him with you, he'll protect you."

[Very quickly the bears start to bite Batman and the actual Sean instructs me to let the bears kill Batman. Little Sean is then alone and tries to find a hiding place, but a bear gets him and has him in its mouth, after which scary wolves do the same, leaving Little Sean dead. He comes alive again and goes home along with Batman who stands guard.]

Sean: [With alarm] "The Angry Man with a torch is coming to hurt Little Sean. [Sean himself plays the Angry Man who sets Little Sean's house on fire. The fire engine comes and puts out the fire.]

Sean: "Look, the Angry Man is coming to set Little Sean on fire" [who is then burnt to a crisp] "and now he's only ash. Quick, go get Doc!"

Me: [as Doc] "Where is Little Sean?"

Sean: [Pointing to the ground] "There he is, that's him there, he's only ash."

Me: [Speaking as Doc] "Oh no, Little Sean isn't here anymore, he's just a pile of ashes. This is so sad, he's disappeared and he's just gone. Now he won't be here with us at Christmas time or when we go on vacation."

[Little Sean comes back to life again and then the Angry Man, played by the actual Sean, burns Batman and Little Sean again so that they are both now ashes.]

Me: "Oh no, Little Sean came back to life, he wasn't ashes anymore, but now he's burned up again into ashes and he's not alive, he's not here at all. He keeps coming alive and then gets burned into nothing."

Sean: [Goes to the toy box and takes out some birds] "Look, they're turning into dinosaurs again and disappearing."

Me: "The birds used to be dinosaurs and they died and became birds instead."

Sean: "You see, you see how this and the other bird are becoming dinosaurs again. The bird doesn't exist anymore."

Me: "The dinosaurs disappeared and became birds, but then the birds turned back into dinosaurs and now the birds don't exist anymore. They're gone like Little Sean who turned into ashes and he disappeared too. That's so scary to disappear, not to exist anymore."

[The play shifts to Little Sean being surrounded by dinosaurs under an impermeable shell, who are now protective and nurturing of Little Sean.]

Discussion

This play sequence beautifully illustrates Sean's experience of his life, played out in innumerable sessions, of having begun his personal evolution into a thriving human being; however, his budding growth was brought to an abrupt halt by the profound neglect of his parents. I believe that my nightmare, coupled with the passage from Tustin about autistic children's fear of predators, permitted me access to the nearly unimaginable horror of non-being. I had my dream the night of a session in which I experienced an almost nauseating feeling of revulsion at coming into contact with Sean's inner world. I was unable to transform that overwhelming affect in the immediacy of the moment and these emotions lay in wait until my alpha function attempted to dream these into a meaningful dream narrative. My dream was like a traumatic dream in which the trauma is repeated and, in this respect, I had taken in Sean's trauma in order to do the unconscious work of transforming it into a more manageable affective experience. As I have written elsewhere (Brown, 2007, 2011a), *countertransference dreams* may serve the function of processing left over affects from the day's session and also are part of the operation of *transformations in O* by which the analyst's dream is processing the untransformed emotional essence (O) of the session that exceeded the analytic couple's capacity to manage while awake. Thus, I gained a newfound appreciation for Sean's struggle to stay alive: to be born, only then to be destroyed and, like Prometheus whose liver was torn out each day, then to endlessly relive this repetition.

The session began in a typical way with Sean being gnashed in the teeth of bears and wolves, but the appearance of the Angry Man, played by Sean himself, who burned Little Sean and Batman, reducing them to ashes, was a new theme. I had already been thinking about the meaning of these predators as something more primeval than persecutory fears and the notion of being reduced to an unidentifiable heap of ashes brought *nonexistence* to my mind. Consequently, my interpretations expressed the terror of disappearing and I was surprised when a little later in the session Sean introduced the word "exist" into the narrative. Little Sean and Batman came alive again after being turned into ashes, but then were burned to ash once more, at which point I said, "He keeps coming alive and then gets burned into nothing."

Remarkably, Sean's attention turned to the toy birds and he said, "Look, they're turning into dinosaurs again and disappearing." In previous sessions, he had mentioned that birds evolved from dinosaurs that had become extinct and so I heard his response to my intervention as a further deepening of the theme of nonexistence: that Sean was terrified that his current state of maturation was under constant threat of devolving into something more primitive. I then linked this story about birds turning back into dinosaurs with Little Sean's fears of turning into ash and he spun out a phantasy of Little Sean being nurtured by protective dinosaurs underneath an impermeable shell. This phantasy seemed to tell the story of his life: that he barely survived extinction and had to rely on what Mitrani (2001) calls "extra-ordinary protections," in which his surviving infantile self was encased in an impervious autistic shell.

So, how did Sean manage to recover from this psychogenic autism? It is reported that in the early months of his life he was developing normally: smiling with good eye contact, thriving and that perhaps his *facilitating environment* (Winnicott, 1965), though deficient, was sufficiently nurturing to support what I assume was a strong constitution. Then the emotional equivalent of a Permian extinction occurred brought on by his parents' severe drug abuse and his father's schizo-affective disorder, creating a deoxygenated, toxic climate that squelched his development and triggered his enclosure in the costly protections of an autistic shell. Fortunately, his grandparents intervened which resulted in Sean's being wrapped in an interpersonally rich environment with his grandparents, nanny and the behavioral therapists that helped him come back from the brink of permanent oblivion. I think being collectively nourished by a replenishing team of loving women was internalized, thereby enabling Sean to gradually let go of autistic protections and also helped to begin the necessary process of mourning his mother (Tustin, 1986), which was continued in the analysis. Moreover, these enriching experiences fostered the rapid growth of cognitive functions and allowed Sean's native exuberance to develop quickly to the extent that when he showed at my office I thought he was the wrong boy.

In our analytic work together, Sean expressed his sense of being broken by introducing Mr. Fixit, but it soon became apparent that our work required much more than a handyman's assistance. Though Little Sean's endless horrific treatment by a collection of tormenters conveyed a boy paralyzed by persecutory fears, for a long time in the analysis I thought of this dynamic as the projection of Sean's rage over his neglect and the absence of any experience of a protective maternal presence. I was also puzzled by the apparent absence of any traces of his earlier autism, except for the short-lived appearance of hugging the arm of a chair, toe-walking and cupping a hard object in his palm. I wondered whether this more typically appearing paranoid-schizoid material was an *apres coup* working through of the earlier trauma, but I could find no apparent link. However, after reading Tustin's discussion of autistic children's fear of predators and having my awful nightmare, a new scenario fell into place: that the persecutory anxieties covered over and subtly conveyed the underlying profound terror of nonexistence. This brings to mind Winnicott's (1974) paper, "Fear of Breakdown," in which he states that patient's fear of breakdown is most often a fear of returning to an *actual* breakdown from early life. He also states in that paper that

> It is wrong to think of psychotic illness as a breakdown, it is a defense organization relative to primitive agony.
>
> (p. 90)

In this connection, Sean's psychotic-like persecutory fears constituted a "defense organization" against "primitive agony" *but also communicated the nature of that agony.* In effect, by my exclusive focus on the persecutory element, I failed to be like the mother Bion (1962a, b) describes, who hears that

> The infant feels fear that it is dying . . . and projects its feelings of fear into the breast . . . [expecting that the breast] would moderate the fear component in the fear of dying that had been projected into it.
>
> (p. 96)

It was not until my nightmare that Sean's fear of dying, which I could not bear to acknowledge, came into focus and allowed me to achieve contact with his "primitive agony" and its resonance in my psyche.

Ogden (2014), in a recent close reading of Winnicott's (1974) paper "Fear of Breakdown," asserts that the breakdown is an event that has never been *emotionally experienced* and therefore leaves the individual feeling that something vital is missing and that "What remains of his life feels to him like a life that is mostly an *unlived life*" (p. 220) [italics added]. Thus, it is *necessary* that the event that has not yet been experienced must be experienced for the first time in the analysis in order for the patient to feel whole. In addition, Ogden states that

> I view this as a universal need – the need on the part of every person to reclaim, or claim for the first time, what he has lost of himself, and in so doing, take the opportunity to become the person he still holds himself to be.
>
> (p. 222)

For a boy like Sean, whose life began with an all-too-brief glow of an infant's smile that nearly dimmed forever, the ordeal of claiming his life "for the first time" is truly a huge undertaking even for a courageous boy like him and an analyst willing to endure the terrifying uncertainty of human life. The analyst in confronting such fears must be on the alert for his own tendency to detach or satisfy oneself with quick solutions, such as my readiness to see Sean as dealing with "typical" problems and to avoid the powerful fears hidden there. In Sean's case, his anxieties about whether he would continue to exist were the true substrate of emotion that was conveyed through his persecutory fears. Paradoxically, Sean had to feel for the first time the horror of imminent death in order to gain a life that was truly lived.

Notes

1 Also referred to as *autistic nuclei* and *autistic enclaves.*
2 This slow disappearance of Little Sean's mother from the play paralleled the diminished frequency of the actual Sean's mother because of her continued drug abuse and inability to manage her life.
3 Bowlby (1969) first described the "fear of predators" he observed in children who had suffered early traumatic geographical separation from their mothers.

CHAPTER TEN

Autistic transformations II

The capacity to tell a joke: reflections from work with Asperger's children

> nonsense in jokes is made to serve the same aims of representation [as in dreams].
>
> (Freud, 1905b, p. 175)

Joke-work as a pathway to representation

I would like to suggest that the capacity to tell a joke is a highly complex interpersonal event that depends upon the maturation of certain developmental achievements that are absent or stunted in children with Asperger's Syndrome. These include, but are not limited to: the capacity for symbol formation, the realization that other people have a separate mind of their own, a sense of the rhythm and timing of interactions, and an empathic ability to place oneself in another's experience. Difficulties in these areas of development leave the Asperger's child in a concrete world in which symbolic play is a puzzling activity, metaphors make little sense and the world of emotions can be an incomprehensible maze of misunderstanding. One 10-year-old boy I saw told me of being teased at school and when I said that I wouldn't want to be in his shoes, he looked at me blankly and said, "But your feet are too big." In my clinical experience, the evolution of the capacity to tell a joke may be an important milestone in the progress of analytic work with some of these young patients and, I believe, offers us a valuable opportunity to observe the unfolding of factors that permit a child to enter, however belatedly, the magical realm of metaphor and play.

In this paper I will be referencing two separate areas of the psychoanalytic literature – the many contributions to understanding humor and those that address the nature of Asperger's children – that comprise a large and fascinating terrain that is much too broad to be encompassed in an individual paper. This contribution assumes a narrower focus that specifically deals with the development of the capacity to tell a joke in Asperger's children. Of necessity, the analytic literature on humor will be discussed but with attention to those studies that examine the developmental factors associated with the ability to understand and tell a joke. Similarly, analytic contributions to the understanding and treatment of Asperger's children are numerous and the focus here is on the elements that impede, and help the growth of, the capacity for abstract thinking upon which a sense of humor rests. I believe that the abilities involved in the capacity to tell a joke, when disturbed, are intertwined with aspects of the nature of Asperger's pathology and that the treatment of these young patients also opens a window to further insights into the evolution of being able to tell a joke. These issues will be illustrated in clinical material from the psychoanalysis of a young Asperger's boy.

Poland (1990) has poignantly written about the "adult gift of laughter" and has discussed how the capacity for humor may unfold in analytic work with adult patients, with a particular emphasis on the emerging ability to deploy humor as a means of softening the inevitable pains and disappointments that occur even in a satisfying life. He goes on to link the gift of laughter with the attributes of the strength of drives and the ability to harness these, frustration tolerance, the capacity for symbol formation and the faculty for play with a range of ideas. Poland considers jokes as "steps toward mature humor" (p. 219), but in my view they are also important achievements in themselves and akin to dreams and reveries in their structure.

In the Introduction to his 1905 book *Jokes and Their Relation to the Unconscious*, Freud stated that jokes play an important role in psychic life but there has not been sufficient attention given them in psychoanalytic thinking. Although he was writing about humor, Freud's primary focus in the book was on the unconscious dynamics and the structure of a joke. Although the subject of humor has received considerable attention in the analytic literature, Freud alone has addressed the *joke as a structure*, akin to a dream, that formed unconsciously and spontaneously. He (Freud, 1900) posited the role of *dream-work* in the construction of a dream and in the *Jokes* book proposed an analogous process, *joke-work*, in the formation of jokes. Both procedures involve the use of *condensation, displacement, faulty reasoning, absurdity* and *turning into the opposite.* For the purposes of our discussion, I want to emphasize that there is an underlying psychological mechanism necessary for each of these factors: the capacity for *symbol formation* or *representation* by which one thing can stand for another. Noting that absurdity and silliness in dreams is one channel of representation, Freud similarly observed that "nonsense in jokes is made to serve the same aims of representation" (1905b, p. 175).

But what is the process by which joke-work produces the joke? Freud states that jokes appear spontaneously and involuntarily in the joke-teller's mind, the appearance of which is preceded by

> an indefinable feeling . . . which I can best compare with an *absence* [the French term], a sudden release of intellectual tension, and then all at once the joke is there – as a rule ready-clothed in words.
>
> (1905b, p. 167)

Furthermore, the *joke* is a product of an instantaneous unconscious process by which a barely recognized (preconscious) thought "plunges into the unconscious . . . seeking there the ancient dwelling-place of its former play with words" (p. 170). *Thus, the joke is a temporary structure that appears unbidden in the joke-teller's mind, like a dream or a reverie, and is one pathway to representing unconscious (or unrepresented) psychic material.*

In the telling of a joke, Freud states that the joke teller begins by posing two seemingly disparate words or situations to create a feeling of "bewilderment" in the listener, which then gives way to a sense of "illumination" (the punch line) and release of laughter by revealing a similarity between things that at first glance appear unrelated and are stitched together by the play of words, double entendres and a likeness in sound. Freud implicitly assumed that each of us possessed a capacity for symbol formation, and therefore an intact and functioning *dream-work* or *joke-work,* but did not consider situations in which these faculties were either damaged or non-existent. In another publication, I (Brown, 1985) wrote that this impairment of symbol formation results in

> the concrete patient's imprisonment in a current situation . . . that casts a shadow of narrow meaning across all experiences. The concrete patient cannot lift himself out of the immediacy of the moment and is trapped in a state of mind that cannot see beyond itself.
>
> (p. 379)

Unlike dreams, which are mainly visual, the joke stays at the level of language and aims to recover "the old pleasure in nonsense" (p. 176) that triggered laughter in childhood. I suspect that a central part of the verbal silliness in young children is the excitement over beginning to master language and also the thrill of linking two objects together[1] in ways that are unusual for that child, which is often an expression of cleverness. That the little boy or girl can evoke laughter in other children or adults through this behavior adds another dimension of pleasure to these verbal antics.[2] I witnessed this recently when my 22-month-old granddaughter told her first joke – "A, B, C, buttons,"[3] which was delivered with a giggle that evoked a response of infectious and absurd silliness in her family audience. According to Freud, this is the long-forgotten childhood territory of verbal, nonsensical zaniness which the joke revives.

However, on a deeper level, this first expression of joke-work likely reaches down into my granddaughter's preverbal (unformulated or unrepresented) experiences having to do with emotions about separation and union as though she was familiar with Freud's (1905b) observation that "nonsense in jokes is made to serve the same aims of representation [as in dreams]" (p. 175). She is to putting together two seemingly unrelated concepts – letters of the alphabet and a button – and this pairing may well serve the aim of representation because the letters, though appearing to be individual elements, hang together as part of a whole (the alphabet) and a button both fastens objects together while also enabling their separation. My granddaughter's joke-work seems to be the equivalent in word play of Freud's (1915b) description of his 18-month-old grandson's *fort-da* ("gone-there") game in which the toddler made a toy on a string disappear by tossing it out of his crib and then reeled it in gleefully to make it reappear: each of these grandchildren in their own way were developing symbolic strategies (one through words and the other through action) to work through and represent early experiences of separation and reunion.

Object relational aspects of capacity to tell a joke

For Freud, though the mechanisms (condensation, displacement, etc.) by which joke-work and dream-work operated were essentially the same, jokes were constructed from verbal psychic material while the roots of dreams reached deeper down into the preverbal layers of the mind. However, he introduced the role of early object relations when discussing the origins of laughter and commented in a footnote that

> the grimace characteristic of smiling, which twists up the corners of the mouth, appears first in an infant at the breast when it is satisfied and satiated and lets go of the breast as it falls asleep.
>
> (p. 146, note 2)

Thus, Freud is suggesting that the *capacity for laughter* begins at the dawn of psychological life with the baby's first smile in response to the pleasurable satisfaction of the infant's hungry tension. Freud's emphasis here is on the economic perspective (the building up and release of tension), which also is a factor in joke-telling: in relating a joke the comedian evokes tension and anticipation of relief by first eliciting a sense of puzzlement in the listener that is then alleviated by the discharge of laughter as the punch-line[4] is delivered.

Playful joking between the mother and her infant offer the baby early experiences of learning to manage levels of excitement alternating with periods of relative quietude. A situation of danger[5] arises from the threat of overstimulation that imperils the early sense of psyche-soma integration: there is a fine line between the pleasurable laughter of a baby being tickled and the terror of disintegration from too much stimulation. This anxiety of disorganizing laughter remains, in my opinion, an element in the adult enjoyment of a joke: a hilarious comic is described as "side-splitting," one who "cracks me up" or makes us "die laughing." Dick Cavett (2013), in his obituary of the late comedian Jonathan Winters, wrote how the comic could cheer people up but "at the risk of injuring themselves, laughing as hard as I was." Regarding this point, Spero (2009) observed that

> From early development onward, powerful states of manic exuberance, laughter, and gleeful aesthetic rapture are experienced as pleasurable *and* painful, requiring sensitive containment lest they overflow and overtake the infant mind.
>
> (p. 195) [italics in original]

Bollas (1995) characterizes the mother as the First Clown to the infant who, through her playful antics, renders herself the Fool of the baby's court, thereby transforming the child's upset and distress into laughter; in essence "Laughing all our cares away, Just you and I."[6] Lemma (1999) additionally sees this interaction as a form of transformation, helping the baby digest what it is unable to manage on its own. This mode of relating lays the groundwork for the later capacity to modulate fear through laughing at one's failings and gaining an appreciation of the human predicament, which Poland (1990) considers the apogee of a mature sense of humor. This First Clown mother is internalized and serves to buffer the baby against fears of fragmentation by inducing laughter to enhance a sense of well-being and integration. This internalized comforting presence was also addressed in Freud's (1927) paper on humor, which up-dated his *Jokes* book from the perspective of the structural theory. There he described how the superego may comfort the injured ego by acting as though it was a benevolent loving parent, which Chasseguet-Smirgel (1988) characterized as the capacity to be a loving mother to oneself. Thus, these early experiences of shared laughter at the edge of bearable excitement and the internalization of a mother/infant digesting these potentially destabilizing states, what Bollas terms "cracking up together" (p. 243), establish an inner sense of well-being and help inoculate the infant against fragmentation.

Spero (2009) approaches the danger of damaging excitation from a different perspective and introduces the notion of a "joke envelope"[7] that is part of the early developmental experiences which wrap the nascent psyche in a protective cover. The joke envelope evolves from what Spero calls early "auditory crises" of overstimulating acoustic experiences that shock the immature psyche which, like a delicate cake baking in the oven, can be readily deflated by abrupt excessive "noise."[8] Spero does not describe the interactional aspects of this early stage of the joke envelope, but I assume the playful teasing, tickling and funny sounds exchanged between mother and infant, Bollas' "First Clown," are its behavioral manifestations. In the mature joke envelope, the psyche is able to harness these primal anxieties with language and thereby further the capacity to tell a joke.

In addition to these factors that underlie the construction of a joke, there are other interactional capacities that must develop in order for the joke-teller to effectively "set up" his audience for the delivery of the punch line. It is commonly said that "*timing* is everything," which is equally true for giving a psychoanalytic interpretation as it is for telling a joke (Lemma, 1999). In both situations, the "punch line" or interpretation is offered at a point of intensity: in the clinical encounter when the transference affects are heightened and within the reach of conscious awareness and, in telling a joke, when the listeners experience an inner tension created by "bewilderment" which is subsequently released through the "illumination" of the punch line. The comic must have the intuitive sense of timing, like that of the analyst or an empathic mother, of the moment at which maximum laughter will be produced: a punch line delivered either too quickly or too long after the body of the joke evokes minimal laughter. This is a situation not unfamiliar to the psychoanalyst, who is no stranger to the comic's lament, "I was dying out there tonight." Sinason (1996, cited in Lemma, 1999) observes that failed jokes – I would say interpretations as well – may be difficult to tolerate because they conjure feelings from early childhood experiences with mother of poorly timed interactions.

The ability to know another's mind goes hand in hand with good timing. Just as the analyst must develop his intuitive skills to know what the analysand is capable of tolerating, so the joke-teller must have the aptitude of reading the mood of his audience and sensing their receptivity to certain material. The capacity to know another's mind, of course, is a complex achievement that depends upon the ability to tolerate one's separateness from, and concern for, the object that emerges in the depressive position, as well as curiosity about the contents of the mother's body which Meltzer (1975) asserts is the wellspring of an infant's fantasies. Finally, the appearance of mature symbol formation in the depressive position is the key that unlocks the infant's mind from the narrowness of a two-dimensional world into the exuberance of a universe of infinite imagined possibilities.[9]

In addition to the dyadic elements of the capacity to tell a joke, Freud (1905b) observed that relating a joke is a three person event: the joke teller, the listener and the subject of the joke. It is this three-person aspect that Lemma (1999) refers to as the *comic perspective*, which, if we are to understand the joke, requires us to stand back and reflect on the comic contrast that the joke has challenged us to think about. She links the idea of comic perspective with Britton's (1998) concept of the "third position," which enables one to tolerate standing alone as an on-looker that underpins the ability to consider situations from different perspectives. We will see in the clinical material that follows how my young patient's ability to appreciate humor was partly fostered by the active involvement of his father, and by me in the transference, to offer a third point of view.

To summarize: joke-work, along with dream-work, is one of the pathways to representation. For Freud, the *true joke* is a temporary structure that appears unbidden in the joke-teller's mind and, sharing similar qualities to a dream, is one pathway to representing unconscious psychic material. While dreams are largely visual in nature and reach down into the darkest depths of the unconscious, Freud (1905b) appeared to view the origin of jokes in the remnants of early experiences that are registered verbally, i.e., what he called the "ancient dwelling place of its [the joke] former play with words . . . [and] the old pleasure in nonsense" (p. 176). However,

I believe that the lineage of the capacity to tell a joke originates in the earliest interactions between mother and baby. *Laughter*, which is released by the punch line of a joke, develops in the first months of life and is linked with rhythmic patterns of increased stimulation followed by sudden quietude, thereby establishing a primordial *joke envelope* that helps gather together the psych-soma into an "emergent self" (Stern, 1986) associated with nascent affects of pleasurable stimulation. As development proceeds, successful experiences in the early oedipal/depressive position that establish the child's ability to tolerate a third position outside of the parental couple enables a growing capacity for empathy and understanding others have a mind of their own separate from the child. These achievements are the necessary bedrock, together with Freud's emphasis on regression to childish play with words, which underlie the capacity to tell a joke.

Asperger's children and the impairment of joke-work

It is well established that Asperger's children typically are concrete, have an underdeveloped sense of humor and experience difficulty in understanding metaphorical language. Often highly intelligent and gifted linguistically, they can recite with encyclopedic accuracy the vast array of *facts* acquired about their favorite subjects yet simultaneously appear "numb and dumb" (Tustin, 1986, p. 27). Their joke-work, which is one pathway to representation/transformation of emotional experience, is either severely damaged or lacking completely. This impairment, of which the incapacity to tell a joke is one example, is reflective of the underlying limitations in their emotional and cognitive development. More specifically, the difficulties these children have with empathy, separation, managing states of "pleasurable excitement" (Tustin, 1983, p. 129) and profound terror lead the child to "autosensual maneuvers" (Mitrani, 1992, 2011) aimed at restoring a semblance of inner control, often through attempting to rigidly command their environment, because "If he fails in this rigid manipulative control, the child feels that he will cease to exist" (Tustin, 1984, p. 147).

For Tustin (1994), autistic states in patients are a means to deal with "the trauma of their catastrophic awareness in infancy of their bodily separateness from the mother's body" (p. 120).

This is a body-to-body closeness whose goal is to adhere as much of the infant's skin surface as possible to the mother's skin surface, what Meltzer (1975) calls an "adhesive identification." In ordinary circumstances, this auto-sensuous connection to the mother promotes the gradual consolidation of disparate sensory experiences in the child that begin to coalesce around a sense of a core self. Premature separation from this state results in an inchoate sense of having one's "skin boundary frontier" (Grotstein, 1984) suddenly peeled away,[10] resulting in

> the experience of impending disintegration of one's sensory surface of one's 'rhythm of safety' resulting in the feeling of leaking, dissolving, disappearing, or falling into unbounded space.
>
> (Ogden, 1989, p. 133)

In addition, the patient may have the sensory experience of a black hole where a core self should exist due to this catastrophic rupture from the mother.

Owing to the unique challenges that confront the Asperger's child, his capacity for humor, especially the aptitude to tell a joke, is extremely limited. Their subjective experience of terror at separation from the mother forecloses the growth of a shared *potential space* (Ogden, 1985; Winnicott, 1971) in which symbols may form, because distance from the mother (as in having a separate mind) is felt as an existential threat. The failure of a potential space to develop strands the child in a two-dimensional terrain that lacks a "third position" (Britton, 1998) and thus there is no opportunity to attain a "comic perspective" (Lemma, 1999). Additionally, empathy in Asperger's children is limited due to the curtailment of their capacity to put themselves in another's shoes (as was the case literally of the boy mentioned earlier in this chapter). Furthermore, since the provenance of autistic phenomena is in the earliest somato-psychic world of infancy, the first boundaries of the self as defined and sustained though various "envelopes" (skin boundary frontier, primitive skin ego, psychic envelopes, joke envelope) always feel under threat of dissolution, so psychic energies are invested in an array of autistic maneuvers that preclude ordinary maturation. With regard to the joke envelope, the capacity for laughter and "pleasurable excitement" remains a particular danger due to the risk of disorganizing over-stimulation.

I have seen a half-dozen child and adolescent patients in psychoanalysis who have either Asperger's or significant autistic enclaves in their personalities. Each of these cases also had noteworthy histories of sensory integration difficulties early in their life: it was as though separation from the sensory buffering mother left them denuded of protection from the glare of light, the abrasiveness of touch and the booming noise of sound. These inborn sensitivities, I believe, likely create some sort of feeling for the infant of having been born prematurely, experienced as being improperly protected by various skin envelopes, and thereby increasing the infant's need for adhesive identification with the mother. This need for a "second skin" (Bick, 1968) from the mother may be so intense that even the most capable mothers are unable to provide the needed protections from sensory overload. In other situations, there may be an interaction between the baby's moderate need for a sensory buffer and a mother who, for a variety of reasons, is not sufficiently available. In either case, autistic defenses may be automatically deployed to manage the infant's onslaught of unbearable somato-sensory overstimulation. Interestingly, Asperger's children are especially intolerant of emotional stimulation and it is my impression that the use of joking as a technique helps to promote a comic perspective which fosters symbolic thinking and advances the capacity for empathy. Furthermore, the laughter engendered by mutual joke telling offers a containing function to help the child manage potentially debilitating overstimulation.

Clinical vignette: Andrew, the teller of jokes

Andrew's parents consulted me regarding longstanding concerns about their son: an only child and now four and a half years old, he was a very anxious boy who needed to control his environment lest he erupt in tantrums. They were also very troubled by his lack of friendships, fearfulness of separations, hitting, spitting and biting. Nevertheless, he could also be warm and cuddly as well as good company at times. When asked about home life, his mother laughed nervously and said that he ate all his meals in the bathtub, which, of course, I was quite shocked to hear and so inquired about this. The parents spoke with much anxiety about numerous pregnancies that had failed in miscarriage, exhaustive medical tests and procedures, all of which came to naught. Finally, with the help of a donor egg impregnated by father's sperm, Andrew came into the world. Consequently, his mother and father appeared to forge an unconscious pact never to expose Andrew to any frustration; thus, if he desired to eat in the bathtub, so be it. The story reminded me of the legend of the Buddha's childhood: that his parents, too, kept their son within the walls of their royal home sheltered from the harsh reality of poverty and sickness lurking just over the ramparts. However, unlike the Buddha who reacted with grief and compassion upon contact with reality, Andrew, terrified and overwhelmed, desperately sought to keep everything rigidly the same. For example, he was terrified of birthdays because he feared growing up meant he would disappear and be unrecognizable to himself and his parents.

Like many children and adults with Asperger's Syndrome, Andrew was highly intelligent with areas of esoteric expertise that felt wooden and pedantic – for example, Andrew knew every imaginable detail about the Titanic but lacked empathy for the human suffering of that tragedy. How are we to understand this lack of empathy? The deficiencies in empathy resulting from a limited ability to experience another mind as separate and to tolerate ideas distinct from one's own are central factors, but in my view there is another level to this enigma having to do with the quality of *representations*, a topic of great current interest in contemporary analytic thinking.[11] In a series of papers, Elizabeth and Elias da Rocha Barros (2000, 2002, 2011, 2013, in press) have explored how dream symbols (representations of affects) develop in complexity as indicators of progress in analysis. In a recent paper,[12] Elias da Rocha Barros (2013) stated that "dream-work becomes an incubator of symbolic forms," which are products of what he and Elizabeth da Rocha Barros (in press) call the *expressive function of the mind*. Following Langer (1942), the Barros' distinguish between *presentational symbolism*, which is expressive of emotions through intuitive processes that evoke affective associations in the listener through projective identification, and *discursive symbolism*, which conveys objective meaning, i.e., the dictionary definition, to the recipient.

I find the distinction between *presentational* and *discursive symbolism* to be very helpful in understanding how the empathic or expressive function of the mind of an Asperger's child operates. With regard to Andrew, his initial communications were almost entirely discursive in nature: he amassed descriptive facts about the Titanic that imparted much knowledge but he was incapable of "incubating" presentational symbols by which to transmit something of the affective human tragedy. His factual recounting of the Titanic communicated little emotionally and felt more like a wall of discursive bricks on which a "stay out" sign was plastered. Consequently, my initial reaction to his recitations of data was fascination followed by boredom, but with no sense of terror or sadness about the catastrophe. I am reminded of Bion's (1992) description of dream images that are not true symbols for the communication of affect, but are proto-symbols that serve as vehicles for (evacuative) projective identification of unprocessed emotional experience. Thus, Andrew's use of evacuative projective identification of discursive and proto-symbols added to other factors that precluded an empathic response in me.

The emergence of presentational symbols and capacity to understand *a joke*

Predictably, as with other Asperger's children, my countertransference was a mixture of boredom, frustration, discouragement and an experience of "reverie deprivation" that Ogden (2003b) describes. In the midst of struggling to make emotional contact with Andrew, an adolescent Asperger's boy I had seen for many years was in my waiting room attempting to come up with a caption for a cartoon in the *New Yorker* weekly caption contest. His unexpected clever suggestions surprised me with their subtle and lively wit that had rarely emerged in our attempts at conversation. Though I did not consciously link this with Andrew's treatment, I noticed a short time later that I had begun to spontaneously engage in word play with him. I also found myself making puns and Andrew was curious what I meant; I explained that I was making a "pun" and soon after he started to invent some of his own. A few sessions later, he arranged the toy cars in three lines, saying they were stuck in traffic and I attempted to speak for the drivers: "Oh this traffic is terrible, I'll be late for work (or getting home)." He said they don't have any feelings and then took out the Freud figure from the toy box, noting that he looked like me, which Andrew then placed motionlessly watching the traffic. I tried to speak for him, commenting that the drivers must be frustrated and Andrew said, "The traffic's frozen, that's all." It then dawned on me that this was an exact representation of what was happening between Andrew and me: that I felt like an on-looker observing our interactions, which were frozen in an inanimate state. This realization enlivened me and I felt encouraged because for the first time he communicated something about our relationship that enabled me to understand him more fully. In addition, he used the Freud figure to stand for me, which signaled Andrew's beginning capacity to form symbols *about an interpersonal situation*. I said that I thought the doctor would like to unfreeze the traffic but didn't know how to do that. Andrew did not reject my statement and appeared to be listening.

A short time later, Andrew came into the office, made a beeline for the window blinds and removed the plastic rod that adjusts the amount of light coming in. Earlier in the analysis, he would play with the blinds by repetitively raising and lowering them to soothe himself, but on this day he stood on the analytic couch and pretended to lift himself with the rod, saying that he was a pole-vaulter. I was stunned and delighted by this sudden appearance of imaginative play, asked if I could join him, then grabbed the rod from the other window and enthusiastically entered the play. I remember thinking, "This is up-lifting," and then realized I had made a pun. I said "This is fun using the rods to pretend we are pole-vaulters," and he responded, "They can also be fishing poles, let's go fishing." We pushed two office chairs together side by side and pretended to be fishing off of a boat, catching imaginary salmon, lobsters, etc. I felt energized by this play and decided to try making a joke: I pretended to struggle reeling in an object, feigned coughing and said, "Oh no, I think I caught a cold!" Andrew laughed and said, "You can't catch a cold in the ocean, that's a funny joke."

How can we explain the apparently sudden appearance of symbolic thinking and Andrew's ability to understand my rather subtle quip about catching a cold with a fishing pole? I think this was the end point of an evolution that began with my seeing the value of comic word play in my adolescent patient, followed by creating puns with Andrew, thereby fostering a mindset in which one thing might stand for another, i.e., the Freud figure for me. In retrospect, I could more easily enlist Andrew in fanciful word play than in pretend play with objects. I believe these off-the-cuff strategies helped to create a shared play space between us and that my use of puns and absurdities made "comic contrasts" (Freud, 1905b, p. 10) that helped to foster the capacity for presentational symbol formation.

Andrew's nascent ability to understand metaphor, fostered by our play with words, gave him the initial tools needed to work through emotional experiences such as separations from me. Andrew, ordinarily a well coordinated boy, stumbled when coming into my office the day before his one week vacation. He said, "I tripped," and I said he's going on a real trip tomorrow with his family and we won't be seeing each other. He laughed and said that was "funny." On the day of his return, Andrew looked sad and commented that I got a new curb [actually true, installed while he was away] in front of my house. I said it makes him sad to see that and he said he didn't know that would happen. I replied, "Maybe when you saw the new curb you wondered whether other things changed, like whether I'd be here or look like me." He said he knew I'd be here and that I always look like me, then commented that he's taller than he used to be. I interpreted, "We haven't seen each other for a week and maybe you're worried I wouldn't know you because you got taller." He responded by opening the office door to check that his mother was in the waiting room and said, "my mother is always there too."

An important session in which Andrew tells *his first joke*

In the week prior to his sixth birthday, Andrew had us playing as farmers who were planting and harvesting potatoes. The day before his actual birthday his mother left me a voicemail saying that Andrew had asked to see her vagina. On his birthday, which landed on the last session of the week, Andrew arrived wearing a Burger King crown. He was very anxious, running back and forth across the office, compulsively touching objects and whisking his sleeve with his hand as though brushing off invisible dust. I said, "It's a very exciting day and you're full of energy," and he replied, "Yes, it's a special day, it's my birthday." I said that it was his sixth birthday today and that birthdays could be exciting and also scary at the same time. Attempting to reassure himself, Andrew replied that "I was born in the nighttime, so I'm not really six years old yet." With pressured speech, he spoke briefly about riding the school bus, which he did not yet do, and this reminded me of some recent play of a school bus crashing. As I was recalling the earlier play, Andrew said, "Wanna hear a joke?" and I asked him to tell me. "Did you hear about the giant who threw up?" he questioned with obvious glee, and before I could finish saying "What happened?" he said in one breath, "It was all over town get it?" He fell back in a chair as we both laughed, asked if I'd like to hear another one, and when I nodded he offered, "What did the necktie say to the hat?" I asked for a moment to think about it, but he quickly told the punch line, again in one breath: "Go on ahead I'll hang around here get it?" As the session drew to a close, Andrew said he'd like us to return to our play of planting and harvesting potatoes and instructed that we were to dig holes, then plant seeds in them. I said, "It's very easy to grow potatoes, but it's much harder to make a human baby." Andrew said he once saw a picture of a baby before it was a baby and "it was like muscles together, it was just muscles." Then he told me a funny story about a bird sitting on an egg and there was such a strong wind that the egg got blown away six times; thus, the mother had to run after it to sit on it again and again.

Apart from the fascinating content in this hour, we can see Andrew's growing capacity to represent his emotional experiences of loss, terror of growing up and curiosity about how human existence comes into being. However, at the outset of the session he was in a near psychotic state: running around the consulting room, having concretized his fear as unseen dust to be whisked away, and falsely believing that he rode the school bus. This evoked my recollecting his play of crashing school buses and also his earlier association of birthdays with disappearing. It was at that moment that Andrew asked if I wanted to hear the two jokes, which seemed to have an organizing effect in the session, partly as a manic defense (saying his birthday was at night), but also and perhaps more importantly, harnessing his overstimulated state by engaging me as a modulating container to laugh along with him. In addition, the content picked up on and expressed what was happening in the session. The joke about the giant who threw up seemed to capture Andrew's psychic state of vomiting up his terror through action and what Bion (1965) calls a *transformation in hallucinosis* (the invisible dust and believing he rode the school bus). The second joke was more organized and appeared to represent the underlying theme of separation and loss ("you go on ahead"), which segued into the latter part of the session characterized by a higher symbolic level.

In the later portion of the hour immediately following the two jokes that helped him manage the excitement and terror of his birthday, Andrew regained his capacity for symbolic (presentational) forms and narrated a fascinating story about prenatal life and the subsequent struggle to be born. I had been thinking about how the entire hour was about growing and surviving; I said that "it's much harder to make a human baby," to which he responded by telling me that he had seen a picture of a baby in utero and "it was like muscles together." I found this comment to be very poignant, conveying a phantasy of himself as formless, and the "funny" story about the mother bird trying to nurture her egg which blew away six times amplified my sad feeling. It was as though he was communicating the fragile sense of his own existence and also, perhaps, some unconscious knowledge of his mother's many miscarriages and difficulty getting pregnant.

In a meeting with his parents around this time, his father revealed that he and Andrew had been reading a joke book together, the first I heard of this. I had not mentioned my use of humor in the treatment, so I inquired how this began and the father said he noticed Andrew was more humorous lately; thus, prompting his purchase of the book. The father described that he explained some jokes to Andrew and why they were funny. I told them that Andrew and I had been using jokes to communicate and the parents said they were unaware of that. Now, having heard of this humorous play with his father, it appeared that Andrew used the relationship with his father and me as a pathway to opening up a comic perspective that enlarged his growing capacity for abstract thought and, significantly, as a channel to tolerate the necessary separation from his mother in order to find a third position with his father (and me) and a mind of his own.

I believe that Andrew's joking with his father and me served as important opportunities in continuing to build a capacity for symbolic thinking and metaphor that are essential for the growth of an inner emotional world. Three dimensional narratives of oneself develop to foster an experience of subjective depth that replaces the clusters of mechanical facts thinly papered over the infinite ink of black holes. In addition, working with Andrew's jokes and other word play contributed to his growing ability to gain a sense of mindfulness, that is, an understanding that others have a mind separate from his, which may also think differently. For example, when Andrew was unable to allow me time to think of the punch line for one of his jokes, it was in essence an inability to recognize that I had a mind of my own (Caper, 2000), which needed time to think. Thus, I let him know that even though he was eager to share his joke, that I needed time to think about it. This brief hiatus also allowed the building up of anticipation of the punch line that brings about the "sudden release of intellectual tension" (Freud, 1905b, p. 167) through laughter. Allowing himself to tolerate *not* telling me the punch line improved his capacity to withstand unpleasant feelings and therefore to represent them.

Discussion and conclusion

A legitimate question may be raised regarding the role that my word play and joke-work had in the significant gains achieved in Andrew's analysis. Put another way, we may wonder about the extent to which these clinical improvements were the result of my analytic approach or whether, instead, his capacity to tell a joke was secondary to other factors. As in any child psychoanalysis, there are many interacting dynamics that combine to create the therapeutic action: the conscious and unconscious dimensions of the analytic relationship, the analyst's interpretations, the inherent potential for growth in the child and work with the parents, to name just a few. Thus, it is difficult to identify the relative weight of each of the elements, which will vary from one treatment to another. However, in analytic work with Asperger's children, the therapist seeks to employ treatment approaches that foster an emotional relationship with the analyst, help to develop empathy, diminish concrete thinking and improve peer relationships. I believe that engaging Andrew in verbal play, including making puns and jokes, played a significant role in his analysis.

In this particular analysis, the approach I adopted included the verbal play Andrew and I engaged in but also involved, especially later in the treatment, more "traditional" interpretive work. However, in order to reach a point at which Andrew was amenable to interpretations, "there is a need for upstream operations to overhaul, sometimes to a considerable extent, the patient's actual apparatus for thinking thoughts [alpha function]" (Ferro, 2009a, p. 18) and fostering Andrew's capacity for telling a joke catalyzed the emergence of abstract thinking. By initially introducing puns, I helped Andrew to get a sense that a word may have more than one meaning, thereby creating a "comic contrast" to enable his awareness that there is meaning beyond the obvious and initiated a nascent ability to think more abstractly. In addition, it seems reasonable to speculate that our lively verbal engagement unconsciously offered Andrew a containing "First Clown" (Bollas, 1995) experience that was lacking in his mother's complete indulgence of his every whim (e.g., eating meals in the bathtub). Furthermore, our word play also seemed to represent his need for a paternal figure that could open up alternative views of reality, i.e., a "third position," beyond the two dimensional one in which he and his mother were encased. All these elements combined to activate a capacity for abstract thinking, including the emergence of presentational symbols that subsequently allowed me to work with Andrew more interpretively.

The growth of a symbolic function enables a child to master various conflicts via the working through of play. Andrew had evolved from play with words to playing out stories with me that were more or less verbatim from books he had read; however, these are no longer mere recitations but are unconsciously picked to convey a difficult situation in his concurrent life and evoke sympathetic feelings (presentational symbols) in me for his dilemmas. Andrew is presently 11 years old and in the seventh year of analysis: his symbolic capacities and the associated ability for interactive play have considerably grown such that his aggression has become our current focus. Now we are, at Andrew's suggestion, two soldiers learning about the science of war and fighting a variety of enemies with an array of potent weaponry. He recently had us create *his* version of the Battle of Dunkirk in which we were instrumental in rescuing the embattled fighters; an apt storyline to describe our long work together to bring him back from the edge of emotional entrapment and psychological disaster.

Notes

1 The word *symbol* derives from the Greek word *symbolon* that suggests throwing things together for contrast and comparison.
2 Trevarthen (2005) observes that parental failure to respond to the infant's attempts to evoke pleasure induces shame in the baby.
3 In effect, this "joke" was employing a mechanism found in more sophisticated humor that offers "a judgment which produces a comic contrast" (Freud, 1905b, p. 10), that, in essence, says, "Isn't it ridiculous to think of A, B and C connected with buttons?"
4 Freud, of course, did not use the words "punch line" since it is an English language term that came into usage in the 1920s or 1930s, many years after his *Jokes* book.
5 See Kris (1938) and Jacobson (1946) regarding the dangers of overstimulation.
6 Lyrics from Chad and Jeremy, *A Summer Song* (1964).
7 Together with Anzieu's (1993) notion of the *skin ego*, Bick's (1986) discussions of the importance of skin in early object relations and Frances Tustin's (1994) work on the *rhythm of safety*, the joke envelope is a central element in this constellation of archaic organizers of the psyche-soma.
8 Perhaps this is one of the sources of humor underlying jokes of flatulence? These reach down into the early unrepresented bodily experiences characterized by sound, the buildup of abdominal pressure and subsequent discharge.
9 Rhode (2011) states that many Asperger children have a sense, albeit not always well developed, of others having an inside in clear distinction from autistic children who lack this capacity.
10 An adult woman I (Brown, 1996) previously reported on felt that she had neither an inside nor an outside and that she was like "a face on a pane of glass" (p. 44). Separations from me reminded her of burn patients with skin grafts: if the bandages were taken off too soon, the new skin would peel off with the gauze.
11 See Levine, Reed and Scarfone's (2013) recent compendium of papers on this subject.
12 Paper given at the Boston Psychoanalytic Institute, December, 2013.

CHAPTER ELEVEN

"Notes on memory and desire"

Implications for working through[1]

> [The analyst] should withhold all conscious influences to his capacity to attend and give himself over completely to his 'unconscious memory.'
>
> (Freud, 1912, p. 112)

Recollecting one's repressed childhood conflicts has been a mainstay of classical psychoanalysis and in "Remembering, repeating and working-through" Freud (1914) discussed how many patients "remember" their early conflicts through actions:

> the patient does not remember anything of what he has forgotten and repressed, but *acts* it out . . . As long as the patient is in the treatment he cannot escape from this compulsion to repeat; and in the end we understand that this is his way of remembering.
>
> (p. 150) [italics in original]

Although these repetitions are a resistance to memory, they simultaneously are a pathway to recovering the forgotten past through the development of a *transference neurosis* by which the analysand's illness becomes "not an event of the past, but as a present day force" (p. 151). Thus, Freud regards the inevitable repetitions as an invaluable tool to help the patient *work through* his infantile past since that troubled history is played out again in effigy through an "artificial illness" (p. 154) in the here and now of the *transference neurosis*. However, the transference neurosis develops slowly as though it had a timetable of its own and the analyst "has nothing else to do than wait and let things take their course" (p. 155). Freud counsels patience with this process and the analyst must curb any tendencies that distract him from paying exclusive attention to what is on the patient's mind in the moment. Freud's advice in this paper elaborates his recommendations two years earlier (1912) that the analyst must adopt a stance in which his unconscious is a "receptive organ" (see Chapter 5) to the analysand's communicating unconscious and that he, the analyst, ought to give himself over to his "unconscious memory."

In my view, there are many aspects of Bion's work that have their origin in ideas that remained inchoate in Freud; partially developed proposals that seeded Bion's genius and he nurtured in creative and unexpected ways. For example, Bion appears to have been greatly influenced by Freud's (1911) paper, "Formulations on the Two Principles of Mental Functioning"[2] (Brown, 2009a, 2011a; Legoretta & Brown, 2015), and significantly reworked the concepts of the *pleasure* and *reality principles* to promulgate a theory of dreaming that broadened Freud's first contributions (Bion, 1962b, 1992; Brown, 2012, 2013; Grotstein, 2009c). Similarly, with regard to clinical practice, though Bion does not refer specifically to "transference neurosis,"[3] he writes as though he has taken Freud's recommendations very seriously and builds on these in unique ways. What is most evident to me in "Notes on Memory and Desire" is Bion's unequivocal emphasis on the here-and-now of the session that is implicit in Freud's (1914) notion of the transference neurosis as a "present day force" (p. 151), but which Bion brings into bold relief as the centerpiece of his technical recommendations. Furthermore, where Freud (1912) advises the analyst "to give himself over completely to his 'unconscious memory'" (p. 112) and "let things take their course" (1914, p. 155), Bion (1967b) speaks of an evolution in the session that emerges effortlessly in which "some idea or pictorial impression floats into the mind unbidden as a whole" (p. 279).

These parallels notwithstanding, Bion parts company with Freud by his seemingly ahistorical approach to the session. Where Freud would stress the important vitality of repetition, Bion (1967b) is concerned that each session should be fresh in order for there to be "less clogging of the sessions by the repetition of material which should have disappeared"

(p. 273), resulting in a livelier analytic pace. Furthermore, Bion states that the analyst following his "rules" will notice that

> The pattern of analysis will change. Roughly speaking, the patient will not appear to develop over a period of time but *each session will be complete in itself*. "Progress" will be measured by the increased number and variety of moods, ideas and attitudes seen in any given session.
>
> (p. 273) [italics added]

To my mind, this raises an important dilemma: if, as Bion says, we must unclog the sessions of repetition and that "each session will be complete in itself," how are we to understand the process of *working through*? And, if *progress* is to be assessed solely through evolution within individual sessions, how are we to regard the established analytic practice of measuring progress by the *working through* of various transference/countertransference configurations over the course of many years? I will now present some analytic material to help us further think about this apparent paradox.

Edward: stuck at a threshold

Edward, a friendless and socially awkward eight-year-old began analysis because of intense panic, which, when he was younger, was manifest as significant separation anxiety. A brilliant student who academically outshone his talented peers, Edward was also a loner whose only reliable companion was his beloved computer. He was eager to display his very impressive knowledge and occasionally I "consulted" him with questions about my computer. One August when he was 11 years old, shortly after my vacation and two weeks before school was to begin, I received a panicked call from his mother that Edward had "melted down." Indeed, that was an apt term because when I saw him he was so terrified that he was barely able to speak, only able to say, "My computer crashed and I lost everything." Although he was consciously referring to the computer's files and documents, the underlying message was clear – that everything holding his world together was gone. I thought, but did not say, that this terror must be the current version of his earlier panic. We were able to talk about how he and his computer were an intertwined unit, like a cyborg that was part human and part machine, and also about his anxiety in starting a new school year. These discussions were very helpful and he was able to regroup emotionally in order to begin school.

I did not share with Edward my association to his earliest separation anxiety for several reasons. Typically, he was exceedingly cerebral and his affects were always muted and/or banished through his impressive intellectual strengths; therefore, finding him in a rare state of emotional vulnerability, albeit one of intense panic, was an opportunity to reach him at a moment of affective aliveness. In addition, more "traditional" interpretations that linked the present with the past were usually dissembled by Edward through arguments that skewered the logical basis of my interventions that had been reduced to a jumble of meaningless words. Thus, I approached each session as a unique experience that enabled the analysis, in certain instances, to be a "lived experience" (Ogden, 2010). Gradually these experiences of "real contact" (Joseph, 1985) in individual sessions accrued over time and created in my mind a more or less coherent sense of Edward's inner world, i.e., what Ogden (2004a, 2004b) terms "dreaming into existence."

Now, three years later, I find Edward, a plump and physically immature 14 year old, standing motionless at the threshold between the waiting room and my office when I open the door for the session. He does not appear frozen with anxiety, but rather seems to be casually standing in place. When I ask what is going on, he says "I'm thinking": he isn't sure whether he will come into the office or not. I comment that his feet are exactly positioned in the middle of the door frame at the threshold of my office as though he can't decide what to do. Edward then steps into the consulting room, lies on the couch and I ask what had just happened. He says he is experiencing the same problem at home: that he feels compelled to stand midway at the doorjamb before he leaves one room to enter another; however, he is not feeling anxious but rather, perched in this in-between place, has a sense of calm. I say that we have been talking about how scared he is to "grow up" and that it seems being stuck at the threshold coming in today expresses his worry about moving out of the relative comfort of being young to the frightening mysteries of being a teenager; that he wants me to see with my own eyes how he is stuck. This comment feels obvious to me and Edward says he thinks I am right, though he shows little emotion. Nevertheless, this "symptom" quickly disappears in a few sessions.

Some weeks later, Edward tells me about the powerful and crippling anxiety he is feeling while doing homework. He then collapses into an anxious mass of tormented tears, self-hatred and impotent rage, saying that his life is over. He is terrified because his panic is so overwhelming that it is difficult to read and he is spending six hours or more each night doing his homework. I also am feeling utterly helpless and that I have little to give him: even when I offer interpretations gingerly, Edward pulls himself into a fetal position and weeps loudly, nearly howling in the grip of some unbearable inner torment. He says he is only able to do his homework when his mother sits next to him and I realize he needs my silent presence as a non-intrusive analyst. I suggest that he bring in a book to read in the session for us to try and get some perspective on his difficulty reading. He brings in Plato's *Republic* that is assigned in one class and reads a portion about the difference between a leader who is a tyrant and the more munificent Philosopher King and suddenly a pall comes over his face accompanied by a chilling shiver. It is the notion of the punishing tyrant that frightens him, and I say I think he lives under constant threat from a tyrant inside him with no gentle Philosopher King inside his mind to protect him. For the first time in many weeks Edward relaxes and, patting the couch like an old friend, stretches out comfortably with an audible sigh of relief.

Edward's anxiety remains very forceful but now, armed with the metaphor of the Tyrant and the Philosopher King, we are able to begin to make sense of what haunts him. Through his tears and panic, he tells me that he only received one B during his school career and all the other grades were As and A+s; now he is terrified that because of his overpowering anxiety his grades will suffer. I say that the tyrant part of him must be very unhappy with that, which brings forth a torrent of plaintive tears and the revelation of his private fear that "it would be the beginning of a slippery slope and I'll end up living in a card board box." I say there's no Philosopher King in his mind to argue against, and protect him from, this cruel tyrant; adding that sitting close to his mother, and reading here with me, gives him the safety and protection he cannot feel when he's alone. He is palpably calmed by this interpretation and there is a sense in the hour that we have arrived at an important emotional truth (Bion, 1965: Grotstein, 2004). In the months that follow, Edward and I learn a considerable amount about the tyrant part of him and his phantasy of being an omnipotent Philosopher King, themes that once contained devastating emotion but whose meaning we are beginning to come to understand.

Discussion

My analytic work with Edward illustrates the apparent paradox about how one works through repetitive painful affective patterns when the focus is on the evolution in each session rather than on the overall arc of the analysis. I condensed nearly seven years of analysis and described the various forms in which his anxiety was manifest: Edward's early separation anxiety, his sheer terror at age 11 when his computer crashed, his getting stuck halfway between the waiting room and my office at 14 years old, and his horror that with one B grade his life would end in ignominy. In my view, there was an important *working through* during this period of time, but a qualitatively different sort than the classical notion of "working through." For Freud, it was an infantile neurosis, organized in early childhood and then repressed, that, under pressure from the repetition compulsion, was replicated over and over in action because it could not be remembered. However, in Edwards' case, there was no structured infantile neurosis but there was instead a periodic destructive threat to his world that looped unpredictably from an unknown corner of the void like an unnamed comet. In this connection, working through consists of a gradual process of helping the patient bring meaning to unrepresented experience in order that, as Bion states, "Out of the darkness and formlessness something evolves" (1967b, p. 272).

Edward's profound anxiety was simply a powerful affect that made an unstructured appearance at certain periods in his life that loosely had something to do with separations and transitions. I realized early on that offering "traditional" interpretations, such as his anxiety about crossing the threshold into adolescence, were typically met with a bland "that could be right" but with no connection to the overwhelming anxieties which persecuted him. I believe that he took great comfort from being near to me, as he was with his mother at his side during homework, and also that I was a containing companion who helped him bear the unthinkable anxieties that tormented him. It was especially vital that I could tolerate, and could share in, Edward's paralyzing helplessness when reading was so difficult for him. It was an experience of at-one-ment Bion (1970) describes that the patient senses and is an important step in the transformation of unrepresented affects into meaningful psychic events. In patients like Edward, I believe this is an essential first step that ultimately leads to the later capacity for the working through that Freud discussed, which requires an organized and symbolically formatted template, i.e., the infantile neurosis that prefigures the transference neurosis.

In a series of papers, da Rocha Barros (2000, 2002, 2011) has explored the connection between dreaming and working through. He notes that Freud's theory of working through was predicated on the assumption that an adequate symbolic capacity was sufficiently intact in the patient to permit the transformation of affects into dream thoughts. Da Rocha Barros (2002) states that

> it is through the process of building up symbols in the dreamwork that part of the process of working through takes place . . . [because] fresh symbols are created that widen the capacity of the person to think about the meanings of his/her emotional experiences.
>
> (p. 1085)

However, these "fresh symbols" created through dream-work, or Bion's (1962b) alpha function,

> are not yet thought processes, since they are expressed in images rather than in verbal discourse and contain powerful expressive, evocative elements.
>
> (2002, p. 1087)

These comments are relevant to the point in Edward's analysis, during our reading of Plato's *Republic*, when the Tyrant and the Philosopher King were discussed in the book. These figures became "powerful expressive, evocative elements" that served as representatives of aspects of his inner object world. In the language of Ferro's (2002a, 2002b, 2006, 2009b) and Civitarese's (2005) work, these were "characters in the field" that signified the affects of the here-and-now emotional field in which Edward and I were immersed. The emergence of the Tyrant and the Philosopher King were the outcome of that component of working through that transformed emotions into what Ferro calls *affective holograms*[4] and these characters gave Edward and me a beginning language to continue the working through process of newly defined themes that had evolved "Out of the darkness and formlessness" (Bion, 1967b, p. 272).

In discussing the "Wolfman's" dream as an example of *Nachtraglichkeit* by which an earlier childhood experience was given psychological meaning by the later dream at four years old, Freud commented that

> *Indeed, dreaming is another kind of remembering, though one that is subject to the conditions that rule at night and to the laws of dream formation.*
>
> [italics added] (1918, p. 51)

This statement seems to suggest a role for dreaming in bringing emotional meaning to dormant experiences that now, having been given representation through "laws of dream formation" (condensation, symbolization, displacement, etc.), may be "remembered." Bion's (1962b) observation that these "laws of dream formation" are continuously active while we are awake and asleep has greatly impacted current psychoanalytic thinking that underscores the omnipresence of a psychic function[5] that constantly transforms raw emotional experience[6] into meaningful psychological events. However, I think it is incorrect to say that previously unrepresented states, now transformed through alpha function, are "remembered," as Freud says, but rather that they are made available for thinking for the first time. In this regard, the appearance of the Philosopher King and the Tyrant in Edward's analysis was a vital step forward because it gave us two meaningful characters (representations) to embody affects that previously were without shape and form, existing only as nameless somato-sensory bombardment. As da Rocha Barros (2002) has stated, these images "are not yet thought processes . . . [but] contain powerful expressive, evocative elements" (p. 1087) that promoted further elaboration in Edward's analysis.

Freud's (1914) concept of working through assumed the existence of an organized infantile neurosis constructed from symbolic elaborations of childhood conflicts and compromise formations. Anna Freud (1970) added that

> Seen from the developmental point of view, the infantile neurosis can represent a positive sign of personality growth; a progression from primitive to more sophisticated reaction patterns.
>
> (p. 202)

However, in patients like Edward, this "progression from primitive to more sophisticated reaction patterns" has not occurred, leaving the analysand vulnerable to invasions of "nameless dread" (Bion, 1962b). In such situations, I believe that working through occurs on both the macro level over a period of time as well as on the micro level in which "each session will be complete in itself" (Bion, 1967b, p. 273). The analysis must first proceed on the micro basis, inhabiting each session as a seemingly isolated outpost, like a string of islands that are later brought together into a unified nation. From the large-scale vantage point, the analytic work aims at containing the anonymous terrors plaguing the patient and helping to build and/or strengthen the "apparatus for thinking" (Bion, 1962b) necessary for symbolization, i.e., to give a face to the analysand's fear. Once accomplished, as when Edward offered the characters of the Tyrant and the Philosopher King, the analytic pair can engage more interpretively with each other and collectively face the pain which now has an identity.

These "isolated outposts" are the building blocks from which the analytic pair can construct a narrative of the patient's emotional life. The initial linking together of these elements occurs within the mind of the analyst as a sort of *construction* (Freud, 1937), a working hypothesis about who the patient is, i.e., "dreaming the patient into existence" (Ogden, 2004a, 2004b). For example, at the beginning of Edward's analysis, I knew from his history that he had been frightened of separations as a young child, but there was no way to access this in the sessions until one hour in which I needed to leave my office for a minute to get some more paper for drawing. Edward grew terrified and asked me not to leave, but he did not know what frightened him. I was able to give a name to the fear, "people going away," that enabled us to speak about it and it was the start of our developing a narrative about his psychic life. Later on, when his computer crashed, I could add that he felt like a cyborg, which was another denotation of his inner experience of himself. Further on in the analysis, when he was stuck in the threshold of my waiting room and office, I added that change was very frightening to him; however, my comment did not have any meaning to Edward emotionally. Nevertheless, it registered quite profoundly for me as I witnessed his paralysis in the moment that facilitated a more complex view in my mind of what was overwhelming him, which could best be described as, "Edward, now heading into adolescence, frozen and terrified of change and separation that could lead to his complete and utter collapse." However, his apparatus for thinking thoughts was still too impaired to tolerate the affects associated with my inner view of him, so my "dream" of him, of necessity, remained my speculation.

Edward's capacity to represent his internal world through reference to the Tyrant and the Philosopher King was a significant leap forward in his growing ability to use symbols to convey his emotional inner life and illustrated da Rocha Barros' (2000) observation that

> What is felt as internal pressure must be transformed at first through images, and then into a broader channel of expression made up of words, in order to become part of our process of thinking.
>
> (p. 1097)

It is important to note that these *characters* (the Tyrant and Philosopher King) were Edward's creation: he brought them into the session and these represented two different emotional currents that initially were "felt as internal pressure" but now signified two discreet internal objects that prefigured later transference manifestations. This forward movement also resulted in the growth of a more deeply enriched analytic process in which both Edward and I were engaged in an unconscious intersubjective exchange (Brown, 2010, 2011a) that spontaneously created new meanings. Thus, he had evolved to a point at which he could form the emotionally evocative image of fearing that he would collapse and end up living in a cardboard box.

Edward's figures of the Tyrant and Philosopher King comprised a vital instance in the analysis and it brought to my mind the work of the Boston Change Process Study Group[7] (henceforth, "Change Group") (2010, 2013) that places great emphasis on analytic encounters that create *now moments* described as

> short subjective units of time in which something of importance bearing on the future is happening in the dyad ... Clinically and subjectively, how analyst and patient know they have entered a new moment, a moment distinct from the usual present moments ... is that these moments are unfamiliar, unexpected in their exact form and timing, unsettling or weird.
>
> (2013, pp. 735–736)

These moments typically produce some turmoil in the on-going mood of the analytic dyad that initiates an action by the analyst, whether an interpretation, an enactment or even a response of silence. The Change Group views such moments as opportunities for change, though the analytic pair may at first wish for a return to the status quo; however, the analytic situation at such times is ripe for the emergence of new patterns of relating that have advanced in a nonlinear way. Indeed, the appearance of the Philosopher King and Tyrant signaled such a pregnant moment that catapulted Edward and me into a new terrain: the emergence of a greater capacity for symbol formation and a "broader channel of expression made up of words" that da Rocha Barros (2000) described.

Much of what the Change Group sees as essential in analysis is consistent with the ideas that I have been discussing, though there are some important differences. Their concept of now moments is a significant contribution that I would relate to Bion's ideas of the importance of the here-and-now as well as his concept of the *caesura* (Bion, 1977; Aguayo, 2013), which marks the sudden change from one mode of being/relating to another; creating an experience of newness and even disorientation. Similarly, Bion's (1966) notion of *catastrophic change*, the calamitous fear that a situation has suddenly and dramatically been altered, appears to link with the Change Group's emphasis on how unsettling the appearance of new ways of relating may feel. In addition, the Change Group's underscoring of nonlinearity is consonant with the perspectives offered in this chapter; however, there are some major differences in how these two points of view diverge – the role of unconscious processes, an appreciation of the subtle intersubjective exchanges that account for the emergence of "now moments," a recognition of different gradients of representations and their role in therapeutic change. I (Brown, 2010, 2011a) have been outlining a model of change that first and foremost hinges on a constant unconscious communication between the psyches of patient and analyst that either aims to uncover repressed unconscious contents or to transform unrepresented affective experience into symbolized and emotionally meaningful experience. Projective and introjective processes are the thoroughfares along which unconscious to unconscious communication travels and alpha function in the analyst and patient is responsible for encoding and decoding unconscious messages. In my view (Brown, 2009a), this process is at work constantly but, since it is unconscious, it is difficult to access except through dreams, one's reveries and countertransference phenomena. Furthermore, working through involves changes in the unconscious, which is comprised of phantasies that may be "registered" as somatopsychic events and exist as yet-to-be-processed emotional experience.

I find that the Change Group tends to underemphasize the role of unconscious processes in their work[8] and that when the unconscious is mentioned (though rarely), it is a different notion than the one promulgated in this book. Instead, they speak of "nonconscious" happenings, "implicit relational knowing" and "implicit relational exchanges"; the latter concept referring to the

> assumption that the patient and analyst are generally working hard to intuitively grasp each other's implicit intentions and directions. Conversation between them occurs continuously.
>
> (Change Group, 2013, p. 729)

This quote conveys an impression that accentuates conscious dialogues, though the wording "implicit relational knowing" seems to suggest an unconscious aspect. Similarly, the Change Group refers to

> Implicit experience [that] is not necessarily dissociated experience, unformulated or repressed, and the goal of working with it is not to transform it into an understanding within the reflective verbal sphere.
>
> (p. 734)

If an experience is not dissociated, unformulated or repressed, then the only other option is that it is a conscious experience or, perhaps, "non-conscious," but it is not clear what the authors mean.

The term, "implicit relational knowing" derives from cognitive psychology and is "one variety of procedural representation . . . [which is about] how to proceed, how to do things" (Change Group, 2010, p. 166), including interactions with others. Procedural representations are not conscious phenomena and neither are they part of the dynamic unconscious, but are non-language based automatic ways of behaving. The Change Group is describing procedures like "knowing how to joke around, express affection and make friends" (ibid, p. 166), but this emphasis seems to leave out so much that is central to the ideas about what constitutes a meaningful psychoanalytic engagement as I have outlined in this book. For instance, as we have seen in Chapter 10, the capacity to tell a joke is an extremely complex intersubjective event; thus, "joking around" is an important development achievement that depends on the successful maturation of several interconnected factors, most of which occur unconsciously.

Conclusion

This chapter has explored the impact on our understanding of the process of working through of Bion's emphasis that each session is an entity unto itself and that the analyst ought to approach each clinical hour without memory and desire. I have suggested that working through, especially when dealing with unrepresented experience, occurs on a micro and macro basis. The micro basis involves working in the immediacy of the clinical here-and-now moments with the assumption that, over a period of time, themes in individual sessions will cohere into meaningful narratives. Working on the macro basis, on the other hand, involves the analyst being mindful of the overall arc of the analysis with an eye on developing transferences and countertransference over a long period of time. Clinical material from Edward's long analysis was discussed to illustrate the process of working through from both points of view – micro and macro. Finally, some similarities and differences between the model proposed in this chapter and the standpoints of the Boston Change Process Study Group have been examined.

Notes

1 Expanded version of a paper given at the International Psychoanalytic Association Congress, Prague, 2013.
2 This work is cited more than any of Freud's other papers.

3 What Bion (1965; Chapter 4) would term a "rigid motion transformation."
4 Or *affective pictograms* according to da Rocha Barros (2000).
5 Alpha function.
6 The reader is referred to the recent book, *Unrepresented States and the Construction of Meaning: Clinical and Theoretical Contributions*, edited by Levine, Reed and Scarfone, for a more detailed discussion of these processes.
7 This group consisted of Nadia Bruschweiler-Stern, Karlen Lyons-Ruth, Alexander C. Morgan, Jeremy P. Nahum, Bruce Reis, Daniel Stern and Louis Sander.
8 The concept, "unconscious," is not listed in the Index of the Change Group's *Change in Psychotherapy, a Unifying Paradigm* (2010).

CHAPTER TWELVE

Conclusion

On Freud's "The question of a Weltanschauung*" – a world of perpetual transformation?*

In this concluding chapter, I want to explore the question of whether the ideas and concepts adumbrated here, as well as their clinical applications, suggest a new and additional *Weltanschauung* for psychoanalysis; a world view that emphasizes constant change, evolution and growth. To be sure, the contemporary world around us is rapidly changing and it often seems like the pace of that change is itself accelerating. Psychoanalysis cannot escape the effect: as our psychoanalytic world has grown more "flat" (Friedman, 2005): there has been an infusion of new perspectives from around the world that have in short time deeply affected our theory and technique. Just as gourmet food emporia offer a wide array of global tastes, so now the analytic world is a sampling of various schools of thought ranging from conservative to cutting edge theories and practices. What does it mean to be a contemporary psychoanalyst? Recently, a colleague in another city teaching at a "contemporary" institute assigned some papers on the Oedipus Complex to a class on development and was roundly criticized for promoting "out-moded" ideas that some found disturbing. One would hope, especially in an institute that calls itself "psychoanalytic," that there would be an openness to all ideas, just as the analyst ought to have the welcome mat out for a variety of possible emotional experiences, both pleasant and painful.

In my view, a contemporary psychoanalyst is one who, as Carl Jung stated, "considers nothing human is alien to himself." This is particularly true if the analyst is going to work with deeply troubled patients and, indeed, help neurotic patients reach the deeper regions of their suffering. Sean (Chapter 9) needed me to have the capacity and courage to dream the nightmare of the life-threatening bear in order to begin a process of transformation that helped enable him to move on with his young life. Another aspect of what I believe is central to a contemporary psychoanalyst is the capacity for reverie, dreaming (while awake and asleep) and to trust one's unconscious as an assistant, guide and oracle in our clinical practice. It's the Obe Wan Kenobe school of psychoanalysis: "Trust your feelings, Luke." Far be it from me to challenge a Jedi Knight, but our emotions are often misleading and we may not have the necessary self-analytic skills to fully comprehend what our subjective experiences are telling us. I think Erikson's concept of "disciplined subjectivity" strikes an excellent balance between wild and excessively constricted use of one's private reactions in the clinical hour. One of the analysts I spoke with who had been supervised by Theodor Reik (Chapter 5) told me that a female patient of Reik's entered his office and noticed that a book on the shelf was upside down. Reik interpreted that the woman was pregnant and she responded with surprise, "How did you know?" This seems like analytic folklore and also an example of *un*disciplined subjectivity; however, it seems true to me that as analysts mature they become more secure in using their private reactions as "an instrument of the analysis" (Freud, 1912).

Note that I have referred to Carl Jung, Theodor Reik, and Freud (and Obe Wan Kenobi!) in answer to the question of "what does it mean to be a contemporary psychoanalyst?" In addition to being open to a wide variety of evoked affects from our patients and the capacity for dreaming and reverie, I strongly believe that a contemporary analyst ought to have a grounding in the sweep of analytic history – the development of its ideas and the important figures. I find it sad that analytic candidates would be dismissive of some conversation about the Oedipus Complex and apparently lack the curiosity about what Freud was attempting to understand. Since studying Bion's (1965) theory of transformations, my interest in the development of psychoanalytic thought has been enhanced by his statement that

> The theory of transformations is intended to illuminate a chain of phenomena in which the understanding of one link, or aspect of it, helps in the understanding of others.
>
> (p. 34)

For example, we may trace the roots of analytic *field theory* to Kurt Lewin's work in Gestalt Psychology in Germany ↔ to England in WWII where Rickman and Bion blended Klein's ideas of unconscious phantasy and Trotter's (1916) observations about the "herd instinct" to form modern group theory ↔ to Uruguay where the Barangers formulated the concept of the shared unconscious fantasy of the couple ↔ to Italy for Ferro and Civitarese to impregnate the Barangers' work with Bion's theories of transformations and dreaming ↔ to American elaborations (Cassorla and Ogden emphasizing dreaming; Brown on intersubjective analytic field). I have used the ↔ symbol in order to emphasize that each of these links is bidirectional. In the forward direction, we trace the development of field theory over the years as it was transformed from its earliest iteration in Lewin's work to subsequent links, each one deepening our understanding of the phenomenon. However, moving in the reverse direction helps us to understand more fully the richness of the earlier link that has inseminated later ones. For example, Ogden's clearly written papers on reverie/dreaming cannot be fully appreciated unless one knows Bion's theory of dreaming and, conversely, familiarity with Ogden's work helps us to understand Bion's contributions more deeply.

I also believe that a contemporary psychoanalyst ought to have a comprehensive understanding of the unconscious and specifically of the nature of *unconscious work*, which I said in Chapter 1 is the "beating heart" of the analytic process. Psychoanalytic treatment occurs on two levels simultaneously: the "timelessness" of the analytic process that unfolds slowly, seemingly at its own pace, and the parallel unconscious work that is instantaneously "dreaming the analysis" (Bion, 1992); constantly at work to give meaning to emotional experience which is subsequently reconfigured, redreamed and re-represented. This is the unceasing work of alpha function, the "engine of transformations" (Chapter 3), that like a busy newsroom is sifting through a constant inflow of data, writing and rewriting the news in a never-ending effort to find meaning in an ever-developing story.

These thoughts bring a memory to mind of doing the research for my dissertation and the excitement I experienced at being able to have the university computer available for the required statistical analyses. It was a huge behemoth of a machine for which one had to create data cards that were fed into its mouth, followed by a long process of metallic gurgling that finally yielded many pages of a printout. A dozen or so years later my latency age daughter and I built our first desktop computer with the assistance of a more knowledgeable friend; a bulky and noisy contraption that seemed to take hours to get online via a dialup connection and then there was little of interest to access. Now my Lilliputian cell phone is gigantic in its capacity to connect to nearly endless sources of information in mere microseconds. These associations to the ease and rapid flow of information at one's fingertips underscore a theme that has been central to the psychoanalytic *Weltanschauung* I have suggested in this book: the incredible capacity of the mind to process emotional data and to create intricately fascinating ways of representing these emotions in the fraction of a second. Another component of this viewpoint is a sense of humility in the face of recognizing the incredible output of one's mind: how alpha function working hand in hand with condensation creates an endless parade of dreams, reveries, characters, quips, etc., that represent the varied emotional currents of a particular situation.

In the last chapter of *New Introductory Lectures on Psycho-Analysis*, Freud (1933) raised the question of whether psychoanalysis offered a new *Weltanschauung*, or world view, in addition to existing perspectives, such as those promoted by religion and philosophy. Although he might have mentioned just a few of the ways in which his work profoundly altered established beliefs, instead he simply said that psychoanalysis was one of the sciences and therefore was devoted to "the truth and the rejection of illusions" (p. 182). Freud was especially critical of approaches that he regarded as illusory or based on intuition and in contrast stated that science is limited to

> what is at the moment knowable and by its sharp rejection of certain elements that are alien to it . . . [and contains] *no knowledge derived from revelation, intuition or divination.*
>
> (1933, p. 159) [italics added]

It strikes me that Freud's insistence that psychoanalysis was a science contributed to his vitriol toward religion and also was a reflection of his "limited attitude to illusion" (Blass, 2004, p. 619); indeed, so much of what is dealt with in analysis is illusory and ephemeral and so his outright rejection of "revelation, intuition and divination" remains puzzling. However, in my view the acceptance and clinical utility of the analyst's reveries, intuitions and oneiric experiences lies at the center of contemporary psychoanalytic theory and technique. As mentioned previously, there are two analytic concepts that I (Brown, 2009b) find capture this current point of view: Erikson's (1964) notion of "disciplined subjectivity" and Bion's idea of "speculative imagination" (1997b), two concepts that speak for themselves. Put another way, the contemporary psychoanalyst must have the capacity to reside in a place between illusion and the truth, fully understanding that sometimes we need a lie to help us begin to bear the truth.

A recent article in the *New York Times* (Schrope, 2015) contains within it some further elements of what I consider a contemporary psychoanalytic perspective. One of the world's oldest books is an eleventh-century book of prayers written on pages of animal skin in Syriac, an ancient dialect of Aramaic in which many early Christian books were written. It was discovered that the text was a palimpsest that covered over an undertext that had been scraped away to "recycle" the pages on which the prayers were later written; however, through the application of spectral imaging the hidden text was revealed. That undertext, likely written in the ninth century in Syriac was itself a copy of the first Syriac translation in the sixth century of Galen's classic medical text, *On the Mixtures and Powers of Simple Drugs*, which he wrote in the second century in Greek. That first (sixth century) translation from the Greek by a Syriac physician and priest was exceedingly tedious because *"He had to create vocabulary* to find Syriac words to correspond to this Greek medical vocabulary" (Schrope, 2015) [italics added]. Thus, Galen's original second-century text written in Greek underwent many subsequent transformations: a sixth-century translation into Syriac, the creation of new Syriac vocabulary words for some original concepts, a ninth-century retranslation into Syriac and its final form as a prayer book. In addition,

> As texts went through multiple rounds of copying, they underwent significant changes.
>
> A scribe might remove parts that seemed unimportant or add material based on new knowledge.
>
> (Schrope, 2015)

In this regard, the "Galen Palimpsest" (the Syriac prayer book that contained the translation of Galen's book) was *"much further removed from the original"* (Schrope, 2015) [italics added] Greek manuscript.

This example may be viewed through several alternating analytic lenses, none of which is more "correct" than the other. The first is a *traditional psychoanalytic model* in which the discovery of the undertext of Galen's book in the eleventh-century hymnal is analogous to making the unconscious conscious: a submerged (repressed) "truth" is unearthed. A second vertex is a model of *the analyst's role in the process* of revealing this hidden truth, just as the scribes altered the texts, in which there are "fingerprints" of the analyst's personality affecting what is discovered. A third lens is *inventing a vocabulary for what is unknown* (i.e., representing): that just as the original translators of Galen's work had to invent new Syriac words to give meaning to some Greek concepts, so there are experiences that affect the analyst and analysand for which they do not have words, e.g., Mr. 72's absorption into a black hole (Chapter 9). A final perspective is the *theory of transformations* (Bion, 1965; Chapter 4) that asserts understanding one link of a chain of phenomena helps in the understanding of other links in that sequence. The beginning of this linkage may fade as further connections are created, yet there is an origin, O, that is often unknown, like the hypothetical East African woman, Lucy, from whom we have all descended. Similarly, the process of transformation from Galen's original Greek to the eleventh-century prayer book occurred over a period of approximately 1,000 years; thus, we are speaking about an evolution that proceeded at a snail's pace and the end point of this progression was far removed in time and meaning from the original manuscript. Thus, the Syriac edition is an approximation, that is, a *representation*, "much further removed from the original." I think all four vertices are part of the armamentarium of the contemporary analyst one might deploy as needed to understand the depth of the analysand's communications.

In retrospect, I've come to regard Chapter 8, "Three unconscious pathways to representing the analyst's experience: reverie, countertransference dreams and joke-work," as one of the central chapters in this book that captures some of the essence of how one's mind can receive, represent/dream (in the Bionian sense) and give meaning to one's emotional experiences almost instantaneously. In the clinical situation, I believe this is among the most important processes for the analyst to try and comprehend. Bion urged the analyst to adopt a mindset of *negative capability* (Mawson, 2015) in order to be maximally receptive to the manifold ways in which we are affected by our analysands. I imagine by now the reader knows how important one's receptivity is in how I think and practice, but I have come to appreciate in recent years how these processes occur in the blink of an eye. It requires us to train ourselves to listen to ourselves, to be somewhat solipsistic regarding what is happening inside of us when listening to our patients. There's a joke about the difference between a Kleinian and a Freudian analyst: in a Freudian analysis, the analyst could die and the analysis would continue (because the patient is used to a silent analyst); whereas in a Kleinian analysis the patient could die and the analysis would continue (because the analyst is so focused on the countertransference). Perhaps we could say that in a Bionian oriented treatment the analysis would die if the clinician's imagination or disciplined subjectivity were brought to a halt?

This joke underscores the importance of being maximally receptive to projections coming from the patient *and to the impact these have upon one's psyche* as discussed in Chapter 5, "The analyst's receptivity: evolution of the concept and its clinical application." In that chapter, one's receptive stance is linked with having trust in one's intuition that is rooted in Freud's recommendation we keep our minds as open as possible without any predetermined agenda as to the outcome of the session. Reik adopted this attitude very seriously; however, this faith in one's intuitive processes as an invaluable tool in the treatment fell by the wayside theoretically with the ascendancy of ego psychology (primarily in the United States) in the 1930s and 1940s, which deemed intuition as "unscientific" (Brown, 2011a; Lothane, 2006). However, it is my impression based on supervisions I have had with some analysts trained in the heyday of ego psychology that they paid great attention to their associations to the analysand's free associations and considered these as relevant to the patient's "material."

I think this apparent paradox – rejecting the value of one's intuition theoretically yet employing one's private associations clinically – reflects the absence at the time of a sophisticated way of understanding *unconscious work,* which I see as the lifeblood of the analytic process. The notion of *unconscious work* derives from Bion's proposal of alpha function (Chapter 3, "Bion's discovery of alpha function: the engine of transformations"), which grew out of his elaboration of Freud's theory of dreaming, that includes the seminal idea that we are always dreaming, while awake and asleep. Put another way, *unconscious work* and *free associations,* whether in the analyst's or the patient's mind, are dreams in the sense that these are in vivo transformations of affective experiences that are alive in the here-and-now of the clinical hour. Thus, when I mentioned the paradox of the previous generation of analysts diminishing the importance of intuition yet valuing their associations to the analysand's "material," I think this was due to the absence of a more comprehensive (Bion's) theory of dreaming. It is my impression, and likely a controversial one, that many of the classical analysts were more at home with using their associations as a pathway to understanding the patient than some present-day clinicians who focus excessively on the factual realities of the analyst/patient interactions.

To dream in Bion's view is to transform an emotional experience into a variety of different manifestations: a night dream, an ordinary thought, a reverie, a countertransference feeling, the "meaningless" thoughts that meander through our minds during a session, etc. He has suggested that we consider the analytic session as if it were a dream. Why? I think he was emphasizing that every element in a session has unconscious meaning and that we ought to treat each of these elements as if they were dream symbols.[1] To orient one's listening in this way underscores the potential unconscious meaning of everything that occurs in the analytic hour. To have an intuition that such-and-such is occurring at a certain point in a session is to have a dream, i.e., a *waking dream thought* in Bion's parlance.

Related to Bion's expansion of what it means to dream is his Theory of Transformations (Chapter 4: "Bion's *Transformations* and Clinical Practice"), another foundational chapter of this book. It is the third of Bion's four major books[2] – notoriously the most challenging to understand – and I had put off reading it for quite a few years, fearful of getting lost in an endless labyrinth without an Ariadne's thread to find my way back. However, I was pleasantly surprised to discover that the book was essentially clinically oriented, despite his musings about mathematics and obscure philosophical questions. His elaboration of the concept of O, the emotional essence of a session or, more generally, the *thing in itself* (Kant), is the critical emotional "stuff" that is transformed into a *representation*, i.e., a dream, reverie, free association, etc., by the activity of the patient's and analyst's respective alpha functions. *Thus, every association of the patient and each thought that passes through our mind is the momentary endpoint of a process of transformational dreaming, which will continue from that point forward.* These thoughts and associations arise from the process of unconscious work that has been quietly on-going internally as well as intersubjectively through unconscious communications between analyst and patient. Furthermore, to the extent that one's reveries are representations (by the patient and/or the analyst) of the emotional climate in the clinical hour, these may also be regarded as *potential or fully formed interpretations.*[3] The joke my analyst told me in the beginning of Chapter 8 came to his mind spontaneously and was a condensation of many themes active at that point in treatment. Though he offered it as casual comment, it proved to be an effective interpretation that is still with me years later.

I have been discussing the complementary bilateral movement in analytic work that is both incrementally slow, yet also astoundingly rapid; a process that occurs within the boundaries of the analytic setting (or frame). The concept of an analytic frame or setting has been central to clinical thinking from Freud's (1912, 1913) original writings onward and in Chapter 6 ("Ruptures in the analytic setting and disturbances in the transformational field of dreams") the focus was on the psychic coordinates of the setting as a place of mutual dreaming that transformed the emotions enlivening that setting. We also saw in that chapter a *unique kind of transformation* by which primitive emotional material too powerful for the analytic pair to deal with in the on-going analytic process was relegated to "non-process" (Bleger, 1967/2013) and then "stored" in the analytic setting until the patient/analyst dyad was capable of managing the powerful affects without being overwhelmed. The nature of that transformation into non-process (and then back again) remains unclear, but the analytic frame holds this primitive material that is rendered into a sort of "freeze dried" state (Brown, 2015c), perhaps analogous to what in information technology is referred to as "the cloud," a place that is not palpable in which material that is potentially accessible is stored; however, when in the cloud (or in the setting) it is inactive. Bleger (1967/2013) was clear in warning us that when the setting is disrupted a "crack" (p. 235) may develop through which a "phantom world" (p. 230) of archaic emotions floods the analytic process as we saw in the analysis of Mr. R. in Chapter 6.

I am writing this segment about the setting/frame two days after the provocative and violent marches by neo-Nazis, KKK members and other fascist groups wreaked havoc in Charlottesville, Virginia, which underscored for me the importance of the setting in situations outside the confines of the analytic office. Suddenly, Bleger's assertion about the release of a "phantom world" into the analytic process when the setting is disrupted took on a fresh and frightening relevance to what had happened that weekend. Freud's (1930) observation, too, comes to mind about the thin veneer of civilization, which directly relates to the absolute necessity for a social framework to be intact in order to keep potential incursions of destructive elements from flooding the everyday rhythm of normal activity. The maintenance and enforcement of the societal setting depends on our leaders to transform behavior inimical to society by strengthening the framework; incarcerating, so to speak, the phantoms to a position in which they are neutralized in a "cloud-like" setting. Indeed, from the perspective of transformational processes, we can say that one of the responsibilities of leadership is to contain the emotions that confront the group (analytic couple, corporation, municipality, nation) and transform these into a narrative that renders the toxic affects more manageable.[4] Of course, if the leadership class regards the usual framework as worthy of demolition and allows or encourages the disruptive emotions in the society to seismically rattle the political setting, then chaos will surely follow.

I hope at this point the definition of the analytic process I gave in the Introduction and discussed further in Chapter 6, which I called "quite a mouthful of psychoanalytic theory, dense and tightly woven," is more meaningful than it was at the outset of this book:

> The active here-and-now process of continuous transformations of affects arising in the intersubjective field to create new meaning, which is achieved through a perpetual, unconscious, joint process of dreaming and Nachträglichkeit (après-coup), made possible through the linked alpha functions of patient and analyst – all of which is enabled by, and depends upon, a stable analytic setting/frame.

But I cannot end here and there is one last point I wish to make and that is about the importance of maintaining what Bion (1965, 1970) calls a "binocular" view, that is for the analyst (and patient) to have the capacity to see one phenomenon from multiple perspectives. For Grotstein (2009a, 2009b), one aspect of *binocular thinking* is that the conscious and unconscious personalities work collaboratively, rather than in opposition as Freud stated, to create a stereoscopic perspective in one's object relations. Grotstein's comment about "resistance" is characteristic of his often pithy way of considering a concept through a binocular point of view:

> When one considers the analysand's utterances and behavior from the dramatic vertex, resistance as a concept and as a phenomenon seems to vanish. *Put another way,* the analysand is always cooperative in the analysis as long as he is attending sessions.
>
> (Grotstein, 2009a, pp. 98–99) [italics added]

With many patients, especially those who are more disturbed, the analyst is frequently challenged by the analysand speaking in different "tongues," each of which may organize their emotional world – and the mood of the analytic hour – through different frameworks. For example, I began in Chapter 9 by relating Mr. B.'s state of mind as governed by an autistic transformation that was dramatically and structurally different from his usual mode of experiencing himself. These sorts of situations require the analyst to be familiar with different pathways to representing emotions and varying channels of communication that are employed. My analytic work with Ms. G. demanded this sort of flexibility.

Analyzing Ms. G.: the importance of staying on one's toes

In his recent book, *The New Analyst's Guide to the Galaxy*, Ferro (2017) addresses what he sees as folly in the psychoanalytic genuflection to past theories:

> We're like a family that has not emptied its closets for 200 years, that hoards as certain psychotic individuals do: hoards and hoards so that we have concepts that are part of the history of psychoanalysis, but have outlived their usefulness. For this reason, a travelling analyst is followed by twenty-four carriages full of trunks, that is no longer useful.
>
> (p. 47)

This year, for the first time, I unexpectedly took off the entire month of August to recover from a mild concussion and some friends invited my wife and me to visit with them for a few days on Cape Cod. Upon telling my patients of my up-coming absence, one said, "Now you're a real psychoanalyst taking all of August off; I guess you're going to Wellfleet[5] on Cape Cod." I had to laugh and said, "Guilty as charged." Despite the tongue-in-cheek humor in Ferro's comment, I think he is making an important point about how often we analysts define ourselves as analysts by taking on the accoutrement of certain prescribed markers to confirm our identity and be part of the group, like a secret handshake. Ferro wisely cautions us to eschew the supposed necessity of, for example, beginning each paper by quoting Freud. Bion, on the other hand, discouraged others from identifying themselves as "Bionian" so that we might instead become our own psychoanalyst that evolves from our in-born predilections, experiences in our families and with teachers, through a process of *entelechy* (Grotstein, 2009b) by which we *become* our inner potential.

Notwithstanding Ferro's proscriptions in the previous paragraph, I had planned to approach the topic of "staying on one's toes" by relooking at one of my papers (Brown, 1996) from about 20 years ago (that I had not read in many years) in which I presented the analytic treatment (four sessions a week face-to-face) of a deeply troubled woman, Ms. G., who related to me in four distinct object relational patterns that appeared at various times, even within the same session. In rereading the paper, I was surprised that I had begun with a discussion of "dual consciousness," an idea promulgated by Breuer and Freud (1893) in *Studies in Hysteria*; what we today would call different organizations; each perceiving, thinking, generating meaning and cordoned off from the other. Regarding each distinct consciousness, Freud said, "their ideational content can . . . reach a more or less high degree of psychical organization" (p. 12). I commented that

> Thus, Freud's first model of the unconscious referred to relatively independent selves dedicated to the illusion that the other did not exist, with each generating its own system of meaning. When external events were ripe,

> the second, hysterical consciousness ascended to become the dominant self, not unlike the sudden coming to political power of a well-organized government in exile.
>
> (p. 22)

Today I would use very different terminology to describe Ms. G.'s alternating states of mind, but 20 years ago Freud's notion of "dual consciousness" offered a scaffolding to understand the shifting interactional patterns in the treatment. Regardless of which psychoanalytic language I brought to characterize the rapid oscillation of varying states of mind in Ms. G. and their impact on me, at the heart of what transpired between us was an experience of O – the shared feeling of instability and uncertainty making "staying on one's toes" difficult, but necessary – that might conceivably be transformed through a variety of psychoanalytic languages (i.e., Freudian, Lacanian, Kleinian, etc.). I think Ferro's earlier hyperbolic quote is a warning to the analyst to consciously stay fresh and jettison what one has learned because those perspectives remain available in our minds as potential frameworks by which to transform the emotional essence of the clinical situation. The capacity for binocular (or multi-ocular) vision depends on the analyst having various transformational lenses available to give meaning to the shared O conjoining patient and analyst.

In working with Ms. G., it was never clear who was coming into my office: *one* presentation was a mature and thoughtful Ms. G. who freely associated, understood metaphors, formed various paternal and maternal transferences; put another way, a classically "neurotic" patient who early on introspectively said, "My father made me sad and my mother made me crazy." On other days, and sometimes within the same clinical hour, a *second* Ms. G. would speak of feeling "drained" or "vacuumed out" while passively telling me that she wanted to die and then refused to leave my office at the end of a session. In Ms. G.'s mind, I had turned into – i.e., been transformed into – the abandoning mother who made her "crazy," an image of her mother with whom I felt identified when I imagined throwing her out of my office. A *third* interactional pattern was expressed through puzzling and bizarre bodily experiences that accompanied her wondering whether she had been sexually abused by her father. In these states, Ms. G. reported feeling that

> her arms and legs were on backwards, that her hands were her father's hands, and that she was walking around with all her body parts clanging disjointedly inside of herself.
>
> (ibid, p. 45)

A *fourth* kind of interaction emerged as she came to recognize how painful separations from me had become, and that

> absences made her feel like what she had heard burn patients go through when new skin is grafted: that if the bandage is removed too soon the new skin will peel off adhered to it . . . [and] that she often felt as though she had neither an inside nor an outside, that she was 'a face on a pane of glass'. . . like the Scarecrow in the *Wizard of Oz* whose insides kept falling out of him.
> (ibid, p. 44)

When Ms. G. spoke these words, I had a chillingly empty feeling, different from my reaction to her fear of being "vacuumed out," her refusal to leave my office or her description of disjointed body parts inside her. I found the image of "a face on a pane of glass" evoked a particularly frightening sense of being two dimensional, without any emotional depth – like a stamp on a postcard with no address. She also refused to leave my office and was filled with blind terror; a very different emotional state than the fear of abandonment in the second version of Ms. G.

I imagine that the reader has his or her own numerous associations and theories about the nature of Ms. G.'s pathology, its connections to her mother and father, its manifestations in the transference and countertransference, hypotheses about what I might have done differently, as well as other approaches. These are important conversations to have, but I want to focus on the nature of the transformations that are occurring, keeping in mind that

> The psychoanalyst's domain is that which lies between the point where a man receives sense impressions and the point where he gives expression to *the transformation that has taken place.*
> (Bion, 1965, p. 46; Chapter 4) [italics added]

Simply put, this "domain" refers to having an emotional experience ("receives sense impressions") and ascribing a meaning ("gives expression to the transformation") to that emotional experience. Implicit in Bion's statement, but not said, is the activity by which a "sense impression" *has been* transformed – unconscious work/dreaming/alpha function. This accounts for the *process* by which the transformation is effected; there are also *different kinds of transformations*, and I will turn to these now in the context of Ms. G's four patterns of interacting with me.

In my view, each of the four interactional patterns in the brief clinical vignettes with Ms. G. are illustrative of different types of transformations: *rigid motion transformations, projective transformations, somatic transformations* and *autistic transformations*. Ms. G.'s initial "neurotic" presentation was a "rigid motion transformation" in that the transference and countertransference were seeded by the repetition of seemingly actual events from her past, which in classical analysis is the repeat of the infantile neurosis in the here-and-now of the transference and the analyst's countertransference is considered a "neurotic" reaction to the infantile aspects of that transference. This scenario assumes a relatively high level of ego functioning including the capacity for representing emotional experience (intact alpha function), metaphorical thinking and communicative projective identification.

In contrast, the "second" Ms. G.'s interaction with me is an example of a *projective transformation* in which experiences of herself and her analyst were greatly shaped by her use of evacuative projective identification, which left her feeling "vacuumed out." Perceiving that she had little left inside, Ms. G. felt empty, abandoned and enraged at me as her transferential mother and planted herself in my office, refusing to leave. This evoked a tendency to enact angrily toward her (throw her out) in response to her aggressive demands to remain after the session. Thus, I had become in phantasy (hers *and* mine) Ms. G.'s abandoning mother and I am quite certain that she sensed my strong desire for her to leave, which surely intensified her rageful passivity. Unlike the rigid motion transformation in which reality distortions are minimal, Ms. G.'s experiences of herself and me were greatly distorted by her evacuative projective identification that left her feeling empty, forgotten and with an analyst painfully like her abandoning mother. In such a patient, the analyst's interpretations (his transformations of what appears to be occurring) need to address the transformational process (massive projections by Ms. G.) by which the patient's distortions are created and, similarly, the ways in which perceptions of the analysand may be misrepresented by the analyst. Addressing the patient's misperceptions is more easily said than done since the analyst's interpretation may be felt as the clinician's forceful projection back into the patient of what he or she had hoped to evacuate out.

I felt completely befuddled when Ms. G. appeared in the third iteration in which she experienced herself as a collection of disjointed body parts and was relieved when she linked this to possible sexual abuse from her father. Making this assertion helped things fall "together" rather than fall "apart" and we both were calmed by having discovered the "answer"; however, a few days later Ms. G. reported a dream in which she was hooked up to an IV in the hospital and the word "Mutilator" was written on the IV bag. When relating the dream to me her thoughts became disconnected and the feeling of her body being dismembered came back. I interpreted that it was as though her dream had alerted us to a force at work within her that was mutilating her thoughts, affects and body. She remembered that her mother would threaten the family that their anger toward her would make her collapse and she would have to be sent back to the State Hospital where she had previously been admitted several times.

These sessions with Ms. G. occurred at the time when the sexual abuse scandal was breaking news in Boston and so I was unsure whether she was in fact abused by her father or perhaps it was a lie[6] that was unconsciously spun. The fact that both Ms. G. and I were relieved when she attributed falling apart to the alleged abuse from her father suggests that this possible "lie" helped organize her and calmed me. However, what I found most striking and difficult to understand was her experience of being broken apart into pieces internally. Now, 20 years later, I am not so convinced that my "mutilator" interpretation was on target: there was a transformational process occurring that oscillated between Ms. G.'s body experienced as dismembered and, only moments later, she was sufficiently integrated to communicate verbally. Bion (1965) hinted at the notion of *somatic transformations* but did not develop this idea; however, he had earlier (1961) speculated that understanding "proto-mental" phenomena, which are primitive states that are neither physical nor mental, could help broaden the study of physical illness. In a related way, Andre Green (2010) conceptualized a *somato-psychic frontier* that is a dividing point between unrepresented somatic stimuli and those stimuli that have been represented in words and this seems to be a useful perspective from which to consider what Ms. G. was experiencing. Furthermore, I find Riccardo Lombardi's (2011, 2013) ideas about somatic phenomena to be very helpful clinically: he emphasizes the importance of addressing the patient's relationship to her body prior to offering a relational interpretation. In retrospect, if I had a time machine to return to that point in working with Ms. G., I would have tried to stay focused on her relationship to her body and to her not having truly crossed the somato-psychic boundary rather than attempting to formulate more standard types of interpretations.

But what to make of the fourth version of Ms. G? I did not feel I was abandoning her when asking her to leave the session as was the case when I felt like tossing her out; instead, I felt protective of this fragile "face on a pane of glass." Writing now, I think of Ms. G.'s experience as an *autistic transformation* (Korbivcher, 2005, 2014; Chapters 9 and 10) in which the self and affect are quite literally flattened out and the patient fears dissolving into non-existence. At the time, I had recently read Ogden's (1989) paper on the "autistic-contiguous position" and realized her need to lean up against me, so to speak, in order to have a sense of an outer boundary that could offer depth and keep her insides from falling out of her. I said to Ms. G., "I know that there is something terrifying you right now that keeps you from leaving, something that has to do with being a 'face on a pane of glass,' that you or I don't have words for." She replied quickly and asked if I ever watched *Star Trek*. I said that I did and wondered why she asked and Ms. G. replied, "You know when they beam someone down to a planet or up from a planet, that the person getting beamed dissolves into something like a mist. That's what it's like for me to leave – that I'll dissolve and there'd be no trace of me."[7] Ms. G. was able to leave the session after this exchange.

I use the term "staying on one's toes" to indicate the necessary awareness of the constant unconscious work in which one's alpha function is engaged to represent and give meaning to the emotions of the intersubjective analytic field of the moment. In addition, one must be alert to the various methods by which the emotions of the field are transformed – rigid motion, projective, somatic and autistic[8] – and, depending upon which is being employed, the analyst must be ready to pivot, perhaps several times within the same session. In place of Bion's types of transformations, I could employ Freud's (1893/1895) idea of a "dual[9] consciousness "[in which] their ideational content can . . . reach a more or less high degree of psychical organization" (p. 12) to explain the changes in Ms. G.'s interactions, which would account for much of the shifts in her perceptions of me and herself. But these are static ideas that require enrichment from Bion's emphasis on how these perceptions change and evolve over the course of the session, and surely over the arc of an analysis. However, Bion's types of transformations have given me a greater appreciation of what Freud was attempting to understand in his hysterical patients; simultaneously, familiarity with Freud's concept of dual consciousness offered me a scaffolding from which to consider Bion's transformations. This seems to me the essence of a contemporary psychoanalyst: being enriched by the past to understand the present more completely and the past more fully; that, like psychoanalysis itself, one is constantly expanding one's horizons in the perpetual search for meaning.

Notes

1 Of course, it is impossible to analyze every element in a dream, just as each segment of a session has innumerable associations that can never be fully explored.

2 *Learning from Experience*, 1962; *Elements of Psychoanalysis*, 1963; and *Attention and Interpretation*, 1970.

3 Discussed in greater detail in Chapter 10.

4 President Franklin Roosevelt's timeless words about the attack on Pearl Harbor, labeling it as a "Day that will live in infamy," and his earlier statement that "We have nothing to fear but fear itself," are but two of many examples.

5 Wellfleet is a town on Cape Cod in Massachusetts rightly known as an August haven for Northeast Coast analysts.

6 A "lie" in the sense that Bion has discussed that serves a defensive purpose to organize and that may or may not be factually true; what he calls a Column 2 phenomenon in the Grid (see Chapter 4).

7 These anxieties of melting, vanishing, etc., are typical of Asperger's children and adult patients with so-called autistic pockets.

8 Bion has hinted that there are additional pathways to transformation, but has left this to future generations to develop, such as Korbivcher's (2005, 2014) idea of "autistic transformations." I would add *transformations in humor*, examples of which were cited in Chapters 8 and 10 here.

9 Or in this case, "four consciousnesses."

REFERENCES

Abraham, K. (1909) Letter to Sigmund Freud, 7 April, 1909. *The Complete Correspondence of Karl Abraham to Sigmund Freud.* Pp. 86–88.

______. (1921) Untitled paper on war neuroses. In S. Ferenczi *Psychoanalysis and the War Neuroses*. Original publisher, Vienna: International Psychoanalytical Press, 1921. Memphis, TN: General Books, 2010.

Ackroyd, P. (2006) *J. M. W. Turner: Ackroyd's Brief Lives*. New York: Doubleday.

Aguayo, J. (2012) Personal communication.

______. (2013) Wilfred Bion's "Caesura": From oral to published text (1975–1977). In H. Levine and L. Brown (Eds.) *Growth and Turbulence in the Container/Contained: Bion's Continuing Legacy*. London: Routledge. Pp. 55–74.

______ & Malin, B. (2013) *Wilfred Bion: Los Angeles Seminars and Supervision.* London: Karnac.

Anzieu, D. (1979) The sound image of the self. *IRPsa*, 6: 23–36.

______. (1993a) The film of the dream. In S. Flanders (Ed.) *The Dream Discourse Today*. London: Routledge. Pp. 137–150.

______. (1993b) Autistic phenomena and the skin ego. *Psa Inq*, 13: 42–48.

Bailey, A. (1997) *Standing in the Sun: A Life of J. M. W. Turner*. London: Tate Publishing.

Balint, A. & Balint, M. (1939) On transference and counter-transference. *IJP*, 20: 223–230.

Balint, M. (1954) Analytic training and training analysis. *IJP*, 35: 157–162.

Baranger, M. & Baranger, W. (2008) The analytic situation as a dynamic field. *IJP*, 89: 795–826.

______ & Mom, J. (1983) Process and non-process in analytic work. *IJP*, 64: 1–15.

Barrows, K. (2008) Experiences with Bion and Tustin. Presentation to the Klein/Bion Study Group of the Massachusetts Institute for Psychoanalysis.

Benton, M. (2003) Wipeout. *New Scientist*, 178: 38.

______. (2005) *When Life Nearly Died*. London: Thames and Hudson.

Bernardi, R. (2008) Letter from Uruguay. *IJP*, 89: 233–240.

Bianchedi, E. (2007) Personal communication.

Bick, E. (1968) The experience of skin in early object-relations. *IJP*, 49: 484–486.

______. (1986) Further considerations on the function of the skin in early object relations. *British Journal of Psychotherapy*, 2: 292–299.

Binswanger, L. (1925) Letter from Ludwig Binswanger to Freud, February 15, 1925. *The Sigmund Freud-Ludwig Binswanger Correspondence 1908–1938*. Pp. 195–178.

Bion, F. (1997) *War Memoirs 1917–1919*. F. Bion (Ed.) London: Karnac.

Bion, W. (1940) The "War of Nerves": Civilian reaction, morale and prophylaxis. In E. Miller (Ed.) *Neuroses in War*, New York: Macmillan & Co., 1945. Pp. 180–200.

______. (1952) Group dynamics: A re-view. *IJP*, 33: 235–237.

______. (1954) Notes on the theory of schizophrenia. *IJP*, 37. Also in *Second Thoughts*. Pp. 23–35.

______. (1957) Differentiation of the psychotic from the non-psychotic personalities. *IJP*: 38. Also in *Second Thoughts*. Pp. 47–64.

______. (1958) On arrogance. *IJP*, 39. Also in *Second Thoughts*. Pp. 86–92.

______. (1959) Attacks on linking. *IJP*, 40: 308–315. Also in *Second Thoughts*. Pp. 93–109.

______. (1961) *Experiences in Groups*. London: Tavistock.

______. (1962a) A theory of thinking. *IJP*, 43: 306–310.

______. (1962b) *Learning from Experience*. London: Heinemann.

______. (1963) *Elements of Psycho-Analysis*. London: Heinemann.

______. (1965) *Transformations*. London: Heinemann.

______. (1967a) *Second Thoughts*. New York: Jason Aronson.

______. (1967b) Notes on memory and desire. In W. Bion (1992) *Cogitations*. London: Karnac Books (extended 1994 version).

______. (1970) *Attention and Interpretation*. London: Heinemann.

______. (1973) *Brazilian Lectures: 1973 Sao Paulo*. London: Karnac, 1990.

______. (1976) Emotional turbulence. In *Clinical Seminars and Other Works*. London: Karnac Books, 1994. Pp. 295–305.

______. (1977) Caesura. *Two Papers: The Grid and Caesura*. London: Karnac Books, 1989. Pp. 35–56.

______. (1979) Making the best of a bad job. In *Clinical Seminars and Other Works*. London: Karnac Books, 1994. Pp. 321–331.

______. (1980) *Bion in New York City and San Paolo*. London: Karnac Books.

______. (1982) *The Long Week-End, 1897–1919: Part of a Life*. Abington: Fleetwood Press.

______. (1984) *Clinical Seminars and other Works*. London: Karnac Books.

______. (1985). *All My Sins Remembered: Another Part of a Life and the Other Side of Genius: Family Letters*. London: Karnac.

______. (1991) *A Memoir of the Future*. London: Karnac.

______. (1992) *Cogitations*. London: Karnac Books (extended 1994 version).

______. (1997a). *War Memoirs: 1917–1919*, F. Bion (Ed.) London: Karnac.

______. (1997b) *Taming Wild Thoughts*. London: Karnac.

______. (2005) *The Tavistock Seminars*. London: Karnac.

Blass, R. B. (2004) Beyond illusion: Psychoanalysis and the question of religious truth. *IJP*, 85: 615–634.

Bleandou, G. (1994) *Wilfred Bion: His Life and Works 1897–1979*. New York: The Guilford Press.

Bleger, J. (1967/2013) Psychoanalysis of the psychoanalytic setting. In *Symbiosis and Ambiguity: A Psychoanalytic Study*. London: Routledge. Pp. 228–241. First published in English as "Psycho-analysis of the psychoanalytic frame," *IJPA*, 48: 511–519.

Boesky, D. (1990) The psychoanalytic process and its components. *Psa. Q*, 59: 550–584.

Bollas, C. (1995) Cracking up. In *Cracking Up: The Work of Unconscious Experience*. New York: Hill and Wang.

Boston Change Process Study Group. (2010) *Change in Psychotherapy: A Unifying Paradigm*. New York: Norton.

______. (2013) Enactment and the emergence of new relational organization. *JAPA*, 61: 727–749.

Botella, C. & Botella, S. (2005) *The Work of Psychic Figurability: Mental States without Representation*. London: Routledge.

Bowlby, J. (1969) *Attachment and Loss: Volume 1: Attachment*. London: Hogarth Press.

Bragg, M. (2016) *The Fighting Temeraire*. In Our Time, BBC Radio Podcast.

Brenman Pick, I. B. (1985) Working through in the countertransference. *IJP*, 66: 157–166.

Britton, R. (1998). *Belief and Imagination*. London: Routledge.

Bromwich, D. (2014) *The Intellectual Life of Edmund Burke*. Cambridge, MA: Harvard University Press.

Brown, L. J. (1985). On concreteness. *Psa Rev*, 72, 379–402.

______. (1996) A proposed demography of the representational world. *J. Melanie Klein & Obj Rels*, 14: 21–60.

______. (2005) The cognitive effects of trauma: Reversal of alpha function and the formation of a beta screen. *Psa Q*, 74: 397–420.

______. (2006) Julie's museum: The evolution of thinking, dreaming and historicization of traumatized patients. *IJPA*, 87: 1569–1585.

______. (2007) On dreaming one's patient: Reflections on an aspect of countertransference dreams. *Psa Q*, 76: 835–861.

______. (2009a) The ego psychology of Wilfred Bion: Implications for an intersubjective view of psychic structure. *Psa Q*, 78: 27–55.

______. (2009b) From "Disciplined Subjectivity" to "Taming Wild Thoughts": Bion's elaboration of the analyzing instrument. *Int Forum Psa*, 18: 82–85.

______. (2010) Klein, Bion and intersubjectivity: Becoming, transforming and dreaming. *Psa Dial*, 20: 669–682.

______. (2011a) *Intersubjective Processes and the Unconscious: An Integration of Freudian, Kleinian and Bionian Perspectives*. New Library of Psychoanalysis Series. New York: Routledge Press.

______. (2011b) Countertransference. In G. Gabbard, B. Litowitz and H. Smith (Eds.) *Textbook of Psychoanalysis, Second Edition*. New York: American Psychiatric Publishing. Pp. 79–92.

______. (2011c) Rickman, Bion and the clinical applications of field theory. *Int For Psa*, 20: 89–92.

______. (2012) Bion's discovery of alpha function: Thinking under fire on the battlefield and in the consulting room. *IJP*, 93: 1191–1214.

______. (2013) The development of Bion's concept of container and contained. In H. Levine and L. Brown (Eds.) *Growth and Turbulence in the Container/Contained*. London: Routledge. Pp. 7–22.

______. (2014) "Packaging Awe: Transformations in O and Religion." Seminar given at the 2014 Bion in Los Angeles meeting, October 2014.

______. (2015a) Notes on Memory and Desire: Implications for Working Through. In H. B. Levine and G. Civitarese (Eds.) *The Wilfred Bion Legacy*. London: Karnac Books. Pp. 333–343.

______. (2015b) Ruptures in the analytic setting and disturbances in the transformational field of dreams. *Psa Q*, 84: 841–865.

______. (2016a) The analyst's receptivity: Evolution of the concept and its clinical application. *Rivista di Psicoanalisi*, LXII: 29–49.

______. (2016b) The capacity to tell a joke: Reflections from work with Asperger's children. *IJP*, 97: 1609–1625.

Burke, E. (1756) *A Philosophical Enquiry into the Origin of Our Ideas of the Sublime and Beautiful*. Oxford: Oxford University Press, 2008.

Busch, F. (2011) The workable here and now and the why of the there and then. *IJP*, 92: 1159–1181.

Caper, R. (1998) *The Clinical Thinking of Wilfred Bion*. London and New York: Routledge.

______. (2000) *Immaterial Facts*. New York: Jason Aronson.
Cassorla, R. (2005) From bastion to enactment: The "non-dream" in the theatre of analysis. *IJP*, 86: 699–719.
______. (2008) The analyst's implicit alpha-function, trauma and enactment in the analysis of borderline patients. *IJP*, 89: 161–180.
______. (2012) What happens before and after acute enactments? An exercise in clinical validation and the broadening of hypotheses. *IJP*, 93: 53–80.
______. (2013) When the analyst becomes stupid: An attempt to understand enactment using Bion's theory of thinking. *Psa Q*, 82: 323–360.
Cavett, D. (2013) Missing: Jonathan Winters. Badly. *NY Times*, May 10, 2013.
Chad and Jeremy (1965) *Summer Song*.
Chasseguet-Smirgel, J. (1988) The triumph of humor. In H. P. Bloom, Y. Kramer and A. D. Richards (Eds.) *Fantasy, Myth and Reality: Essays in Honor of Jacob A. Arlow*. Madison, CT: International Universities Press.
Civitarese, G. (2005) Fire in the theater: (Un)reality of/in the transference interpretation. *IJP*: 85: 1299–1316.
______. (2011) Aesthetic conflict and the α function. In *The Violence of Emotions: Bion and Post-Bionian Psychoanalysis*. London: Routledge. Pp. 119–157.
______. (2014) Bion and the Sublime: The origins of an aesthetic paradigm. *IJP*, 95: 1059–1086.
______. (2015) *Losing Your Head*. New York: Rowman & Littlefield.
______ & Ferro, A. (2013) The meaning and use of metaphor in analytic field theory. *Psa Inq*, 33: 190–209.
Corrao, F. (1981) Polyadic structure and gamma function. *Gruppo e Funzione Analitica*, n. II–2.
da Rocha Barros, E. M. (2000) Affect and pictogram: The constitution of meaning in mental life. *IJP*, 81: 1087–1099.
______. (2002) An essay in dreaming, psychical working out and working through. *IJP*, 83: 1083–1093.
______. (2013) On the expressive function of the mind. Paper given at the Boston Psychoanalytic Institute, December, 2013.
______ & Rocha Barros, E. L. (2011) Reflections on the clinical implications of symbolism. *IJP*, 92: 879–903.
______. (In press) Reverie, symbolization and the expressive function of the mind. Reflections inspired on Bion's work. *IJP*.
D'arcy Wood, G. (2014) *Tambora: The Eruption that Changed the World*. Princeton, NJ: Princeton University Press.
Dylan, B. (1966) Visions of Johanna. In *Blonde on Blonde*. Columbia Records.
Eliot, T. S. (1943) *The Four Quartets*. New York: Harcourt Press.
Elkins, J. (2011) Against the sublime. In R. Hoffmann and I. Whyte (Eds.) *Beyond the Finite: The Sublime in Art and Science*. New York: Oxford University Press. Pp. 75–90.

Erikson, E. (1964) *Insight and Responsibility*. New York: WW Norton.
Faimberg, H. (2014) The paternal function in Winnicott: The psychoanalytic frame. *IJP*, 95: 629–640.
Ferenczi, S. (1909) Letter from Sandor Ferenczi to Sigmund Freud. November 22, 1909. *The Correspondence of Sigmund Freud and Sandor Ferenczi. Volume I.* 1908–1914. Pp. 65–66.
______. (1911) Letter from Sandor Ferenczi to Sigmund Freud, February 7, 1911. *The Correspondence of Sandor Ferenczi and Sigmund Freud Volume 1, 1908–1914*. P. 253.
______. (1921) Untitled paper on war neuroses. In S. Ferenczi *Psycho-Analysis and the War Neuroses*. Original publisher Vienna: International Psychoanalytical Press, 1921. Memphis, TN: General Books, 2010. Pp. 4–16.
Ferro, A. (2002a) *In the Analyst's Consulting Room*. New York: Brunner-Routledge.
______. (2002b) Some implications of Bion's thought: The waking dream and narrative derivatives. *IJP*, 83: 597–607.
______. (2005) *Seeds of Illness, Seeds of Recovery*. New York: Brunner-Routledge.
______. (2006) Clinical Implications of Bion's Thought. *IJPA*, 87: 989–1003.
______. (2009a) *Mind Works: Technique and Creativity in Psychoanalysis*. New York: Routledge.
______. (2009b) Transformations in dreaming and characters in the psychoanalytic field,. Int. J. Psycho-Anal., 90: 209–230.
______ & Civitarese, G. (2015). *The Analytic Field and Its Transformations.* London: Karnac.
______ & Forest, G. (2008) "Objects" and "characters" in psychoanalytic texts/dialogues. *Int. Forum Psa*, 17: 71–81.
Ferro, A. & Nicoli, L. (2017) *The New Analyst's Guide to the Galaxy*. London: Karnac Books.
Fliess, R. (1942/2007) The metapsychology of the analyst. *Psa Q*, 11: 211–227. Also in *Psa Q*, 76: 679–695.
Freud, A. (1970) The infantile neurosis: Genetic and dynamic considerations. *The Writings of Anna Freud, Volume VII*. New York: IUP. Pp. 189–203.
Freud, S. (1894) Draft H. Paranoia. *The Complete Letters of Sigmund Freud to Wilhelm Fleiss.*
______. (1900) The interpretation of dreams. *SE*, 4–5.
______. (1905a) Fragment of an analysis of a case of hysteria. *SE*, 7: 3–122.
______. (1905b) Jokes and their relation to the unconscious. *SE*, 8.
______. (1909) Letter to Sandor Ferenczi, October, 22, 1909. *The Correspondence of Sigmund Freud and Sandor Ferenczi Volume 1, 1908–1914*. Pp. 84–86.
______. (1910) The future prospects of psycho-analytic therapy. *SE*, 11: 139–151.

______. (1911a) Letter from Sigmund Freud to C. G. Jung, December 31, 1911. *The Freud/Jung Letters: The Correspondence between Sigmund Freud and C. G. Jung*. Pp. 475–476.

______. (1911b) Formulations on the two principles of mental functioning. *SE*, 12: 215–226.

______. (1912) Recommendations to physicians practicing psycho-analysis. *SE*, 12: 109–120.

______. (1913a) Letter to Ludwig Binswanger, February 20, 1913. *The Sigmund Freud- Ludwig Binswanger Correspondence 1908–1938*. Pp. 112–113.

______. (1913b) The disposition to obsessional neurosis, a contribution to the choice of neurosis. *SE*, 12: 311–326.

______. (1913c) On beginning the treatment. Further recommendations on the technique of psycho-analysis. *SE*, 13: 191–198.

______. (1914) Remembering, repeating and working-through. *SE*, 12: 147–156.

______. (1915a) The unconscious. *SE*, 14: 159–215.

______. (1915b) Letter from Sigmund Freud to Sandor Ferenczi, September 1. 1915. *The Correspondence of Sigmund Freud and Sandor Ferenczi, Vol. 2, 1914–1919*. P. 77.

______. (1918) From the history of an infantile neurosis. *SE*, 17: 1–124.

______. (1920) Beyond the pleasure principle. *SE*, 18: 3–64.

______. (1921) Introduction. In S. Ferenczi *Psycho-Analysis and the War Neuroses*. Original publisher, Vienna: International Psychoanalytical Press, 1921. Memphis, TN: General Books, 2010. Pp. 1–4.

______. (1922) Dreams and telepathy. *SE*, 18: 195–220.

______. (1923) The ego and the id. *SE*, 18: 3–66.

______. (1926) Inhibitions, symptoms and anxiety. *SE*, 20: 77–174.

______. (1927) Humour. *SE*, 21: 161–166.

______. (1930) Civilization and its discontents. *SE*, 22: 57–146.

______. (1933) New Introductory lectures on psycho-analysis. *SE*, 22: 1–182.

______. (1937) Constructions in analysis. *SE*, 23: 255–270.

Friedman, T. (2005) *The World Is Flat: A Brief History of the Twenty-first Century*. New York: Ferrar, Strauss and Giroux.

______. (2016) *Thank You for Being Late: An Optimists Guide to Thriving in the Age of Acceleration*. New York: Ferrar, Strauss and Giroux.

Fromm, M. G. (1989) Impasse and transitional relatedness. In M. G. Fromm and B. Smith (Eds.) *The Facilitating Environment: Clinical Applications of Winnicott's Theory*. Madison: International Universities Press. Pp. 179–204.

Gerzi, S. (2005) Trauma, narcissism and the two attractors in trauma. *IJP*, 86: 1033–1050.

Glover, E. (1927) Lectures on technique in psycho-analysis. *IJP*, 8: 311–338.

Goethe, J. (1810) *Theory of Colors*. Mineola, NY: Dover Publications.

Graves, R. (1929) *Good-bye to All That*. Penguin Modern Classics, 2000.

Gray, P. (1996) Undoing the lag in the technique of conflict and defense analysis. *PSC*, 51: 87–101.

Green, A. (1975) The analyst, symbolization and absence in the analytic setting (On changes in analytic practice and analytic experience) – in memory of D. W. Winnicott. *IJP*, 56: 1–22.

______. (1999) On discriminating and not discriminating between affect and representation. *IJP* 80: 277–316.

______. (2005) *Key Ideas for a Contemporary Psychoanalysis: Misrecognition and Recognition of the Unconscious*. New York: Routledge Press.

______. (2010) Thoughts on the Paris School of Psychoanalysis. In M. Aisenstein and E. Rappoport de Aisemberg (Eds.) *Psychosomatic Today: A Psychoanalytic Perspective*. London: Karnac. Pp. 1–45.

Grinberg, L. (1990) *The Goals of Psychoanalysis: Identification, Identity and Supervision*. London: Karnac Books.

Grotjahn, M. (1950). About the "third ear" in psychoanalysis: A review and critical evaluation of Theodor Reik's "Listening with the Third Ear: The Inner Experiences of a Psychoanalyst." *Psa Rev*, 37: 56–65.

Grotstein, J. (1977) The psychoanalytic concept of schizophrenia: I. The dilemma. *IJP*, 58: 403–425.

______. (1980) A proposed revision of the psychoanalytic concept of primitive mental states – Part I. Introduction to a newer psychoanalytic metapsychology. *Cont. Psa.*, 16: 479–546.

______. (1984) A proposed revision of the psychoanalytic concept of primitive mental states, Part II—The borderline syndrome-section 3 disorders of autistic safety and symbiotic relatedness. *Contemp. Psa.*, 20: 266–343.

______. (2000) *Who Is the Dreamer Who Dreams the Dream?* Hillsdale, NJ: Analytic Press.

______. (2004) The seventh servant: The implications of a truth drive in Bion's theory of "O." *IJP*, 85: 1081–1101.

______. (2005) "Projective transidentification": An extension of the concept of projective identification. *IJP*, 85: 1051–1069.

______. (2007) *A Beam of Intense Darkness: Wilfred Bion's Legacy to Psychoanalysis*. London: Karnac.

______. (2009a) *". . . But at the Same Time and on Another Level . . .", Volume I. Psychoanalytic Theory and Technique in the Kleinian/Bionian Mode*. London: Karnac.

______. (2009b) *". . . But at the Same Time and on Another Level . . .", Volume II. Clinical Applications in the Kleinian/Bionian Mode*. London: Karnac.

______. (2009c) Dreaming as a "curtain of illusion": Revisiting the "royal road" with Bion as our guide. *IJP*, 90: 733–752.

______. (2012) Personal communication.

______. (2014) Bion crosses the Rubicon: The fateful course – and curse – of O in psychoanalysis and the furies left in its wake. Paper give at the 2014 Los Angeles Bion Conference. October, 2014.

Hamerton, P. G. (1879) *Life of Turner*. Boston: Roberts Brothers.

Hankey, D. (1917) *A Student in Arms*. London: Andrew Melrose.

Harrison, T. (2000) *Bion, Rickman, Foulkes and the Northfield Experiments*. London: Jessica Kingsley.

Heimann, P. (1950) On counter-transference. *IJP*, 31: 81–84.

Hinshelwood, T. (2011) Making sense of Bion's nomadic journey. Paper given at the Psychoanalytic Center of California, April 9, 2011.

Isakower, O. (1957/1992) Preliminary thoughts on the analyzing instrument. Paper presented to the New York Psychoanalytic Institute. *J Clin Psa*, 6: 184–194.

______. (1963/1992) The analyzing instrument: States of consciousness and the dream psychology of Dr. Bertram Lewis. *J Clin Psa*, 6: 204–215.

Jacobs, T. (1983) The analyst and the patient's object world: Notes on an aspect of countertransference. *JAPA*, 31: 619–642.

______. (1986) On countertransference enactments. *JAPA*, 34: 289–307.

______. (1991) *The Use of the Self: Countertransference and Communication in the Analytic Situation*. New York: International Universities Press.

______. (1999) Countertransference past and present: A review of the concept. *IJP*, 80: 575–594.

______. (2007) Review of "The metapsychology of the analyst" by Robert Fliess. *Psa Q*, 76: 715–724.

Jacobson, E. (1946) The child's laughter – theoretical and clinical notes on the function of the comic. *Psa Study Child*, 2: 39–60.

Jones, E. (1921) War shock and Freud's theory of neuroses. In S. Ferenczi *Psycho-Analysis and the War Neuroses*. Original publisher, Vienna: International Psychoanalytical Press, 1921. Memphis, TN: General Books, 2010. Pp. 32–44.

Joseph, B. (1975) The patient who is difficult to reach. In M. Feldman and E. Spillius (Eds.) *Psychic Equilibrium and Psychic Change: Selected Papers of Betty Joseph*. New York: Routledge, 1989. Pp. 75–87.

______. (1985) Transference: The total situation. *IJPA*, 66: 447–454.

Kahn, M. (2012) Personal communication.

Kant, I. (1799, English version) *Of the Distinct Objects of the Feeling of the Beautiful and Sublime*.

Kernberg, O. (1965) Notes on countertransference. *JAPA*, 13: 38–56.

______. (1967) Borderline personality organization. In *Borderline Conditions and Pathological Narcissism*. New York: Jason Aronson, 1975. Pp. 3–47.

Khan M. (1963). The concept of cumulative trauma. *PSC*, 18: 286–306.
Klein, M. (1945) The Oedipus complex in the light of early anxieties. In *Love, Guilt and Reparation*. Pp. 370–419. Delacorte Press, 1975
______. (1946) Notes on some schizoid mechanisms. In *Envy and Gratitude*. London: Hogarth Press, 1975. Pp. 1–24.
Klein, S. (1980) Autistic phenomena in neurotic patients. *IJP*, 61: 395–402.
Korbivcher, C. (2005) The theory of transformations and autistic states. Autistic transformations: A proposal. *IJP*, 85: 1595–1610.
______. (2014) *Autistic Transformations*. London: Karnac.
Krauss, L. (2012) A blip that speaks of our place in the universe. *NY Times*, July 9, 2012.
Kris, E. (1938) Ego development and the comic. *IJP*, 19: 77–90.
Langer, S. (1942) *Philosophy in a New Key*. Cambridge, MA: Harvard University Press.
Langs, R. (1978) Validation and the framework of the psychoanalytic situation – thoughts prompted by Hans H. Strupp's "Suffering and Psychotherapy." *Cont Psa*, 14: 98–124.
Latane, D. (1983) Samuel Rogers "The Voyage of Columbus" and Turner's Illustrations to the Edition of 1834. *The Wordsworth Circle*, 14: 108–112.
Legorreta, G. & Brown, L. J. (2016) *On Freud's "Formulations on the Two Principles of Mental Functioning."* International Psychoanalytic Association series, *Contemporary Freud: Turning Points and Critical Issues*. London: Karnac.
Lemma, A. (1999) *Humour on the Couch*. London: Whurr Publishers.
______. (2014) The body of the analyst and the analytic setting: Reflections on the embodied setting and the symbiotic transference. *IJP*, 95: 225–244.
Levine, H. (2011) "The consolation which is drawn from truth": The analysis of a patient unable to suffer experience. In C. Mawson (Ed.) *Bion Today*. New York: Brunner-Routledge, 2011. Pp. 188–211.
______. (2012) The colourless canvas: Representation, therapeutic action and the creation of mind. *IJP*, 93: 607–629.
Levine, H. & Brown, L. J. (2013) *Growth and Turbulence in the Container/Contained: Bion's Continuing Legacy*. New York and London: Routledge.
Levine, H., Reed, G. & Scarfone, D. (Eds.) (2013) *Unrepresented States and the Construction of Meaning: Clinical and Theoretical Contributions*. London: Karnac Books.
Lewin, K. (1935) *A Dynamic Theory of Personality*. New York: McGraw-Hill.
Llewellyn, N. & Riding, C. (Eds.) *The Art of the Sublime*. Tate Research Publication, January 2013.
Lombardi, R. (2011) The body, feelings, and the unheard music of the senses. *Cont Psa*, 47: 3–24.

______. (2013) Object relations and the ineffable bodily dimension. *Cont Psa*, 49: 82–102.

Lothane, Z. (2006) Reciprocal free association: Listening with the third ear as an instrument in psychoanalysis. *Psa Psychol*, 23: 711–727.

Marquez, G. (1995) *Memories of My Melancholy Whores.* New York: Alfred A. Knopf, Inc.

Mawson, C. (2015) On the concept of *negative capability*. Paper given at the Regional Bion Symposium, Los Angeles, March, 2015.

______. (2016) *The Complete Works of Wilfred Bion*. London: Routledge.

Meltzer, D. (1975) Adhesive identification. *Cont. Psa.*, 11: 289–310.

______. (1986) *Studies in Extended Metapsychology: Clinical Applications of Bion's Ideas.* Strath Tay, Perthshire: Clunie Press.

______ & Williams, M. H. (2008) *The Apprehension of Beauty*. London: Karnac.

Meslay, O. (2005) *Turner: Life and Landscape*. New York: Abrams.

Mitchell, S. (1998) The analyst's knowledge and authority. *Psa Q*, 67: 1–31.

Mitrani, J. (1992) On the survival function of autistic maneuvers in adult patients. *IJP*, 73: 549–559.

______. (2001) "Taking the transference": Some technical implications in three papers by Bion. *IJP*, 82: 1085–1104.

______. (2011) Trying to enter the long black branches: Some technical extensions of the work of Frances Tustin for the analysis of autistic states in adults. *IJP*, 92: 21–42.

Modell, A. (1984) Self preservation and the preservation of the self. *Ann Psa*, 12: 69–86.

Money-Kyrle, R. (1956) Normal countertransference and some of its deviations. *Int. J. Psych.*, 37: 360–366.

Moyle, F. (2016) *The Extraordinary Life and Momentous Times of J. M. W. Turner*. New York: Penguin Press.

Newton, I. (1672) *Discovery of the Dispersion of Light and the Nature of Color.*

Nietsche, F. (1886) *Beyond Good and Evil*. Wilder Publications, 2008.

Ogden, T. (1985) On potential space. *IJP*, 66: 129–141.

______. (1989) On the concept of an autistic-contiguous position. *IJP*, 70: 127–140.

______. (1994) The analytic third: Working with intersubjective clinical facts. *IJP*, 75: 3–19.

______. (2003a) What's true and whose idea was it? *IJP*, 84: 593–606.

______. (2003b) On not being able to dream. *IJP*, 84: 17–30.

______. (2004a) This art of psychoanalysis: Dreaming undreamt dreams and interrupted cries. *IJP*, 85: 857–877.

______. (2004b) The analytic third: Implications for psychoanalytic theory and technique. *Psa Q*, 73: 167–195.

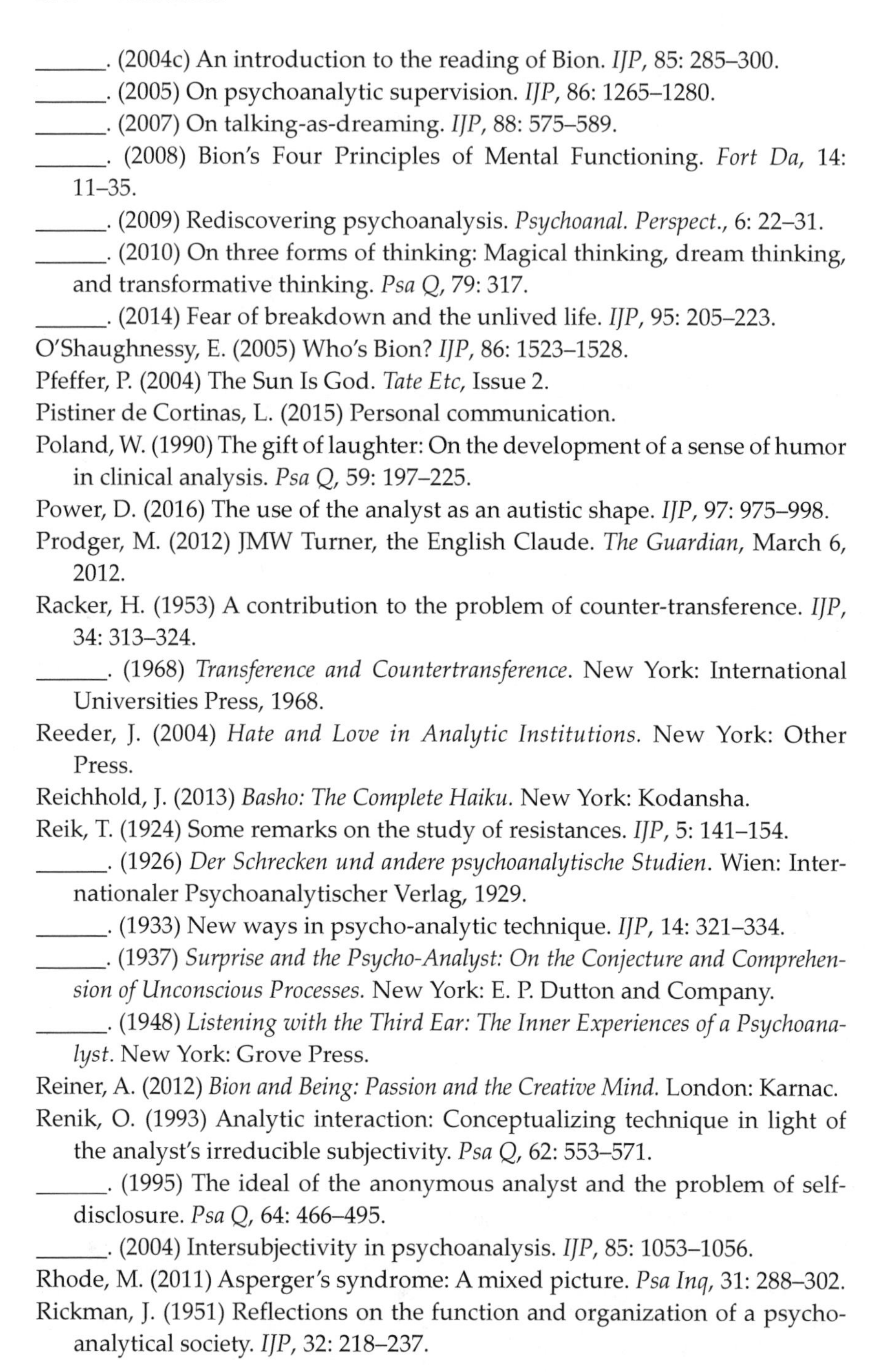

______. (2004c) An introduction to the reading of Bion. *IJP*, 85: 285–300.

______. (2005) On psychoanalytic supervision. *IJP*, 86: 1265–1280.

______. (2007) On talking-as-dreaming. *IJP*, 88: 575–589.

______. (2008) Bion's Four Principles of Mental Functioning. *Fort Da*, 14: 11–35.

______. (2009) Rediscovering psychoanalysis. *Psychoanal. Perspect.*, 6: 22–31.

______. (2010) On three forms of thinking: Magical thinking, dream thinking, and transformative thinking. *Psa Q*, 79: 317.

______. (2014) Fear of breakdown and the unlived life. *IJP*, 95: 205–223.

O'Shaughnessy, E. (2005) Who's Bion? *IJP*, 86: 1523–1528.

Pfeffer, P. (2004) The Sun Is God. *Tate Etc*, Issue 2.

Pistiner de Cortinas, L. (2015) Personal communication.

Poland, W. (1990) The gift of laughter: On the development of a sense of humor in clinical analysis. *Psa Q*, 59: 197–225.

Power, D. (2016) The use of the analyst as an autistic shape. *IJP*, 97: 975–998.

Prodger, M. (2012) JMW Turner, the English Claude. *The Guardian*, March 6, 2012.

Racker, H. (1953) A contribution to the problem of counter-transference. *IJP*, 34: 313–324.

______. (1968) *Transference and Countertransference*. New York: International Universities Press, 1968.

Reeder, J. (2004) *Hate and Love in Analytic Institutions*. New York: Other Press.

Reichhold, J. (2013) *Basho: The Complete Haiku*. New York: Kodansha.

Reik, T. (1924) Some remarks on the study of resistances. *IJP*, 5: 141–154.

______. (1926) *Der Schrecken und andere psychoanalytische Studien*. Wien: Internationaler Psychoanalytischer Verlag, 1929.

______. (1933) New ways in psycho-analytic technique. *IJP*, 14: 321–334.

______. (1937) *Surprise and the Psycho-Analyst: On the Conjecture and Comprehension of Unconscious Processes*. New York: E. P. Dutton and Company.

______. (1948) *Listening with the Third Ear: The Inner Experiences of a Psychoanalyst*. New York: Grove Press.

Reiner, A. (2012) *Bion and Being: Passion and the Creative Mind*. London: Karnac.

Renik, O. (1993) Analytic interaction: Conceptualizing technique in light of the analyst's irreducible subjectivity. *Psa Q*, 62: 553–571.

______. (1995) The ideal of the anonymous analyst and the problem of self-disclosure. *Psa Q*, 64: 466–495.

______. (2004) Intersubjectivity in psychoanalysis. *IJP*, 85: 1053–1056.

Rhode, M. (2011) Asperger's syndrome: A mixed picture. *Psa Inq*, 31: 288–302.

Rickman, J. (1951) Reflections on the function and organization of a psycho-analytical society. *IJP*, 32: 218–237.

Riviere, J. (1924) Translator, *Sigmund Freud Collected Papers* (Five Volumes). New York: Basic Books, 1959.

Rolnik, E. J. (2008) "Why is it that I see everything differently?" Reading a 1933 letter from Paula Heimann to Theodor Reik. *JAPA*, 56: 409–430.

Roper, M. (2009) Nameless dread. In M. Roper *The Secret Battle: Emotional Survival in the Great War.* Manchester: Manchester University Press. Pp. 243–275.

______. (In press). Remembering and containing: The First World War memoirs psychoanalytic thought of Wilfred Bion. In S. Alexander and B. Taylor (Eds.) *Clio's Dream. Encounters between History and Psychoanalysis.* Basingstoke: Palgrave.

Rosenblum, R. (1961) The abstract sublime. In S. Morley (Ed.) *The Sublime.* Cambridge, MA: MIT Press. Pp. 108–112.

Ross, W. D. & Kapp, F. T. (1962) A technique for self-analysis of countertransference – use of the psychoanalyst's visual images in response to patient's dreams. *JAPA*, 10: 643–657.

Sandler, J. (1960) The background of safety. *IJP*, 41: 352–356.

______. (1976) Countertransference and role-responsiveness. *Int Rev Psa*, 3: 43–47.

______ & Rosenblatt, B. (1962) The concept of the representational world. *PSC*, 17: 128–145.

Sandler, P. (2000) What is thinking – an attempt at an integrated study of W. R. Bion's contributions to the processes of knowing. In P. Bion Talamo, F. Borgogno and S. Merciai (Eds.) *W. R. Bion: Between Past and Future.* London: Karnac Books.

______. (2003) Bion's war memoirs: A psychoanalytic commentary: Living experiences and learning from them: Some early roots of Bion's contributions to psychoanalysis. In R. Lipgar and M. Pines (2003) *Building on Bion: Roots*. London: Kingsley.

Sandler, J. (1960) The background of safety. *IJP*, 41: 352–356.

Schafer, R. (2007) On "The metapsychology of the analyst" by Robert Fliess. *Psa Q*, 76: 607–714.

Schmidt-Hellerau, C. (2012). Personal communication.

Schrope, M. (2015) Medicine's hidden roots in an ancient manuscript. *New York Times*, June 2, 2015.

Searles, H. (1960) *The Nonhuman Environment in Normal Development and Schizophrenia*. New York: IUP.

Shaw, P. (2006) *The Sublime*. New York: Routledge.

Sherman, M. H. (1965) Freud, Reik and the problem of technique in psychoanalysis. *Psa Rev*, 52: 19–37.

______. (2012) Personal communication.

Sinason, V. (1996) But psychotherapists don't laugh, do they? *Psa Psychother in South Africa*, Summer, pp. 19–31.

Solms, M. (2012) Personal communication.

Souter, K. M. (2009) The *War Memoirs*: Some origins of the thought of W. R. Bion. *IJP*, 90: 795–808.

Spero, M. H. (2009) The joke envelope: A neglected precursor of the psychic envelope concept in Freud's writing. *PSC*, 64: 193–226.

Spillius, E. (2007) Melanie Klein revisited: Her unpublished thoughts on technique. In *Encounters with Melanie Klein: Selected Papers of Elizabeth Spillius.* New York: Routledge.

Spillius, E., Milton, J., Garvey, P., Couve, C. & Steiner, D. (2011) *The New Dictionary of Kleinian Thought*. London and New York: Routledge.

Steiner, J. (2017) *Lectures on Technique by Melanie Klein: Edited with a Critical Review by John Steiner.* London: Routledge.

Sterba, R. (1934) The fate of the ego in analytic therapy. *IJP*, 15: 117–126.

Stern, D. (1986) *The Interpersonal World of the Infant.* New York: Basic Books. New York: Routledge.

Symington, J. & Symington, N. (1996). *The Clinical Thinking of Wilfred Bion.* New York: Routledge.

Szykierski, D. (2010) The traumatic roots of containment: The evolution of Bion's metapsychology. *Psa Q*, 79: 935–968.

Tarantelli, C. (2011) Personal communication.

Trevarthern, C. (2005) First things first: Infants make good use of the sympathetic rhythm of imitation, without reason or language. *J Child Psychother*, 31: 91–113.

Trotter, W. (1916) *Instincts of the Herd in Peace and War.*

Turner, J. M. W. (1925–1820) *Death on a Pale Horse*. www.tate.org.uk/art/research-publications/the-sublime/joseph-mallord-william-turner-death-on-a-pale-horse--r1105617.

Tustin, F. (1980) Autistic objects. *Int Rev Psa*, 7: 27–39.

______. (1981) *Autistic States in Children*. London: Routledge.

______. (1983) Thoughts on autism with special reference to a paper by Melanie Klein. *J Child Psychother*, 9: 119–131.

______. (1984a) Autistic shapes. *Int Rev Psa*, 11: 279–290.

______. (1984b) The growth of understanding. *J. Child Psychother*, 10: 13–7149.

______. (1986) *Autistic Barriers in Neurotic Patients.* New Haven: Yale University Press.

______. (1994) Autistic children who are assessed as not brain-damaged. *J Child Psychother*, 20: 103–131.

Vermote, R. (2011) On the value of "late Bion" to analytic theory and practice. *IJP*, 92: 1089–1098.

Weiss, E. (1970) *Sigmund Freud as a Consultant*. New York: Intercontinental Medical Book Corporation.

Weiss, H. (2012) Personal communication.

Whyte, I. (2011) The Sublime. In R. Hoffman and I. Whyte (Eds.) *Beyond the Finite: The Sublime in Art and Science*. New York: Oxford University Press.

Winnicott, D. (1949) Hate in the countertransference. *IJP*, 30: 69–74.

______. (1955) Metapsychological and clinical aspects of regression within the psycho-analytic set-up. *IJP*, 36: 16–26.

______. (1960) The theory of the parent–infant relationship. In *The Maturational Processes and the Facilitating Environment*. New York: IUP, 1965. Pp. 33–55.

______. (1965) *The Maturational Processes and the Facilitating Environment: Studies in the Theory of Emotional Development*. London: Hogarth Press.

______. (1971) *Playing and Reality*. New York: Basic Books.

______. (1974) Fear of breakdown. *Int Rev Psa*, 1: 103–107.

Wyman, H. M. & Rittenberg, S. M. (1992) The analyzing instrument of Otto Isakower, M. D. Evolution of a concept. *J Clin Psa*, 1: 165–316.

INDEX

Note: numbers preceded by *n* are chapter endnote numbers.